THE QUEBEC ACT

THE
QUEBEC ACT

A Study in Statesmanship

BY

SIR REGINALD COUPLAND

OXFORD
AT THE CLARENDON PRESS

Oxford University Press, Ely House, London W. 1

GLASGOW NEW YORK TORONTO MELBOURNE WELLINGTON
CAPE TOWN SALISBURY IBADAN NAIROBI LUSAKA ADDIS ABABA
BOMBAY CALCUTTA MADRAS KARACHI LAHORE DACCA
KUALA LUMPUR HONG KONG TOKYO

FIRST PUBLISHED 1925
REPRINTED LITHOGRAPHICALLY IN GREAT BRITAIN
AT THE UNIVERSITY PRESS, OXFORD
BY VIVIAN RIDLER
PRINTER TO THE UNIVERSITY
1968

PREFACE

No student of Canadian history can fail to recognize his debt to Dr. A. G. Doughty, Keeper of the Public Records, and his fellow workers on the Archives at Ottawa; and the preparation of this essay would have been an infinitely longer and more difficult task if the printed collection of constitutional documents from 1759 to 1791, admirably edited by Dr. Shortt and Dr. Doughty, had not been available. The author's obligation to other workers in the same field, especially to Dr. C. W. Alvord, Dr. V. Coffin, and Sir Charles Lucas, will be evident from the references in the foot-notes.

Of the friends who have kindly assisted him from time to time with criticism and advice, the author would specially mention Mr. H. E. Egerton, his predecessor in the Beit Chair, Mr. E. M. Wrong, lately Beit Lecturer in Colonial History, Mr. H. F. Angus, and Professor Basil Williams. He would also like to take this opportunity of recording his indebtedness to the very useful library of the Royal Colonial Institute and to the courtesy of its honorary librarian, Mr. Evans Lewin, and his staff.

R. C.

WOOTTON HILL,
April, 1925.

ABBREVIATIONS USED IN THE FOOT-NOTES

IV A.A.   *American Archives* : edited by P. Force.   Fourth Series. Washington, 1840.

B.K.   *Selected Speeches and Documents on British Colonial Policy, 1763–1917* : edited by A. Berriedale Keith ; 2 vols., Oxford, 1918.

C.D.   *Canadian Archives : Documents relating to the Constitutional History of Canada, 1759–1791* : edited by A. Shortt and A. G. Doughty.   Canadian Sessional Paper, No. 18 of 1907.   Second edition, Ottawa, 1918.

C.H.R.   *The Canadian Historical Review.*   Toronto, 1920 onwards.

E. & G.   *Canadian Constitutional Development, shown by selected speeches and dispatches* : edited by H. E. Egerton and W. L. Grant.   London, 1907.

K.   *Documents of the Canadian Constitution, 1759–1915* : edited by W. P. M. Kennedy.   Toronto, 1918.

N.S.D. i.   *Selections from the Public Documents of the Province of Nova Scotia.*   Halifax, 1869.

N.S.D. ii.   *Nova Scotia Archives II, being the Calendar of two Government Letter-Books and a Commission Book.*   Halifax, 1900.

P.H.   *Parliamentary History.*

R.C.A.   *Reports on Canadian Archives* : edited by the Dominion Archivists (D. Brymner, A. G. Doughty).   Ottawa, annually from 1872.

For the convenience of students, where documents cited may be found in more than one published collection, alternative references are given in square brackets.

CONTENTS

Until we come to respect what stands in a respectable light with others, we are very deficient in the temper which qualifies us to make any laws and regulations about them.

Burke, on the Irish penal laws, in 1782.

United Canada is a great accomplished fact to-day. And it has become so without loss of individuality in the several and very diverse states which compose it and without violence being done to their distinctive character and traditions.

Lord Milner, at Winnipeg, in 1908.

INTRODUCTION

I

THERE is, perhaps, no more important fact in modern history than the fact that the British people, after having signally failed to keep together in one political society those of their race who had settled overseas and those who had remained in the mother country, were given the rare privilege of a second chance—a chance to build on the ruins of the British Empire a greater, a better, and a more lasting British Commonwealth. To many, indeed, in that black February of 1783, when Parliament perforce accepted the most mortifying treaty a British Government has ever signed, it seemed as if the record of British colonial expansion, so triumphantly sustained in the previous war only twenty years before, was now closed. But the gloom of those debates was not wholly unbroken. It was fitting that Chatham's son, in the course of defending the inevitable treaty as Chancellor of the Exchequer in the Shelburne Government, should solemnly attest the passing of 'the memorable era of England's glory'; but it was also fitting that the younger Pitt should sound a note of hope. 'Let us examine what is left', he said, 'with a manly and determined courage. Let us strengthen ourselves against inveterate enemies and reconciliate our ancient friends. The misfortunes of individuals and of kingdoms that are laid open and examined with true wisdom are more than half redressed.'[1] Nor was this a mere flight of rhetoric, a young man's defiance of misfortune. There *was* something left—some groundwork for the second chance, some British soil

[1] Speech of February 21, 1783, *War Speeches of William Pitt the Younger* (ed. R. Coupland, Oxford, 1915), pp. 3–5.

overseas where white men could live and thrive, some foot-hold in North America itself. New British colonies were presently to be established in more distant continents in southern seas ; but the greatest of the Dominions in the British Commonwealth, as we now know it, was to spring and spread from that piece of North America that was ' left ' in 1783.

2

The thirteen colonies which secured their independence in 1783 were not the only British colonies in North America. Twenty years earlier, in the ' era of England's glory ', a vast territory in the north and centre of the continent, hitherto claimed and partly colonized by France, had been ceded to Great Britain by the Treaty of Paris. ' His Most Christian Majesty ', ran the terms of cession, ' renounces all pretensions which he has heretofore formed or might have formed to Nova Scotia or Acadia in all its parts, and guaranties the whole of it, and with all its dependencies, to the King of Great Britain ; Moreover, his Most Christian Majesty cedes and guaranties to his said Britannick Majesty, in full right, Canada, with all its dependencies, as well as the island of Cape Breton, and all the other islands and coasts in the gulph and river of St. Lawrence. . . .'[1] As the wording of the clause implies, the first of the territories mentioned had already been acquired by the British Crown. Nova Scotia, or Acadie as the French called it, had been ceded to Britain in 1713 by the Treaty of Utrecht, when also a great forest district in the North, which the fur-traders of the Hudson's Bay Company had explored, had been recognized as British territory. But while the French had relinquished the peninsula part of Acadia, they had continued to claim and to occupy the adjacent territory on the mainland which was afterwards, under British rule, to

[1] Treaty of Paris, Article IV.

be separated from Nova Scotia and constituted a separate
province (New Brunswick). By the new treaty the mainland as well as the peninsula had been indisputably ceded.
The French tenure of the Island of Cape Breton, too, had
not been unbroken; its fortress of Louisbourg had been
captured in 1745 by the colonial militia of New England;
but in 1748 by the Treaty of Aix-la-Chapelle it had been
returned to France in exchange for Madras. Now, together
with Île St. Jean (afterwards known as Prince Edward
Island), it had become finally British. In Canada proper,
on the other hand, Britain had never won a hold; and
it was Canada 'with all its dependencies' that constituted
by far the greatest part of the territory acquired in 1763.
It consisted, first, of the colonized district lying along
both sides of the St. Lawrence from near its mouth
to the point at which the Ottawa joins it, with a relatively large and almost wholly French population,
settled in a long straggling line of agricultural villages.
About half-way along it stood the town of Quebec, at its
western end the town of Montreal, and between these the
town of Three Rivers (Trois Rivières).[1] Beyond this settled
portion of the province lay a wide forest tract surrounding
the Great Lakes, traversed only by Indian tribes and
French or half-breed trappers, with here and there a military
outpost or trading settlement to which the merchants of
the eastern towns came to buy their furs. The boundaries
of this area had never been strictly defined, but the French
had treated as part of Canada all the country, as far west
as the upper waters of the Mississippi, into which the
traders of the province had penetrated.[2] Southwards,

[1] Three Rivers was the centre of an administrative district under the
French and British régime, but its population in 1762 was only 672
(C. D., p. 89).
[2] General Gage, military governor of the district of Montreal, judging
from the trade authorized by the French Governors of Canada, reported
(March 1762) 'not only the lakes, which are indisputable, but the whole
course of the Mississippi from its head to its junction with the Illinois to

finally, from Canada right down to the Gulf of Mexico, stretched the long-debated strip of unsettled country between the Alleghany Mountains and the Mississippi, all claim to which had been finally ceded to Britain ' in order to re-establish peace on solid and durable foundations and to remove for ever all subject of dispute with regard to the limits of the British and French territory on the continent of America '.[1]

Thus the Treaty of Paris had added at one stroke to the colonial field of the British Empire an area far greater than that of all its previous American colonies together ; and at the same time it had removed the obstacle which the French occupation had presented to further expansion. Beyond the western limits of the ceded territory, beyond the Great Lakes and the Mississippi, lay the central belt of the prairies, and beyond that the Rocky Mountains and the sea. No Europeans save a few adventurous explorers had penetrated as yet into this immense domain. Only sparsely occupied by roaming Indian tribes, it stood open to the unborn generations of those European peoples who held the eastern seaboard and the entry of the St. Lawrence : and·it was inevitable that the great migration which had crossed the Atlantic from Western Europe should push on in course of time across the American continent to the Pacific. No one in 1763 or in 1783 could have foreseen what the future world-position of North America would be —with the growth of population, with the development of man's power over nature, with the shrinking of space and time and the closing together of the peoples of the world.

have been comprehended by the French in the Government of Canada ' (C. D., p. 96). The Lords of Trade informed Lord Egremont (June 8, 1763) that ' Canada, as possessed and claimed by the French,' included ' the whole lands to the westward indefinitely which was the subject of their Indian trade ' (C. D., p. 140).

[1] Treaty of Paris, Article VII. New Orleans was left to France. East Florida was ceded to Britain by Spain, to whom, by way of compensation, France ceded her claim to the undefined *hinterland* beyond the Mississippi.

But, in fact, the opening of the continent mainly to it by the Treaty of Paris was a decisive event for the destiny of the Anglo-Saxon race ; and the retention of the northern part of the continent within its bounds by the Treaty of Versailles was a decisive event for the destiny of the British Empire.

It is the purpose of this essay to explain how it happened that, when the thirteen southward colonies severed their old-standing ties with Britain, the great colony in the North, very recently acquired and by conquest, not by settlement, continued in its new allegiance.

I

THE FRENCH-CANADIAN QUESTION

I

THE acquisition of French Canada had thrust British statesmen into a new field of colonial policy. Before the Seven Years' War the expansion of the British Empire in the western world had been effected almost wholly by settlement rather than by conquest. Only one or two small insular or seaboard colonies such as Jamaica, Nova Scotia, and New York had hitherto been annexed as the result of war. British colonial policy had therefore been concerned mainly with the government of Britons. But British statesmen had now upon their hands a large and old-established colony, stretching far into the continent, whose white population was almost exclusively French. They had already had to deal with French subjects of the British Crown, as will be seen, in Acadia, as also with Dutch subjects in New York ; but in both these cases the populations concerned were relatively small.[1] It was in Canada that the problems raised by the inclusion in the British Empire of a colony peopled by a foreign European nation were first raised on a large scale : and in the treatment of those problems in Canada the first step was taken towards the future development of the Empire into a world-wide Commonwealth of many nations.

[1] At the time of its capture, New York, then called New Amsterdam, the capital of the Dutch settlement in North America, 'consisted chiefly of small thatched houses, and was so poor and so mean that the English general complained that he was unable to find in the town bedding for his soldiers' (Lecky, *History of England in the Eighteenth Century*, vol. ii, p. 235. For the Acadian population, see pp. 11, 15; below).

If this was practically its first appearance in the colonial field, the question of nationality, as every one knows, was not new to the mother country. Geography had imposed on the four nations of the British Isles the need of solving in the interests of each and all of them the old problem of unity and freedom. For the English, Welsh, and Scots it had been solved, but not for the Irish. And the failure in Ireland might well seem to tell against the chances of success in Canada. In all the elements of nationality the French-Canadians were at least as different from Englishmen as the Irish and far more different than the Scots. There was the same marked distinction of race as in Ireland, and a stronger, because more equal, rivalry of language. There was a similar difference in legal and social traditions. Above all, there was the same difference in religion—which in Ireland had proved for more than a century past and for more than a century to come was still to prove the greatest obstacle to peace and harmony with Britain. And there was one last discordant factor in Canada, closely associated with nationality, yet not inseparable from it, which was not present in Ireland. The problem raised by the subjection of the French-Canadians to the British Crown was not only how to govern a people whose tongue and faith and customary ways of life were not those of their rulers or of their neighbours in the British colonies, but also how to govern a people whose civic and political ideas had already been moulded and hardened by a system of government radically different from and in principle hostile to the British system. How, in a word, could New France be smoothly fitted into the same political fabric as England Old and New ?

2

Of the three main elements of French-Canadian nationa-lity—the Roman Catholic religion, the French language, and a peculiar system of law—the Roman Catholic religion was the most vital, and on its treatment the success or the failure of British policy in Canada was chiefly to depend. Happily, in the course of the eighteenth century, a belief in religious toleration, partly on moral, partly on practical grounds, had been steadily growing in the mother country. The weaknesses of the Revolu-tion settlement in the matter of religious liberty were still indeed embodied in the statute-book; but public opinion had shown itself increasingly ready to allow the cir-cumvention or neglect of the illiberal laws it shrank from positively repealing. The Test Act still denied Noncon-formists civic equality with Anglicans; but many of them were enabled to hold office in national and municipal administration by the illogical contrivance of annual Indemnity Acts. The English Roman Catholics, similarly, lived under the shadow of the penal laws, deprived of all share in the political or civic life of their own country. But the harsher provisions of the penal code were more and more rarely enforced;[1] and it did not prevent the English Catholics from growing steadily in numbers, from maintain-ing their own chapels and worshipping without secrecy and with their own priests, from bringing up their children in their own faith and bequeathing them their

---

[1] Offences against the law could always be denounced by private informers for motives of personal enmity or in order to obtain the statutory reward, which in the case of the celebration of mass by a priest, for instance, was as high as £100. The judges did what they could to check the enforce-ment of the law by this means by demanding complete and unimpeachable evidence (see p. 10, n. 1, below); and it was also decided that informers who prosecuted for the sake of the reward should pay their own costs. On the whole subject see Lecky, *History of England in the Eighteenth Century*, vol. i, pp. 344-356; vol. iv, pp. 301-307.

property. Only in one respect, apart from their exclusion from all public service, were they really and regularly ' persecuted ' : a double land-tax was exacted from them by an annual law. In Ireland, of course, the position of the Catholics was far worse : but even in Ireland the vigour of the penal laws was beginning to be relaxed by the second half of the century, and from the first it had been obviously impracticable to enforce those laws which forbade three-quarters of the Irish people to worship in their own manner. There was no lack of Catholic priests in Ireland, and even bishops were known to be secretly performing the functions of their office. The Protestant tyranny, in fact, did not attempt the impossible task of suppressing Roman Catholicism : it was content with the easier achievement of excluding Catholics from all political and civic functions and deadening and degrading their social, their intellectual, and especially their economic life. It was a general subjugation of an alien and conquered people rather than a particular repression of their faith.[1] Religious persecution, as such, had never indeed been a settled principle of British policy or a natural reflection of the British temperament. It was the *political* character, the *political* danger, of the Roman Church that had inspired the penal laws both in England and in Ireland and that so long prevented their repeal.[2] In the middle of the eighteenth century the conflict of religions, though weaker now than in previous wars and cut across by the conflict of national and dynastic interests, was still a factor in the struggle against French ascendancy. Romanism and Jacobitism, moreover, were not unjustly regarded as

[1] Lecky, *History of Ireland in the Eighteenth Century*, vol. i, pp. 136–169 ; vol. ii, pp. 181–217.

[2] Religious persecution in France and Spain, though there also political motives were behind it, was more directly religious and far more drastic and cruel than in England or Ireland. When the Treaty of Paris was concluded (1763) the French Government was keeping men in the galleys and women in prison merely for the offence of attending Protestant meetings (Lecky, *History of England*, vol. i, p. 337).

inseparable allies, and at the time of the Seven Years' War the dark days of 'Forty-Five were not far distant. There were reasons, therefore, for British Governments desiring to preserve the legal existence of an instrument of repression which could be left on the shelf in normal times but quickly taken down to meet a dangerous emergency. Nor was it unnatural that the ignorant and uneducated should still cherish the prejudices which had bitten so deep into English history, still rank all English and, of course, all Irish Papists with the foreign enemies of England, still easily be kindled, as the Gordon Riots were to show as late as 1780, to the extremes of passion and violence by the old ' No Popery ' cry. None the less, as the neglect and evasion of the penal laws were themselves evidence enough, the idea was growing that circumstances no longer justified the fears and hatreds of Elizabeth's or James II's days. The instinctive willingness of the normal Englishman, when undisturbed by panic or pugnacity, to tolerate his neighbour's personal opinions, to ' live and let live ', was beginning to assert itself. And by cynic and idealist alike the rightness and wisdom of religious tolerance as a general principle were becoming more and more widely recognized. Burke, the greatest orator and political theorist, and Mansfield, the greatest lawyer of the age, emphatically proclaimed it : [1] and as early

[1] Speaking in the House of Lords in 1780, Mansfield said : ' Conscience is not controllable by human laws, nor amenable to human tribunals. . . . What bloodshed and confusion have been occasioned from the reign of Henry IV, when the first penal statutes were enacted, down to the revolution in this kingdom, by laws made to force conscience ! There is certainly nothing more unreasonable, more inconsistent with the rights of human nature, more contrary to the spirit and precepts of the Christian religion, more iniquitous and unjust, more impolitic than persecution. It is against natural religion, revealed religion, and sound policy ' (Campbell, *Lives of the Chief Justices*, London, 1849, vol. ii, pp. 512–513). Mansfield was foremost among the judges in discouraging the enforcement of the penal laws. On one occasion he saved a priest from conviction on a clear case by suggesting ingenious doubts and difficulties in the evidence and so giving the jury an excuse for acquitting him (Lecky, *History of England in the Eighteenth Century*, vol. iv, p. 305).

as 1739 a leader of the Anglican Church, Bishop Warburton, had declared that 'with religious errors as such the state has no concern ', that it must not restrain a religion unless it produces grave ' civil mischiefs ', and that the penalization of Roman Catholics is not directed against the errors of their faith but against the dangerous ' political usurpations of the Court of Rome '.[1] Thus by the date of the conquest of Canada the ideas which inspired the liberal *renaissance* of the later part of the century had manifestly begun to leaven English thought.

From far earlier times, moreover, English statesmen had proved themselves willing to extend the toleration they denied to Irishmen and even to Englishmen at home to those of their fellow subjects who lived at a safer distance overseas. From the days of Charles I onwards a refuge was allowed in the American colonies for those whom the law refused the free practice of their faith at home, and for Roman Catholics as well as Protestant dissenters.   And by the Treaty of Utrecht in 1713 a precedent had been created more closely analogous to the case of Canada than the precedents of Maryland or Pennsylvania.   In Article XIV it was ' expressly provided ' that such of the French inhabitants of Acadia, now ceded to Britain, as are ' willing to remain there and to be subject to the Kingdom of Great Britain, are to enjoy the free exercise of their religion according to the usage of the Church of Rome, as far as the laws of Great Britain do allow the same '.[2]   The numbers involved were far smaller ; there were some two or three thousand Acadians in 1713 as against some seventy thousand Canadians in 1763 ;[3] but in other respects, in the simple conservative character of the illiterate peasant-population,

---

[1] Lecky, *History of England in the Eighteenth Century,* vol. vi, p. 21.

[2] Treaty of Utrecht, Article XIV.

[3] The Acadians were roughly reckoned at 500 families of 5 persons in 1714.   Colonel Vetch to the Lords of Trade, November 24, 1714, N. S. D. i, p. 5.

in their devotion to their faith and their dependence on its priests, as well as in their race and speech, the cases were much alike. But this example of the policy of toleration, applied so recently, so near at hand and under such similar conditions, was by no means encouraging. The experiment had failed completely and its close had been a tragedy.[1]

3

The failure had not been due to any lack of earnestness or perseverance on the part of the British Government at home or on the spot. Article XIV of the Treaty had stipulated that those of the population who desired to leave Acadia should be free to do so within a year ; and strong pressure was exercised by the French in the neighbouring province of Île Royale (Cape Breton) to persuade the Acadians to emigrate. A few families did so at the outset ; but the great majority, deeply attached to their old homes and discouraged by the British authorities who did not wish to see the colony depopulated, stayed where they were. For many years their lot was not unhappy. The pledge of religious freedom was strictly observed ; and the British authorities went far beyond their treaty obligations in their efforts to reconcile them to British rule, knowing as they did that the conflict with France in North America had not yet reached its final issue and bent on strengthening their new

[1] The chief English documents on this controversial subject are to be found in *Selections from the Public Documents of the Province of Nova Scotia* (Halifax, 1869), cited as N. S. D. i. See also the Calendar of two Government Letter-Books and a Commission Book, published as *Nova Scotia Archives*, ii (Halifax, 1900), cited as N. S. D. ii ; the Calendar of Nova Scotia documents in R. C. A. 1894 ; and the documents, both French and British, given in M. Placide Gaudet's study of the genealogy of the Acadian families, R. C. A. 1905, vol. ii, part iii. Parkman, in *Montcalm and Wolfe* (London, 1901) and in *A Half Century of Conflict* (London, 1907), E. Richard in *Acadia, A Lost Chapter in American History* (edited and expanded by H. d'Arles, Paris, 1916–1921), and E. Lauvrière in *La Tragédie d'un Peuple* (Paris, 1922) are open in different degrees to charges of partiality. A new scientific treatment of the whole subject, based on the documents in London, Paris, and Ottawa, is much needed.

strategic position on the flank of the remaining French colonies. For more than thirty years no attempt was made to augment the British population by immigration ; and the British Governors at Annapolis, a meagre outpost with a garrison of barely two hundred, left the Acadians to live as they pleased. No new or oppressive taxes were intro-duced. Only those feudal dues were exacted which had been paid in kind to the previous French administration. When they refused to take a full unconditional oath of allegiance to the British Crown, although the guarantee of religious freedom in the Treaty had only applied to those Acadians who were willing ' to be subject to the Kingdom of Great Britain ', no consistent effort was made to force the oath upon them by penal measures.[1] The British policy in fact was a wholehearted, if self-interested, policy of toleration, as French observers at the time confessed ; and yet it proved a miserable failure. The reason is not far to seek. The French Government, which in the Treaty had solemnly recognized the Acadians who chose to remain in Acadia to be British subjects,[2] did everything in its power to persuade them to continue to regard themselves as subjects of the King of France. To this end the Roman Catholic Church was set to play its old unseemly part as a political agency. So long as the British Government on its side was faithful to its word, French priests would not be excluded from Acadia ;[3]

[1] The Nova Scotia documents are full of the Governors' complaints as to the refusal of the oath. For a case of limited oath, see N. S. D. i, p. 84. On the other hand, it is incontestable that the Acadians were allowed the free exercise of their religion. La Jonquière, Governor of Canada and no friend of the British, reported (1750) that they did not obstruct the priests in the performance of their duties : and in an order of Louis XV (1751) it is admitted that the Acadians have enjoyed liberty of religion. See Parkman, quoting from documents in the Paris Archives de la Marine et des Colonies, in *Montcalm and Wolfe*, vol. i, pp. 99–100. See also the letter of M. Roma, a French officer at Cape Breton (1750), the text of which is given by Parkman, *op. cit.*, vol. ii, Appendix B.

[2] Articles XII and XIV.

[3] Only Recollets of the Province of Paris were shut out. Some priests were expelled, but only on the ground of their seditious activities. Two

and they laboured tirelessly to prevent their simple and credulous parishioners from making any truce with their heretic rulers. Left to themselves, these easily contented peasants must soon have yielded to the conciliatory advances and the demonstrable good faith of the British authorities : [1] it was their priests who urged them to hold aloof, to refuse the oath of allegiance, to be ready at the first hint of war to rise in arms for France and the true faith. And the Church enforced its teaching by other than spiritual weapons. The priests did not scruple to intimidate the Acadians by threats of letting loose on them the neighbouring tribes over whom the notorious missionary, Le Loutre, had acquired an extraordinary personal ascendancy.[2]

Some thirty years after the acquisition of Acadia the British Government made an important change of policy. Hitherto it had left Acadia severely alone : it had kept it as it found it, a colony of Frenchmen. But now it decided to strengthen its hold on it by settlement, and in 1749 the colony of Halifax was founded and populated with British

of these, when questioned by the Governor's Council, were openly contumacious : ' Je suis ici de la part du Roy de France' (I am here on the business of the King of France), said one, and the other spoke to the same effect (Minutes of Council, May 18, 1736, N. S. D. i, p. 103. See also N. S. D. ii, pp. 100, 105–106, 108). These two priests were frankly supported by the Governor of Île Royale (N. S. D. ii, pp. 110–111) ; for the subsequent trouble with one of them, de St. Poncy, who was at first allowed to remain in Acadia at the request of his parishioners, was finally expelled, and then returned without permission, see N. S. D. ii, pp. 114, 132, 140, 145, 149, &c. The Letter-Books in N. S. D. ii are largely taken up with this question of the priests ' encroaching little by little ', as a British official writes in 1741, ' and endeavouring to become the commanders of the parishes in which they reside ' (p. 144).

[1] Governor Nicholson was neither conciliatory nor scrupulous, but he only remained in the colony a very short time and left no permanent mark on its administration.

[2] In a letter to Le Loutre (the authenticity of which is not beyond dispute), the Bishop of Quebec protested against the severity of his methods in refusing the sacraments to the Acadians and threatening them with the hostility of the Indians. He also warned him against the consequences of his political activity. ' I reminded you a long time ago', he wrote, ' that a priest ought not to meddle with temporal affairs ' (N. S. D. i, p. 241).

emigrants. Their arrival did little to adjust the balance
of numbers ; for the Acadians were exceptionally prolific
and had by now increased to at least 12,000 souls. Nor was
the French Government diverted from its previous course
by this proof of British determination to retain Acadia.
It continued to act as if the possession of the province were
still an open question, and the priests were stimulated to
further and greater efforts. The Indians were encouraged
to molest the new British settlers and were paid by Le Loutre
himself for British scalps.[1] The unhappy Acadians were
incited anew with homilies and threats to hate and to betray
the British ; and over two thousand were now persuaded,
some of them under actual compulsion from the Indians,
to emigrate to the neighbouring French islands or to the
adjacent Acadian mainland, still claimed as French territory.[2]
For a few years longer the British continued their efforts
to bind the Acadians to their side ;[3] but when the unceasing
quarrel with France was clearly about to pass once more
from diplomatic strife to open war, when both Governments
were sending troops to North America while pretending to
be still at peace in Europe, when regular fighting had actually
begun on the disputed isthmus between the Acadian peninsula and the mainland, it was difficult to persevere in a policy
of patience which had always been wholly ineffective and now
seemed dangerous. So in 1755 it was decided that those

[1] The evidence for the French priests' use of the Indians against the
British is unimpeachable. See the dispatches from La Jonquière to the
Colonial Minister and especially the Royal Instruction of April 24, 1751,
printed by Parkman in *Montcalm and Wolfe*, vol. ii, Appendix B. As to
the payment for scalps, Prévost, Intendant at Louisbourg, wrote to the
Minister (August 16, 1753) : ' Les Sauvages ont pris, il y a un mois,
18 chevelures anglaises, et M. Le Loutre a été obligé de les payer 1800 *l.*,
argent de L'Acadie, dont je luy ay fait le remboursement ' (*ibid.*).

[2] For the miserable conditions and heavy mortality among these
emigrants, see Parkman, *Montcalm and Wolfe*, vol. i, pp. 114–115. Some
wished to return but were threatened by Le Loutre with excommunication
(p. 127).

[3] See especially Governor Cornwallis's addresses to the Acadians in 1750,
N. S. D. i, pp. 185–192.

Acadians who still refused to swear their full allegiance to
the lawful ruler of the land could not be suffered to remain
there in such a time of uncertainty and peril. In a circular
letter to his fellow Governors in the other colonies, Governor
Lawrence explained the decision. While pretending to be
neutral, he pointed out, the Acadians had constantly helped
the French and the Indians against the British. When the
fort of Beauséjour was captured, 300 of them were found
among its garrison. If they refused the oath when a British
fleet and additional troops from New England were at hand,
what might they not attempt in the coming winter when
the ships were gone and the garrison reduced? Their
removal, in fine, was 'indispensably necessary to the
security of this colony'.[1]

The Acadians, therefore, were given a last chance.
Deputies representing nine-tenths of the population were
assembled and requested to take the usual oath. They
were warned that on refusal they could no longer
be regarded as British subjects and would be removed
from the country. They were told to weigh the consequences and to take their time. To a man they refused.
Thereupon, with the aid of colonial troops from New
England, over 6,000 Acadians were taken from their homes,
set on shipboard, and transported to the British colonies
along the Atlantic coast.[2] The New England troops

---

[1] The circular letter (August 11, 1755) is in N. S. D. i, p. 277. The
question of deportation as a remedy had been raised before. The responsibility for the eventual decision was Lawrence's. The Lords of Trade
(Lord Halifax was President of the Board) wrote on March 25, 1756 :
' We have laid that part of your letter which relates to the removal of
the French inhabitants, and the steps you took in the execution of this
measure, before His Majesty's Secretary of State ; and as you represent
it to have been indispensably necessary for the security and protection of
the Province in the present critical situation of our affairs, we doubt not
but that your conduct herein will meet with His Majesty's approbation '
(N. S. D. i, p. 298).

[2] Some of the Acadians who escaped deportation by hiding in the woods
and others who succeeded in finding their way back to Acadia were not
molested after the war, and their descendants are now living there.

behaved, with some grievous exceptions, as humanely as
their task allowed : but the harrowing scene still haunts our
imaginations ; and however justifiable the act may have
seemed a century and a half ago, in view of the flagrant
dishonesty of the French Government, the open treason
of the priests, the blind and thankless docility of their
Acadian parishioners, and the danger of leaving them at
large as long as they refused to promise the full allegiance of
British subjects to the British Crown in the imminent war, it
has left a stain on the record of the British Commonwealth.
It has always been easy to argue that ' necessity knows no
law ' ; it has always been harder to prove the necessity.[1]

4

In a very few years' time a different tale was to be told.
The pitiful outcome of the policy of toleration in Acadia,
the grim proof it had afforded of the readiness of the Roman
Catholic priesthood to use their religious liberty as a means
of insidious political attack upon the Government which
granted it, the pathetic submission of the French peasantry
to their control—none of these things deterred the British
Government from trying the same policy again when the
circumstances were reproduced on a larger scale in Canada.
From the very beginning it made its purpose clear. In
the public documents which marked the first steps of the
conquest, the British representatives in Canada promised
the Canadians the same religious toleration as the Acadians
had enjoyed. Liberty to practise the Roman Catholic faith
was granted in the Articles of the Capitulation of Quebec in
1759,[2] and, in more explicit terms, in those of the Capitula-

---

[1] The case against ' necessity ' is briefly (1) that the Acadians had often
promised to be neutral and only refused the oath because it would oblige
them to fight for the British; (2) for some twenty years a form of oath
without that obligation had been tolerated ; (3) that they had only fought
for the French, as at Beauséjour, under compulsion.   In fine, was a
promise of neutrality a sufficient safeguard ?

[2] Article VI ; given in Appendix A, p. 197, below.

tion of Montreal in 1760.¹ Similarly, in the course of the
peace negotiations in 1761, Pitt stated the intentions of his
ministry in the following words : ' As to what concerns the
public profession of the Roman Catholic religion in Canada,
the new subjects of his Britannic Majesty shall be maintained in that privilege without interruption or molestation.'²
In religious matters, therefore, the policy of suppression was
once more ruled out at the start ; and it was soon apparent
that, as in Acadia after the Treaty of Utrecht, the promise
of toleration was no merely formal pledge, no mere diplomatic
counter thrown into the scale to turn the balance of negotiation. The intentions of the British officers who signed the
Capitulations were as genuinely conciliatory as those of the
British ministers who negotiated the subsequent treaty.
Had it been otherwise, had the men who conquered Canada
felt and acted as conquerors too often do, had they treated
the French-Canadians as a beaten and subjected people,
had they been arrogant and cruel, derided their foreign
ways, shown no more respect especially for their religion
than was required by the letter of their obligations, then,
however wise the decisions of ministers in London might
have been, however generous the terms of the coming
treaty, the prospects of welding the new colony happily
and firmly into the frame of the British Commonwealth
would have been gravely, perhaps irreparably, injured.
What did in fact occur may be gathered from the dispatches
of the military governors of Canada in the interval between
the conquest and the establishment of a civil administration.
' I feel the highest satisfaction ', reported General Gage,

¹ Articles XXVII to XXXV ; given in Appendix A, pp. 198–201, below.
² ' Papers relating to Mr. Pitt's negotiation for peace between England
and France ' (P. H., vol. xv, p. 1062). General Murray's report from
Quebec (June 6, 1762) confirmed the Government's policy. ' The Canadians ', he wrote, ' are very ignorant and extremely tenacious of their
religion. Nothing can contribute as much to make them staunch subjects
to his Majesty as the new Government giving them every reason to imagine
no alteration is to be attempted in that point ' (C. D., p. 71).

who was in charge of the district of Montreal, in 1762, ' that
I am able to inform you that, during my command in this
Government, I have made it my constant care and attention
that the Canadians should be treated agreeably to His
Majesty's kind and humane intentions. No invasion on their
properties or insult on their persons has gone unpunished.
All reproaches on their subjection by the fate of arms, revil-
ings on their customs or country, and all reflexions on their
religion have been discountenanced and forbid. No distinction has been made betwixt the Briton and the Canadian,
but [they have been] equally regarded as subjects of the
same Prince.' ¹ In a similar strain wrote Colonel Burton
from the district of Three Rivers : ' The inhabitants and
chiefly the peasantry seem very happy in the change of their
masters. They are protected in the free exercise of their
religion ; they begin to feel that they are no longer slaves,
but that they do enjoy the full benefit of that indulgent and
benign Government which constitutes the peculiar felicity
of all who are subjects to the British Empire.' ² Still more
remarkable testimony to the spirit of British rule is proffered
by the report, dated June 6, 1762, in which General Murray,
Governor of Quebec, describes the treatment and the sentiments of the *habitants* or ' Order of Peasantry '.

' They [the former French Government] took particular
pains to persuade them the English were worse than brutes,
and that if they prevailed the Canadians would be ruled
with a rod of iron and be exposed to every outrage. This
most certainly did not a little contribute to make them so
obstinate in their defence. However, ever since the conquest,
I can with the greatest truth assert that the troops have
lived with the inhabitants in an harmony unexampled even
at home. I must here, in justice to those under my command in this Government, observe to Your Lordship that,
in the winter which immediately followed the reduction of

¹ C. D., pp. 91–92.   ² *Ibid.*, p 87.

this Province, when from the calamities of war and a bad
harvest the inhabitants of these parts were exposed to all the
horrors of famine, the officers of every rank, even in the
lowest, generously contributed towards alleviating the distress of the unfortunate Canadians by a large subscription;
the British merchants and traders readily and cheerfully
assisted in this good work; even the poor soldiers threw in
their mite and gave a day's provisions or a day's pay in the
month towards the fund. By this means a quantity of provisions were purchased and distributed with great care and
assiduity to numbers of poor families, who without this
charitable support must inevitably have perished.'[1]

Deeds are better than words; and the conduct of the
British army, officers and men, towards their vanquished
enemies, revealing as it did the British character at its best
and kindliest, seemed to promise the Canadians as surely
as any treaties or capitulations the liberty they craved to
continue their old life. At the close of his report Murray
confidently affirmed that the behaviour of the British army
of occupation had transformed their previous attitude and

[1] C. D., p. 80. The British treatment of the French-Canadians during
the preceding war had been similarly humane. Outrages were promptly and
severely punished: and special protection was given to the convents (G. M.
Wrong, *The Fall of Canada*, Oxford, 1914, pp. 56, 68, 201). On the night
of the capitulation of Montreal, Amherst wrote to a friend, 'I have as much
pleasure in telling you Canada belongs to the King as I had in receiving
the capitulation of it this day. . . . I entered the inhabited country with
all the savages and I have not hurt the head of a peasant, his wife or his
child, not a house burnt, or a disorder committed; the country people
amazed; won't believe what they see; the notions they had of our
cruelties from the exercise of their own savages, drove them into the woods;
I have fetched them out and put them quiet in their habitations, and they
are vastly happy.' His subsequent order to the army contained the
following: 'The General is confident that, when the troops are informed
this country is the King's, they will not disgrace themselves by the least
appearance of inhumanity, or by any unsoldierlike behaviour of seeking
for plunder; but that, as the Canadians are now become British subjects,
they may feel the good effect of his Majesty's protection.' Compare
Amherst's Proclamation of September 22, 1760 (ordering *inter alia* payment
in money and at regular rates for all goods and for the use of horses, carts,
and sleighs) (C. D., p. 38).

that, convinced ' that the free exercise of their religion will be continued to them once Canada is irrevocably ceded by a Peace, the people will soon become faithful and good subjects of his Majesty '.[1]

Their expectations were quickly realized. On February 10, 1763, the Treaty of Paris was concluded, and in its fourth Article his Britannic Majesty solemnly agreed ' to grant the liberty of the Catholick religion to the inhabitants of Canada ' and undertook ' to give the most precise and most effectual orders, that his new Roman Catholick subjects may profess the worship of their religion according to the rites of the Romish church, as far as the laws of Great Britain permit '.[2] The official instructions to General Murray, who was appointed first civil Governor of Canada, directed him to ' conform with great exactness to the stipulations of this clause '.[3]

5

In thus renewing their policy of toleration British ministers had not shut their eyes to the lessons of their experience in Acadia. They were determined that the free exercise of the Roman Catholic religion should not again be used as a cloak for asserting the authority of the Church in political affairs and intriguing for the recovery of Canada by France. Writing to General Murray in the autumn of 1763 to inform him of his appointment, the Secretary of State, Lord Egremont, warns him that the French may try to take advantage of the concession of religious freedom to the Canadians ' in order

[1] C. D., p. 80.

[2] The full text of the clause is given in Appendix A, p. 206, below.

[3] Instructions to Governor Murray, par. 28, C. D., p. 191 [K., p. 31 ; E. & G., p. 11]. A concise account of the *Régime Militaire* is given in chap. iv of W. P. M. Kennedy's able study of Canadian constitutional development (*The Constitution of Canada*, Oxford, 1922). The old tradition that the *Régime* was tyrannical survives in F. X. Garneau (*Histoire du Canada*, 5th edition, Paris, 1920, vol. i, p. 297) ; but it has been corrected by modern French-Canadian scholars, e. g. T. Chapais, *Cours d'Histoire du Canada* (Quebec, 1912), vol. i, pp. 7–8. For contemporary French-Canadian opinion, see p. 73, below. See also p. 23, n. 1, below.

to keep up their connexion with France, and by means of the priests to preserve such an influence over the Canadians as may induce them to join, whenever opportunity should offer, in any attempt to recover that country '. Murray is therefore advised to keep a close watch on the priests and promptly to remove any of them ' who shall attempt to go out of their sphere and who shall busy themselves in any civil matters '. Egremont then explains the qualifying phrase— *as far as the laws of Great Britain permit*—attached in the treaty to the pledge of religious freedom. To the casual reader this phrase might seem to nullify the concession altogether, since at this date, as has been seen, the laws of Great Britain did not permit the free exercise of the Roman Catholic religion at all. But the great body of penal legislation in Britain was intended to apply only to Roman Catholicism in England and Scotland, as the Irish penal laws to Roman Catholicism in Ireland. On one point, however, the laws of Great Britain were of universal application in every part of the British Commonwealth ; nowhere on British soil could the ' political usurpations ' of the Roman Church be countenanced. Thus Egremont defines the laws in question as those which prohibit absolutely all Popish hierarchy in any of the dominions belonging to the Crown of Great Britain. ' This matter ', he continues, ' was clearly understood in the negotiation of the Definitive Treaty. The French ministers proposed to insert the words, *comme ci-devant*, in order that the Roman religion should continue to be exercised in the same manner as under their government ; and they did not give up the point, till they were plainly told that it would be deceiving them to admit those words, for the King had not the power to tolerate that religion in any other manner than *as far as the laws of Great Britain permit.*' [1]

---

[1] Egremont to Murray, August 13, 1763, C. D., p. 169. The letter concludes with instructing Murray, while ' attending with the utmost

On this vital question, then, of the political pretensions and activities of the Roman Church there was to be no ambiguity : the Pope was to exercise no authority whatever, spiritual or temporal, in Canada : but, apart from that, in the profession and practice of their faith Catholics in Canada were to be as free as Protestants. It soon appeared, moreover, that in civil life they were to be relieved, in some degree at any rate, of the disqualifications imposed by law on Catholics in the British Isles. Already in the period of military rule between the conquest and the establishment of civil government, French-Canadians had been temporarily appointed without reference to their religion to act as judges and to hold commissions in the Canadian militia.[1] And Murray had not been long in office before he found that in a country, in which the Roman Catholics outnumbered the Protestants by 350 to 1, justice could not be done unless the former could sit on juries as freely as the latter. In 1764, with the unanimous agreement of his council, he promulgated an ordinance, establishing the civil courts, which allowed ' all his Majesty's subjects in this colony to be admitted to juries without distinction ',[2] granting thereby to Roman Catholics in Canada a share in the functions of British citizenship which was denied by law to all their co-religionists in Britain till

vigilance to the behaviour of the priests ', to act with great caution in this ' delicate ' matter of religion and to ' avoid anything that can give the least unnecessary alarm or disgust to His Majesty's new subjects '. Not unnaturally an exception was to be made in the case of Le Loutre, who was to be refused the right to remain in the province. Kingsford, *History of Canada* (Toronto and London, 1892), vol. v, p. 172.

[1] ' The governors are authorised to nominate to all posts vacant in the militia, and may begin by signing commissions in favour of those who have lately enjoyed such posts under His Most Christian Majesty' (Proclamation by General Amherst, September 22, 1760, C. D., p. 40. Judge Allier's Commission, January 16, 1760, *ibid.*, p. 36). No office under the Crown, civil or military, was tenable by Catholics in the British Isles.

[2] Ordinance of September 17, 1764, C. D., p. 205 [K., p. 37]. For the unanimity of Council, see Murray to the Lords of Trade, October 29, 1764 (*ibid.*, p. 231).

1791 and to those who were unwilling to swear an oath denouncing the civil power of the Pope till 1846. The same ordinance extended to the Canadian legal profession the right to practise in the Court of Common Pleas, though not in the superior Court of King's Bench. These concessions were not indeed to pass unquestioned. They were vigorously denounced as violations of the laws of Great Britain and an unwarrantable and 'unconstitutional' extension of the liberty promised in the Treaty by the British Protestant immigrants, to whom, as will be seen, the policy of toleration was by no means acceptable.[1] And Murray himself seems to have been uncertain as to whether the Government at home would regard these measures as strictly legal. Commenting on the copy of the ordinance which he sent to London, he declares that, if two hundred Protestants are to be made perpetual judges of the lives and property' of the eighty thousand French-Canadians, many of the latter will take advantage of the provision of the Treaty of Paris allowing them freely to emigrate to France or elsewhere.[2] 'I flatter myself', he writes later to the Board of Trade, ' there will be some remedy found out even in the laws for the relief of this people . . . a race, who, could they be indulged with a few privileges, which the laws of England deny to Roman Catholics at home, would soon get the better of every national antipathy to their conquerors

[1] The Presentments of the Grand Jury of Quebec (October 16, 1764) declared that Roman Catholics ' by the laws are disabled from holding any office, trust or power, more especially in a judicial capacity ', and cited 3 James I, chap. v, as forbidding them to practise law. In a paragraph added later the jurymen denied that they desired to ' remove every Roman Catholic from holding any office ', and limited their complaint to the admission of Roman Catholics ' as jurors in a cause betwixt two Protestants '. In a counter-statement the French jurymen argued that 3 James I, chap. v, ' only refers to Catholics who may enter the Kingdom ' (C. D., pp. 212–223).

[2] Article IV. The time allowed was eighteen months from the ratification of the treaty. Sale of estates and removal of property were to be permitted : see text, p. 207, below. For Murray's comment on the ordinance, see C. D., p. 206, nn. 2–5.

and become the most faithful and most useful set of men in this American Empire.'[1] The Home authorities, it seems, were of Murray's mind. The ordinance remained in force.

6

The religion of the French-Canadians was the most important element in their nationality ; but there were two other elements which were equally endangered by foreign conquest and to which they clung with a devotion as simple and habitual and scarcely less intense—the language of their fathers and the system of law on which their rights of property were based. From the standpoint of the British Government these questions of language and law were quite as difficult as the question of religion. It was not as if the new colony could permanently retain its previous character as a purely French community : its inclusion within the British Commonwealth implied the free entry and the steady increase of a British population. The prospects of Canada as a field for British settlement and trade had been the chief argument of those who had urged its retention at the close of the war ; and after the cession the Government did everything in its power to encourage immigration. It was recognized, indeed, that Nova Scotia and the Acadian coast-line, being more thinly populated by French colonists than the banks of the St. Lawrence, were more suitable for British settlement than Canada : and for this reason a new boundary line for Canada was drawn so as to include in the colony of Nova Scotia the territory contained at the present day in the province of New Brunswick.[2] But it was none the less intended from the first

[1] Murray to the Lords of Trade, October 29, 1764, C. D., p. 231 [K., p. 40]. The question was soon to be settled by an 'opinion' of the Crown lawyers : see p. 51, below.
[2] The Lords of Trade reporting to Egremont on the general character and prospects of the new colonies, pointed out that 'the new settlers upon this tract of land will with greater facility be made amenable to the

to foster British settlement in Canada as well. In their report to the Secretary of State on the colonies acquired by the Treaty the Lords of Trade stated that, while the number of French inhabitants in Canada must ' greatly exceed for a very long period of time ' that of any British immigrants and while the ' ancient inhabitants ' should be secured ' in all the titles, rights and privileges granted to them by treaty ', the number of British settlers should be as much as possible increased.[1] Detailed instructions were therefore given to Governor Murray for the preparation and regulation of new settlements. The whole province was to be surveyed with this object as soon as might be convenient ; and in the meantime townships were to be laid out, if possible with access to the St. Lawrence ; towns planned, with special attention to sites for fortifications, barracks, and a church, and with the allotment of a sufficient acreage for the maintenance of a minister and a schoolmaster ; careful provisions framed for granting lands in proportion to the settler's capacity to cultivate them ; and a proclamation as to these land-grants, containing an advertisement of ' the natural advantages of the soil and climate and its peculiar conveniences for trade and navigation ', published at Murray's discretion ' in all the colonies in North America '.[2]

jurisdiction of Nova Scotia than to that of Canada '. They also urged that ' the utmost attention should immediately be given to the speedy settlement of this tract of country ' (June 8, 1763, C. D., p. 142).

[1] Ibid., p. 142. Cf. Egremont's reply, p. 149.

[2] Instructions to Governor Murray, pars. 44–56, C. D., pp. 194–198. In the light of these instructions, which, as is clear from the paragraphs referring to the local features of Canada such as the timber between Lake Champlain and the St. Lawrence and the iron mines at St. Maurice, were not merely an unconsidered copy of instructions sent to other governors, it is difficult to accept the report of the Lords of Trade of November 3, 1763 (suggesting that, as Canada has a large French population, it is unnecessary to make other provisions or offer other encouragements for settlement ' for the present, than what are contained in the draft of the instructions, &c.'), as proof of a definite policy of segregating the French from the British. Similarly, as regards the omission of Canada when Nova Scotia is mentioned as a colony in which settlements should be fostered (Lords of Trade, August 5, 1763, C. D., p. 153). See C. W. Alvord,

Schemes of land-settlement are apt to outrun the limits of practical possibility, and these projects of 1763 were to prove as premature as 'booms' of a later day. But it is important to remember that British ministers approached the problems of French-Canadian nationality with the definite purpose in their minds of a considerable British immigration into Canada. Clearly, in that event, the perpetual maintenance of national differences was bound to increase the difficulties of government. Clearly it would be easier to organize and control a community whose members all spoke the same tongue, possessed the same system of law, and followed the same legal procedure. It has always been the tendency of autocratic Governments to make such uniformity their aim and to secure it, if need be, by rigorous coercion. And to adopt such a course in Canada British statesmen had the power if they had the will. The French language might have been, as far as possible, ignored and handicapped,[1] and the legal system replaced entirely by the English. In other words the French-Canadians might only have been accepted as fellow subjects of the British Crown on condition that they spoke the English language and conformed to the English pattern of law. Many of the Canadians would in that case have sold their lands and goods and left the country : but those who remained could doubtless have been forced more or less effectively into the British mould—for a time.

Such a course was not to be expected from the men who had committed themselves to a liberal policy of toleration

The Mississippi Valley in British Politics (Cleveland, U.S.A., 1917), vol. i, p. 174 and p. 208. Nova Scotia was certainly preferred, but Canada was by no means ruled out. For further comment, see p. 34, n. 1, below.

[1] By prescribing English as the only language for all official or legal purposes, as was done in Cape Colony in 1827. A more positive and systematic suppression of a language seems to belong rather to nineteenth-century nationalism than to eighteenth-century ideas. Such a policy was adopted by the Dutch at the Cape towards the French Huguenot immigrants after 1685, but they only numbered about 200.

in religion ; and from the outset no attempt was made to restrict in any way the use of the French language, nor was a knowledge of English rendered obligatory even for official purposes. Difficulties were indeed inevitable, especially in legal procedure, difficulties which tended to make the educated French-Canadians needlessly sensitive and suspicious of British designs against their language.[1] But Murray was well aware of the difficulties and did all he could to ease them. When the French members of the Grand Jury of Quebec ask the Governor and Council for an official translation of the presentment drawn up by their British colleagues, it is at once conceded.[2] The admission of French-Canadian lawyers to practise in court is regarded as a necessity because, so Murray says, ' we have not yet got one English barrister or attorney who understands the French language.'[3] And it is significant that the official *Quebec Gazette*, the first printed publication in Canada, is produced at a considerable increase of labour and cost in parallel columns of French and English.[4]

[1] For examples of inevitable confusion, see the statement of the French members of the Grand Jury, C. D., pp. 216–219.

[2] C. D., p. 216.

[3] Writing to the Lords of Trade (October 29, 1764) Murray declares that ' the greatest part of this valuable people ' will emigrate if they are not allowed ' judges and lawyers who understand their language ' (C. D., p. 231). The French jurymen point out that the admission only of English lawyers involves the use of interpreters ' who would scarcely ever give the exact meaning of the matter in hand ' (*ibid.*, p. 221).

[4] Kingsford, *History of Canada*, vol. v, p. 152. Official publications in the Union of South Africa are similarly printed both in Dutch and in English, in accordance with par. 137 of the Act of Union (1909) which runs as follows : ' Both the English and Dutch languages shall be official languages of the Union, and shall be treated on a footing of equality, and possess and enjoy equal freedom, rights, and privileges ; all records, journals, and proceedings of Parliament shall be kept in both languages, and all Bills, Acts and notices of general public importance or interest issued by the Government of the Union shall be in both languages.'

7

The question of the legal system was far more intricate. To the substitution of English for French *criminal* law there could be small objection. The English criminal law was still and for years to come a brutal law, but it was almost lenient in comparison with the French. Torture, for example, had always been regarded as foreign to English practice and its use for a long time past had been reprobated by public opinion ; but such barbarous penalties as ' breaking on the wheel ' were regularly imposed in France till the time of the Revolution.[1] The introduction of the English criminal law, therefore, could scarcely be regarded as a hardship by most French-Canadians, though they might at first be somewhat puzzled, and the aristocratic temper of their *seigneurs* somewhat shocked, by a device so strange to them and so democratic in principle as trial by jury. But it was otherwise with the *civil* law, concerned as it was so much more closely with their normal life and particularly with the ownership of property. ' The Custom of Paris ', as the code was called, had come from old France long ago. The sentiment and usage of generations had endeared it to them : its very singularity marked it as their most distinctive national possession. Yet it was far from an ideal code. No one sympathized with the traditions of French Canada more earnestly than Murray ; but Murray himself in deploring ' the litigious disposition' of the French-Canadians

---

[1] ' Whereas the certainty and lenity of the criminal law of England ' was the wording of the Quebec Act (see p. 214, below). In the debate on this Act Lord North described is as ' a more refined and a more merciful law ' (Cavendish, *Debates on the Canada Bill in 1774* (London, 1839), p. 12 [K., p. 87]). The torture known as the *peine forte et dure* was not abolished in England till 1772 ; but it had not been used since one case in 1726 and not as a method of execution since 1658 (Maitland, *Constitutional History of England*, p. 212). Macaulay, in preparation for his Indian penal code, studied the old French criminal law and was horrified at its unfairness and cruelty ; for his lively comments see Sir G. O. Trevelyan, *The American Revolution*, vol. ii, p. 74, note.

expressed his belief that ' the many formalities in their procedures and the multiplicity of instruments to be drawn up on every occasion seem to encourage this disposition '.[1] Cumbrous, intricate, old-fashioned, it was clearly inadequate for the needs of a progressive community. How then could British colonists, whose immigration was to be encouraged, how especially could British traders, be expected to endure it ? Yet how could it be superseded without undermining the whole existing system of property in Canada and plunging the legal relations of its people into chaos ? By such considerations British ministers were not unnaturally perplexed, and the difficulty was not lightened by a change in the administration at Whitehall. In August, 1763, on the sudden death of Lord Egremont, the duties of Secretary of State for the Southern Department, which embraced the American colonies, had been taken over by Lord Halifax ; and in September the young Lord Shelburne, who already, unlike most British statesmen, had read widely and thought deeply on colonial problems, had been succeeded after a few months in office by Lord Hillsborough as President of the Board of Trade. The notorious Proclamation of October 7, which formally inaugurated civil government in Canada, was thus mainly the work of men new to their posts and uninstructed in the details of colonial policy, hurriedly adapting to their purposes the materials their predecessors had bequeathed them.[2] Under such circumstances no adequate consideration was or could be given to this intricate and highly technical question of law. The result was the framing of the following clause in the Proclamation : ' All persons inhabiting in or resorting to our said colonies may confide in our royal protection for the enjoyment of the benefit of the

[1] Report of the State of the Government of Quebec, June 5, 1762, C. D., p. 53.

[2] See vol. i, chap. viii, of Alvord's valuable *Mississippi Valley in British Politics*, based on detailed study of contemporary documents ; and also his earlier paper, *The Genesis of the Proclamation of 1763* (Michigan Pioneer and Historical Society, December 13, 1907).

laws of our realm of England ; for which purpose we have given power under our Great Seal to the Governors of our said colonies respectively to erect and constitute . . . courts of judicature and public justice . . . for hearing and determining all causes, as well criminal as civil, according to law and equity, and *as near as may be agreeable to the laws of England.*'[1]

It would seem as if in the matter of law as of religion the policy of the British Government was to depend on the interpretation of a qualifying phrase. But if that was the intention the use of these particular words was unfortunate. For the same or a similar formula had usually been inserted in the constitutions and charters of the earlier colonies in America ; and since in those colonies, being ' settled ' colonies of Englishmen, the maintenance of the main body of English law had been a matter of course, the formula had simply been intended to allow for a certain elasticity in the application of English law to local conditions. Evidently the same formula as applied to a ' ceded ' colony, already peopled by men whose race, language, and traditional system of law were not English but French, might be otherwise interpreted. But the Proclamation was not addressed to the colony of Quebec alone : it embraced the other new colonies of East Florida, West Florida, and Grenada, in which the European population, though also foreign, was small and in which there could be no question of permanently maintaining a foreign system of law. That for all four colonies, moreover, the authors of the Proclamation intended at least the main body of law to be English law was evident from the explicit promise of its ' benefit '. as an encouragement to British immigration. There were passages, moreover, in Murray's Commission and Instructions which seemed to imply that English law would be in force : lands, for example, were to be granted under English forms.[2]

---

[1] C. D., p. 65 [K., p. 19 ; B. K., p. 6].

[2] C. D., pp. 179, 195–196. See also the British-Canadian complaint, *ibid.*, p. 514 : and the alteration of the Instructions, p. 71, below.

In the absence, therefore, of any more specific orders Murray naturally took the qualifying phrase to mean what it had always meant, and, not without misgivings, construed the Proclamation as prescribing the replacement, subject to necessary minor adjustments, of the whole system of French-Canadian law by the English. He made this clear enough when in his ordinance of September 17, 1764, establishing the civil courts he provided that the French ' laws and customs ' should be recognized in the Court of Common Pleas in all cases ' between the natives of this province, where the cause of action arose *before October* 1, 1764 '.[1]

If this was indeed their deliberate intention, there were serious reasons, apart from the question of expediency, why British ministers should have hesitated to make so drastic a decision. It was a moot point, not decided till Lord Mansfield's famous judgement in 1774, whether the King-in-Council could alone and without Act of Parliament abolish the legal system of a ' ceded ' colony. Mansfield decided that the King did possess this power, but in the same judgement he stated the unquestionable rule that ' Articles of capitulation, upon which the country is surrendered . . . are sacred and inviolate ',[2] and in its practical results the abolition of French-Canadian law might be regarded as an infringement of the terms on which the Marquis de Vaudreuil had surrendered Montreal in 1760. His request, indeed, that ' the French and Canadians shall continue to be governed according to the Custom of Paris and the laws and usages established for this country ' had been set down in Article XLII as answered by ' the preceding articles and particularly by the last ' ; and Article XLI had firmly stated that the people who remained in the colony ' become subjects of the

---

[1] C. D., p. 207 [K., p. 38].
[2] Lord Mansfield's judgement in Campbell *v.* Hall, given in C. D., p. 522 [K., p. 79].

King '. But, although in none of the articles was the maintenance of French-Canadian law explicitly provided for, Article XXXIV had granted that the religious communities should retain their possessions, including ' the property and revenues of the seigniories and other estates ', and Article XXXVII had promised that *les seigneurs des terres* and all other French-Canadians should suffer no loss or damage to their property on any pretence. Now the old feudal dues were as much an essential part of the *seigneurs'* property as of that of the religious communities : and how could they be paid in either case if the whole system of French-Canadian law were overthrown ? Would any property, indeed, be safe from loss or damage unless the laws ' by which that property was created, defined, and secured,' were continued in force ? [1]

Five years later, when the deplorable results of the Proclamation as interpreted by Murray had long been known to any one who knew anything of Canada, Lord Hillsborough disclaimed any intention on the Government's part of doing what had in fact been done. ' Whatever the legal sense conveyed by the words of that Proclamation may be ', he wrote, ' I certainly know what was the intention of those who drew the Proclamation, having myself been concerned therein ; and I can take upon me to aver that it never entered into our idea to overturn the laws and customs of Canada with regard to property.' Their idea, he explained, had been that French-Canadian customs should be recognized in Canada in the same way as certain local customs such as ' Gavel-kind ' and ' Borough English ' were recognized in parts of England.[2] An ingenious excuse, but

[1] Report of Attorney-General Thurlow in 1773, C. D., p. 443. Masères also makes this point in his evidence before the H. of C., K., p. 118 : cf. p. 83; n. 1, below. See Munro, *The Seigniorial System in Canada* (New York, 1907), pp. 189–190. The text of the Articles is given in Appendix A, p. 198, below.

[2] Hillsborough to Carleton, March 6, 1768, C. D., p. 297 [K., p. 57].

with an air about it of being wise after the event ; and even
then not over-wise.   For to suppose that Canadian laws and
customs with regard to property could be maintained by
treating them like some trivial anachronism which had
survived in Kent was utterly to misconceive the situation
in Canada.   The truth seems to be that ministers, preoccupied in the first instance with the problem of the Indian
territories, which the outbreak of Pontiac's War had
rendered so grave and so urgent and to which a large part
of the Proclamation was devoted, and secondly with their
desire to promote British immigration into all the newly
acquired colonies, overlooked in their haste, perhaps also
in their ignorance, the peculiar needs of Canada, and
prescribed the general introduction of English law in the
comfortable belief that, if indeed it should occasion any
difficulties in Canada, they might somehow or other solve
themselves by virtue of the qualifying phrase.[1]   But
it is also true beyond a doubt that ministers did not
deliberately and in full knowledge of the facts set out to
destroy the whole fabric of Canadian law.   Their treatment
of the religious question had shown that their primary
object was to conciliate the French-Canadians and win their
allegiance to the British Commonwealth.   The increase of
the British population in the province was important,
but not so important.   Obviously they did not mean to
jeopardize the attainment of their first object in pursuit
of the second.   To combine the two at all was a delicate

---

[1] Alvord propounds the attractive theory that the Proclamation,
the draft of which was left unfinished by Shelburne, was originally meant
to apply only to the other three colonies with their small foreign populations, and not to Quebec, which was to be separately dealt with in the
Commission and Instructions to the Governor ; and that the inclusion
of Quebec in the same Proclamation was a sheer blunder on Hillsborough's
part (see *The Mississippi Valley in British Politics*, vol. i, chap. viii, and
the essay on the Proclamation, cited p. 30, n. 2, above).   But this theory
is largely based on the supposition that it had been decided *not* to encourage
British settlement in Quebec ; and the evidence for this is not convincing.
See p. 26, n. 2, above.

and difficult task ; they had attempted it in the matter of the legal system without adequate knowledge or reflection ; and they had made a serious blunder.

8

The difficulties which were bound to arise from the introduction of British settlers into French Canada were soon to appear in the matter of constitutional as well as civil law. Could a form of government be set up in the province of Quebec suited equally to its old and new inhabitants ?

The Proclamation of October 7, 1763, with the attendant Governors' Commissions and Instructions established practically the same constitutional system for each of the four new colonies. The supreme civil authority was vested in a Governor, appointed as usual by the British Government and subject to control by the Secretary of State, and Murray's commission was that of ' Captain-General and Governor-in-Chief in the province of Quebec '. In civil matters the Lieutenant-Governors, who were similarly appointed for the districts of Montreal and Three Rivers, were subordinate to him ; but in the command of their troops they claimed and exercised an independent authority, on the ground that in his military capacity Murray was under the orders of the Commander-in-Chief of all the British forces in North America.[1] In the exercise of both executive and legislative functions the Governor was to be assisted by a Council of twelve members, all of whom, like the Governor himself, were not only to take the same oaths of abjuration in support of the Protestant succession to the Crown but also the same declaration against transubstantia-

---

[1] The friction inevitable from this arrangement was increased when General Gage, Lieutenant-Governor of Montreal, succeeded General Amherst as Commander-in-Chief. Murray protested to Halifax (see his letter of October 15, 1764, C. D., p. 210), but the system remained unchanged.

tion and other Roman Catholic doctrines as were required
by statute from members of the British House of Commons.[1]
In this respect, therefore, a similar political disability was
imposed on Roman Catholics in Canada as in the mother
country. The twelve members of Council were to include
the two Lieutenant-Governors, the Chief ·Justice of the
Province, and the Surveyor-General of Customs for the
northern district of America—all officials appointed directly
by the Home Government. The other eight members were
also to be appointed in London, but on the nomination of the
Governor, who would have power, normally but not necessarily with Council's consent, to suspend a member from his
duties pending a decision on the case from Whitehall.[2]
The Governor was empowered ' by the advice ' of Council
(not necessarily, therefore, ' with its consent ') to make rules
and regulations, or in other words to legislate by ordinance
and proclamation, ' for the peace, order and good government ' of the province, ' taking care that nothing be passed
or done that shall any ways tend to affect the life, limb or
liberty of the subject or to the imposing any duties or
taxes ; and that all such rules and regulations be transmitted to us, by the first opportunity after they are passed
and made, for our approbation or disallowance '.[3] While
the Quebec Government could not raise revenue itself, the
Governor was of course enabled, with the advice *and* consent
of Council, to expend ' for the support of the Government '
the funds yielded by taxes already in existence or imposed by
Parliament.[4] In levying and employing troops the Governor
could act alone.[5] Thus in the executive and legislative field
the Governor or the Governor-in-Council were to enjoy the
usual wide powers of what is known as ' Crown Colony '

---

[1] Commission, C. D., p. 174 ; Instructions, par. 3, *ibid.*, p. 182 [K., p. 28;
E. & G., p. 3].

[2] Instructions, pars. 2 and 7, *ibid.*, pp.182–183 [K., pp. 27–28; E. & G., p. 3].

[3] Instructions, par. 11, *ibid.*, p. 185 [K., p. 28; E. & G., p. 5].

[4] Commission, C. D., p. 179.   [5] Commission, *ibid.*, p. 177.

government; and the whole personnel of the administration were directly or indirectly responsible to the Home Government and all its actions were subject to their supervision and correction. As to the judiciary, apart from the Chief Justice of the province who was directly appointed from England, the Governor, with the consent of a majority of Council, could appoint judges or magistrates, but they were to hold office ' during pleasure only '.[1]

The contrast between the relatively autocratic government thus provided for Canada and the self-governing institutions of the neighbouring British colonies is manifest at once. But there were obvious reasons for it. The Canadians, after all, were the enemies of yesterday; however effective the policy of conciliation might prove to be, it was clearly premature to give straightway the same confidence to these new members of the Commonwealth as to the old, and to trust them with the same measure of self-government as the inhabitants of the ' settled ' colonies, British subjects from their birth, enjoyed as a matter of right. The Canadians, moreover, were Roman Catholics; and tolerant as British ministers had proved themselves to be in Canada, they were not yet prepared to establish in any part of George III's dominions a little Catholic parliament.[2] And lastly, the Canadians had had no experience whatever in self-government; they knew nothing about it even in theory; and they were quite incapable as yet of fulfilling its responsibilities. To them in fact a simple transition from French to British autocracy would seem natural and no hardship; and since in a ' ceded ' colony the law allowed the Crown to establish any form of government it chose, there was nothing to prevent the King of England from stepping straight into the shoes of the King of France, and ruling Canada, not indeed with the same absolute personal power as the Bourbon autocrats, but

[1] Instructions, par. 20, C. D., p. 188 [K., p. 30; E. & G., p. 9].
[2] See the debate on the Quebec Act, p. 99, below.

without allowing the Canadian people any more voice than before in the control of their affairs.   But if this is what was done and rightly done in 1763, the maintenance of an autocratic form of government could not be regarded as a permanent policy.   For a time the French-Canadians might remain contented or indifferent ; but although the *régime* of Murray and Carleton might be more or less as illiberal in form as the *régime* of Duquesnes and Vaudreuil, they could not but find it different in spirit ; they would breathe a freer air on British soil than French, and sooner or later a day would come when they would aspire to the same political liberty as other members of the Commonwealth possessed.

But British ministers had a more immediate reason for conceiving the system established in 1763 as by no means a permanent form of government for Canada.   The British colonists whose immigration they had decided to foster would relish the maintenance of the political traditions of French Canada as little as that of its laws.   Neither contentment nor indifference, ministers were well aware, could be expected from Britons born and bred if they were deprived for any length of time of rights which they regarded as an inalienable heritage.   Thus the Lords of Trade, who had reported all the new colonies to be favourable for settlement and needing it, had written to Halifax to point out that ' it will give confidence and encouragement ' to immigrants ' that an immediate and public declaration should be made of the intended permanent constitution and that the power of calling Assemblies should be inserted in the first Commissions '.[1]   Accordingly the Proclamation of October 7 declared that the Governors of the free colonies had been instructed that ' *as soon as the state and circumstances of the said colonies shall admit thereof,* they shall, with the advice and consent of the members of our Council, summon and

---

[1] Lords of Trade to Halifax, October 4, 1763, C. D., p. 156.

call General Assemblies ' ; [1] and Murray was authorized in his Commission to constitute, when the time should come, a General Assembly in the province of Quebec of persons ' elected by the major part of the freeholders '.[2] Before they took their seats members of the Assembly were to take the oaths and declaration which have been mentioned above as required from members of the Council.

This last provision may well have seemed to the drafters of the Proclamation almost a matter of course. A Roman Catholic Assembly was, as has already been remarked, inconceivable as yet to British statesmen. It was one thing to allow Catholics in Canada the free exercise of their religion and to absolve them from the oppressive payments and penalties prescribed by law in England : it was quite another thing, considering the political record of their Church, to give them direct political power as members of the legislature—a power which was not for generations to be conceded to Catholics at home. But, if Catholics were disqualified, could ministers have seriously intended to establish an Assembly in Canada at all—at least within any measurable time ? They doubtless hoped for a steady increase in the British population, but their advisers had warned them that for a long period to come the French population must in any event continue to exceed it.[3] Did they really contemplate, then, the reproduction in Canada of the Protestant ascendancy in Ireland, the subjection of a Catholic majority to a legislature representing only a Protestant minority ? It is surely more probable that their hasty pursuance of a double object had led them to a second blunder ; that, as in their sudden abrogation of French-Canadian law, so in this promise of a Protestant Assembly, they were thinking first and last of the promotion of immigration ; and that in holding out a prospect of representative government in the

[1] C. D., p. 165 [K., p. 19; B. K., p. 6].
[2] Ibid., p. 175.   [3] See p. 26, above.

same manifesto and in the same terms for all four colonies they had either overlooked or set aside for future consideration the peculiar conditions of Quebec.[1]

The main lines of the first attempt of British statesmen to handle the French-Canadian question were thus laid down in 1763. In its general intention and in its more important features it was an earnest and wise attempt at reconciling a conquered people to the commonwealth which now contained them. In religion the primary claims of French-Canadian nationality had been conceded : and by that alone a long step had been taken towards avoiding in Canada a re-enactment of the Irish tragedy. The French language had been similarly respected. In the legal and constitutional settlement, if injustice had been done directly or prospectively, it had been due not to any deliberate departure from the policy of conciliation, but to the intrusion of a secondary policy and to the failure through ignorance or haste or weak procrastination to think out clearly the consequences of applying it to Canada. But in any case the settlement of 1763 was only a provisional settlement. it was the work of King George III in Council, the principal responsibility for it was confined to Grenville as head of the Government and to Hillsborough and Halifax as the ministers directly concerned : and it was soon to be evident that the government of Canada could not be established on a permanent footing without the authority of Parliament.

---

[1] Alvord's thesis provides, as before, an alternative explanation ; see references, p. 34, n. 1, above.

II

MURRAY AND CARLETON

I

THE character of the permanent settlement was to be largely determined by the personality and opinions of the Scotsman and the Irishman who were the first and second Governors of Quebec.[1] Guy Carleton was a greater man than James Murray, but they had much in common, and in training and habits of mind they were closely akin. Both were distinguished soldiers, members of the British landed gentry who had taken the lead in many parts of the world in fighting and winning Chatham's wars. Both shared the shortcomings of their class—a strictly conservative outlook, a belief in good family and broad acres as the natural qualifications for the exercise of political power, an aloof and patronizing attitude towards plebeian 'persons' and pursuits, a somewhat peremptory manner. But they also possessed its virtues—its honour, its courage, its common sense and practical ability, and, with these, a quality more rarely found in men of their breed and time, a capacity to escape in some degree from national prejudices, to appreciate and sympathize with a foreign people and their culture, to treat them with the same instinctive fair play as members of their own race and creed. Than Murray and Carleton— the latter an intimate friend of Wolfe and his Quartermaster-General at the siege of Quebec—the British Government, committed as they were to a policy of conciliation, could

[1] Murray was born in 1719, the fifth son of the fourth Lord Elibank. Carleton was born in 1724 at Newry, County Down, of a Protestant North of Ireland family. Biographies : *Life of Murray* by Major-Gen. R. H. Mahon (London, 1921), *Lord Dorchester* by A. G. Bradley (London, 1908).

not have chosen better men to maintain in the government of Canada the example set by the men who conquered it.

If the new province could have remained as of old a country of French-Canadians alone, their task would have been easier. The results of the Government's attempts to foster British immigration were, it is true, disappointing : something more was needed than the encouragements held out in the Proclamation of 1763 to divert settlers from the warmer climate and less alien character of the southern colonies. It has been reckoned that between 1763 and 1775 emigrants from the British Isles, mainly from Ireland and the Scottish Highlands, crossed the Atlantic to North America to the average number of 20,000 a year :[1] but scarcely any of these went to Canada. Except for a little settlement in 1763 of Frasers and Montgomeries, who had served in the army of conquest, at Murray Bay on the north bank of the St. Lawrence, the British immigrants into Canada at this period came mainly from the neighbouring American colonies and settled mainly in the towns of Quebec and Montreal. Thus the two or three hundred British residents in Canada in 1764 had grown two years later to not much more than five hundred, and ten years later had made very little further increase.[2] But small as it was the influx accentuated from the outset the problem of nationality. Those particularly of the new-comers who hailed from New England were the least likely of men to fit smoothly into the life of New France.[3] Their national antipathies and their

[1] S. C. Johnson, *A History of Emigration from the United Kingdom to North America, 1763–1912* (London, 1913), pp. 1–3. From five Ulster ports alone 43,720 people sailed for America in the years 1769 to 1774.

[2] An official return for the province in 1770 gave about 360 *male* Protestants ; and as there were only two or three French Protestants in Canada, ' Protestant ' was practically equivalent to ' British '. By 1774 the number had diminished. See Carleton to Shelburne, November 25, 1767, C. D., p. 284, and his evidence before the H. of C., Cavendish's *Debates on the Canada Bill* (London, 1839), p. 103 [K., p. 104], and p. 124, n. 2, below.

[3] An official analysis of the origin of the British population in the district of Montreal in 1765 gives only 12 out of 136 men as *born* in the

uncompromising Protestantism had been accentuated by
a century of barbarous border warfare which had burnt
into their hearts a hatred of the Church of Rome and of
the Frenchmen in Canada who had used or served it, more
bitter and enduring than was easily comprehensible to
Englishmen in far-off comfortable London, removed by
leagues of ocean from the haunting fears and unforgettable
tragedies of life in a colonial frontier village. If British
statesmen had doubts about the status of a Roman Catholic
in a British colony, the men of New England had none
whatever. In their eyes he was *ipso facto* disqualified from
the privileges of citizenship. For them there could be no
hesitation as to the rightness and wisdom of applying to
Canada the principles which had inspired the Protestant
ascendancy in Ireland. To them it seemed obvious that the
conquest of Canada involved the political subjection of the
Canadians ; as obvious that civic rights must be withheld
from Roman Catholics and Frenchmen in this new province
of the British Empire as that civic rights must be conceded
to Protestants and Britons, however disproportionate their
numbers.

To men of this temper impartiality between the two
races and the two religions seemed little short of treason ;
and naturally they soon fell foul of Murray, who in fulfilling British treaty obligations and carrying out his instructions from home did not conceal, but made it indeed somewhat provocatively clear, where his personal sympathies
lay. Unrestrained abuse of his policy, underhand intrigue
against his authority, were rife from the outset in the
little British community at Quebec and Montreal ; and
its leading members were not long in making a direct

American colonies as against 98 *born* in the British Isles. But it is clear
that most of the British-born had lived in the older colonies before moving
on into Canada, and the most vigorous and outspoken members of the
British community in Canada were certainly ' American ' in training and
outlook. See the arguments in V. Coffin, *The Province of Quebec and the
Early American Revolution* (Madison, Wis., 1896), pp. 303–305.

and public attack on his administration. The Ordinance of September 17, 1764, allowing French-Canadians despite their religion to sit on juries and to practise in the Court of Common Pleas, evoked a formal protest from the fourteen British members of the Grand Jury of Quebec.[1] And in this remarkable document the complaint on the religious question figured as but one of many grievances. Reforms of varying importance—the establishment of a public Protestant school, the due observance of the Sabbath, the removal of petty-trading stalls from the market-place, regulations for cleaning streets and sweeping chimneys, and so forth—were demanded of Government. And not content with this irregular use of their office as an opportunity for political agitation, these fourteen British jurymen claimed to be regarded henceforth as a sort of legislative chamber for the province. 'We represent', they wrote, 'that, as the Grand Jury must be considered at present as the only body representative of the colony, they, as British subjects, have a right to be consulted before any ordinance that may affect the body that they represent be passed into a law; and as it must happen that taxes be levied for the necessary expenses or improvement of the colony, in order to prevent all abuses and embezzlements or wrong application of the public money, we propose that the public accounts be laid before the Grand Jury at least twice a year to be examined and checked by them and that they may be regularly settled every six months before them.'[2]

This vigorous assertion of minority-rights was followed in the next year by a petition of twenty-one ' British merchants and traders ' to the King. Its signatories asserted that since their settlement in the country they had striven to promote its commercial prosperity with substantial advantage to the mother country. ' With peace ', they declared, ' we trusted to enjoy the blessings of British liberty and happily reap the

[1] See p. 24, n. 1, above.   [2] C. D., pp. 153–155.

fruits of our industry.' But they had been debarred from
open trade in the Indian territory ; and they had suffered
from the enactment of ' ordinances, vexatious, oppressive,
unconstitutional, injurious to civil liberty and to the Protestant cause '. Above all they complained of the behaviour
of the Governor, his ' rage and rudeness of language and
demeanour ', his deliberate attempt to ' keep your Majesty's
old and new subjects divided from one another by
encouraging the latter to apply for judges of their own
national language ', his ' discontinuing the Protestant
religion by almost a total neglect of attendance upon the
service of the Church '. ' The burden of these grievances
from Government ', it was explained, ' is so much the more
severely felt because of the natural poverty of the country '
and the consequent confinement and distress of trade.
The lives, in fact, of the loyal British subjects in the province
had been rendered ' so very unhappy ' that they will be
obliged to leave it, ' unless timely prevented by a removal
of the present Governor '. They therefore prayed for the
appointment of a Governor ' acquainted with other maxims
of government than military only ' and for the establishment
of a House of Representatives as in the other colonies,
to be composed of ' loyal and well-affected Protestants ', for
whose election, however, the ' new subjects ' might be allowed
to vote without being burdened ' with such oaths as in their
present mode of thinking they cannot conscientiously take '.[1]
  In a battle of words Murray could give as good as he got.
' Little, very little ', he wrote home, ' will content the new
subjects, but nothing will satisfy the licentious fanatics
trading here but the expulsion of the Canadians.' [2] Later on,

[1] Petition of the Quebec Traders, C. D., pp. 232–234 [K., p. 41]. A group
of London merchants interested in the Canadian trade presented a petition
supporting the charges made in the Quebec petition and the claim that
the government in Canada should be put ' on the same footing ' as in the
other American colonies (ibid., p. 235).
[2] Murray to Lords of Trade, Oct. 29, 1764, ibid., p. 231 [K., p. 40]. In
a postscript to this letter he describes the British residents who are seeking

when he was back in England, he described his old opponents as mostly ill-educated camp-followers or disbanded soldiers. ' All ', he said, ' have their fortunes to make, and I fear few of them are solicitous about the means when the end can be obtained. I report them to be in general the most immoral collection of men I ever knew, of course little calculated to make the new subjects enamoured with our laws, religion, and customs, far less adapted to enforce those laws and to govern.' ¹ Murray had a hot temper ; and these very sweeping charges are clearly the language of an angry man. It must be remembered that the most active members of the British community had acquired their political habits of mind in an atmosphere in which criticism of the British system of colonial government was, not without reason, a perennial growth. It must be remembered, too, that the immigrants into Canada remained in touch with the fellow colonists they had left behind, whose relations with the Home Government, especially on the question of taxation, were just at this time beginning to be strained : and it is significant that in the summer of 1764 an inter-colonial movement was already afoot to oppose the imminent Stamp Act. In Canada, moreover, as in the older colonies, ill feeling had been accentuated by friction between the immigrant colonists and British military officers, whose conduct towards them was far more arrogant and offensive than towards the French-Canadians. Attorney-General Masères, concerned as he was with numerous cases of assault, wrote feelingly in a letter home of ' the violent gentlemen of the army '.² Thus an attitude of aggressive

to get appointed members of Council as follows : ' The first is a ¡notorious smuggler and a turbulent man, the second a weak man of little character, and the third a conceited boy. In short it will be impossible to do business with any of them.'
  ¹ Murray to Shelburne, August 20, 1766, printed in Kingsford, vol. v, pp. 188–190.
  ² This friction came to a head in the case of Mr. Walker, an Englishman by birth, who had emigrated to Boston and had now come to Montreal

independence or positive hostility on the part of the British immigrants towards the Quebec Government was intelligible enough, and it is absurd to suppose that there were no honest or disinterested men among them. Most of them, however, had come to Canada to make their fortunes in the fur trade : and, while their vigorous business-methods and the impetus they gave to trade were ultimately helpful to the population as a whole, they tended at the outset to regard the new province and its old inhabitants as primarily a field of exploitation. Their attitude, in fact, was dangerously akin to that of the Protestant colonists in Ireland ; and unhappily their views were all too widely shared by the little pack of subordinate officials which the British Government, in accordance with the worst traditions of the old colonial system, had sent out to man the civil service with little other qualification than the desire to make money. On these men, on their numbers, their incompetence, their conduct, Murray's strictures were quite as severe as on the colonial traders.[1]

2

It was the behaviour of the British community towards the French-Canadians that condemned them most in Murray's eyes. It cut at the roots of his own policy. This assumption of racial superiority by a handful of self-seeking

where he had been appointed a justice of the peace. On the question of billeting troops, which had made trouble at Montreal as elsewhere, Walker's attitude was highly obnoxious to the military, and on his committing a certain Captain Payne to prison for refusing to obey his order to vacate rooms he had occupied, he was seriously assaulted by a group of officers. Murray and Carleton after him took a very firm line and did everything in their power to bring the culprits to justice. The prosecution was conducted by Masères. The Secretary of State, Conway, vigorously supported Walker's case. See *The Masères Letters, 1766–1768* (Toronto, 1919, ed. W. S. Wallace), pp. 44–45, 69, 124, and for a full account of the case, Wallace's introduction, pp. 14–18, and Kingsford, vol. v, pp. 163–169. The more important documents are given in R. C. A. 1888, p. 1.

[1] Murray to Shelburne, cited p. 46, n. 1, above. Murray's judgement on the British community, especially the colonials, is contested by Coffin, *op. cit.*, pp. 303–324.

immigrants, this contempt of the old inhabitants and their ways, this bigoted hostility to their faith, were precisely what the soldiers who had conquered Canada had so scrupulously avoided. Such conduct was bound in some degree to counteract the Government's efforts to win the friendship and allegiance of the French-Canadians; it was bound to create the very atmosphere which in later days and many lands was to prove the worst and most persistent obstacle to successful treatment of the delicate problem of nationality; it was bound to make the French-Canadians more self-conscious and susceptible, more suspicious of designs on their traditions, more vociferous in defence of them. Naturally the protest of the British jurymen against their admission to jury-box and bar had evoked a counter-protest. ' The leniency of the existing Government ', declared the French members of the Grand Jury, ' has made us forget our losses and has attached us to His Majesty and to the Government ; our fellow-citizens make us feel our condition to be that of slaves.' [1] To make matters worse the change in the legal system resulting from the Proclamation of 1763 was now beginning to operate, and in January 1765 a petition was addressed to the King by ninety-five of ' the principal inhabitants of Canada ', complaining of the difficulty of understanding the new legal constructions and of settling their family affairs without the aid of obstructive lawyers ' who know neither our language nor our customs and to whom it is only possible to speak with guineas in one's hand ',[2] and praying for permission to conduct their family business in accordance with their old customs and for the publication of a code of law in French. Not unnaturally,

[1] Statement of French Jurors, October 26, 1764, C. D., pp. 227–229. It was explained in this document that those French jurors who had signed with the British the main part of the previous Presentment, had done so without fully understanding its contents.

[2] ' A qui on ne peut parler qu'avec des guinées à la main ' (Petition of January 7, 1765, C. D., p. 224).

moreover, the introduction of English law and the costly
tyranny of British lawyers were connected in the petitioners'
minds with the attack made by the British jurymen on their
religion. The greater part of the document was an answer
to this attack and a plea for the confirmation of Murray's
concessions to their faith despite the protests of those who
held that it disqualified them for any office in the country.
' Who are those ', they ask, ' who wish to have us proscribed ? About thirty English merchants. Who are the
proscribed ? Ten thousand heads of families who feel
nothing but submission to the orders of your Majesty.'
Already there is a touch of rhetoric, a note of exaggeration,
worse still, a strain of bitterness, in the language of French-
Canadian nationalism : and, if this was partly due to the
haste or ignorance of British ministers, it was mainly due
to the arrogance and selfishness of British immigrants.

The French-Canadians need not have been afraid that the
Government would easily be deflected from the policy of
conciliation : ministers were anxious, indeed, to undo what
in haste or ignorance they had done to wound the national
sentiment and suppress the national traditions of French
Canada. The news that the Proclamation of 1763 had
already resulted in the supersession of the existing civil
law came as a complete surprise to political circles in
London. ' I have heard from the King in general ', wrote
Lord Mansfield to Grenville in December 1764, ' and
afterwards more particularly, but very distinctly, from some
persons who visited me last night, of a complaint concerning
a civil government and judge sent to Canada. Is it possible
that we have abolished their laws and customs and forms
of judicature all at once ?—a thing never to be attempted
or wished. The history of the world don't furnish an
instance of so rash and unjust an act by any conqueror
whatsoever ; much less by the Crown of England, which
has always left to the conquered their own laws and usages,

with a change only so far as the sovereignty was concerned.'
' For God's sake ', he added, ' learn the truth of the case,
and think of a speedy remedy.'[1] Ministers were as much
dismayed as Mansfield, but they were determined in remedy-
ing their mistake to avoid both the haste and the ignorance
through which they had committed it. It was already clear
that the provisional settlement of 1763 must be reconsidered
as a whole and recast in a more complete and permanent
form. The question of law took its place, therefore, in the
careful and prolonged inquiry into the whole Canadian
problem which the Government now set on foot. It was
inevitably a slow business ; and fifteen months had passed
since Mansfield's outcry before it was echoed by the Law
Officers of the Crown in their formal report on the French-
Canadian grievances.[2] In the meantime ministers closed
their ears to the protests of the British minority in Canada
and supported Murray in his attempts to alleviate for the
time being the confusion and the hardships of the legal
situation. No question was raised on the ordinance ' for
quieting people in their possessions ', issued by Murray on
November 6, 1764, which provided that tenures of land
and rights of inheritance, as held and practised before the
Treaty of Paris, ' according to the custom of this country '
should ' remain to all intents and purposes the same ' until
August 10, 1765.[3] Another palliative measure was the
dismissal, early in 1766, of Chief Justice Gregory and
Attorney-General Suckling, whom Murray had reported to
be ' entirely ignorant of the language of the natives ',
' needy in their circumstances and, though perhaps good

[1] *Grenville Papers* (London, 1852–3), vol. ii, p. 476.
[2] See p. 55, below.
[3] C. D., p. 229 [K., p. 43]. In 1767 Carleton, Murray's successor, submitted
a draft ordinance for restoring the French-Canadian law in matters of tenure,
inheritance, and alienation of land, which was approved by the Secretary
of State but set aside to await the permanent settlement of the province.
See Hillsborough to Carleton (March 6, 1768), C. D., p. 298. The draft
ordinance is given in C. D., p. 292.

lawyers and men of integrity ', readier to ' create difficulties than remove them ', and their replacement by William Hey and Francis Masères.[1] Nor, of course, was there any idea of revoking the notorious ordinance which had admitted French-Canadians to legal functions. The vital question of the application of the laws of Great Britain to Roman Catholics in Canada was submitted for decision to the Law Officers of the Crown ; and in June 1765 they delivered the opinion that ' his Majesty's Roman Catholic subjects residing in the countries ceded to his Majesty in America by the Definitive Treaty of Paris are not subject in those colonies to the incapacities, disabilities and penalties to which Roman Catholics in this kingdom are subject by the laws thereof '.[2] Fortified by this decision, ministers obtained, early in the following year, the approval of the King-in-Council to the issue of Additional Instructions, which, so far from revoking the ordinance in question, directed Murray to alter those of its provisions ' which tend to restrain our Canadian subjects in those privileges they are entitled to enjoy *in common with our natural born subjects*'. Accordingly on July 1, 1766, an amending ordinance was published proclaiming in the terms laid down in the Instructions that ' His Majesty's Canadian subjects ' are henceforth permitted to practise professionally ' in *all or any* of the courts ' in the province of Quebec, and that all British subjects without distinction are entitled to sit as jurors ' in *all* causes civil and criminal cognizable by *any* of the courts or judicatures within the said province '. A proviso was added that, if it be required by either of the parties concerned, in cases between British disputants only or Canadians only the jury should be wholly British or wholly Canadian and in cases between British and Canadians an equal number of

[1] C. D., pp. 256–257, notes.
[2] Opinion of Attorney-General Norton and Solicitor-General De Grey, June 10, 1765, C. D., p. 236.

each race should be empanelled—a wise and equitable proviso under the circumstances, but sorry evidence of a race-antagonism in Canada already so strong as to necessitate in the interests of justice its formal recognition and embodiment in the machinery of government.[1]

But ministers had afforded a far more striking proof than this ordinance of the sincerity of their policy of religious toleration—a proof which could be immediately appreciated by every Roman Catholic in the province. Since the death of Monseigneur de Pontbriand, the last Bishop of Quebec under the old *régime*, in 1760 the episcopal functions had been exercised by three grand vicars. Naturally the French-Canadian churchmen had regarded the appointment of a bishop as a necessity, and in 1763 M. Montgolfier, one of the grand vicars, had gone to England in order to make arrangements for his consecration in some Roman Catholic country on the Continent. Naturally also the British Government let it be known that they could not permit the appointment of a bishop in Canada. For a bishop could only be consecrated and instituted by the direct authority of the Pope ; and the exercise of any papal authority, spiritual as well as temporal, was the one forbidden thing in any dominion of the British Crown, the one element in the practice of the Roman Catholic religion which the laws of Great Britain, in the well-known treaty-clause, did not permit. M. Montgolfier wisely accepted the decision and returned to Quebec. But the question could not be closed. Only a bishop could ordain priests, and without new priests the Church could not long survive. Murray recognized the dilemma. He suggested that aspirants for priesthood should be trained in Canadian seminaries and sent to Europe for consecration at the public expense.

[1] C. D., pp. 249–250 [K., p. 48]. As Murray had left Canada, the ordinance was published by Colonel Irving, President of the Council and Acting-Governor from June 28 to September 24, 1766.

But, of course, this rather clumsy expedient did not satisfy the Canadian churchmen. They argued that a bishop was an essential element in their Church, that without a bishop the Roman Catholics of Canada could not be properly described as free to practise their religion ; and Murray was presently convinced that generosity was again the wiser course. Despite the limitation in the treaty, despite the well-known interpretation of it by Egremont and his successors, despite the clause in his own Instructions forbidding him to ' admit of any ecclesiastical jurisdiction by the See of Rome ', Murray advised the Home Government that, in some form or other, the claim for a duly appointed head of the Church in Canada should be conceded. Doubtless this decision was made easier by the fact that the Quebec chapter had chosen M. Briand as its candidate for the bishopric instead of M. Montgolfier. For Murray regarded the latter as a proud and imperious priest who was bound to give trouble to the Government, whereas he was on excellent terms with the moderate and tactful M. Briand to whose influence, indeed, his policy may have been largely due. M. Briand, therefore, proceeded to London, with Murray's recommendations ; and there for fourteen months he waited while successive ministries wrestled with the obvious difficulties of the case. At last the Rockingham Government, probably influenced in some degree by Burke, adopted a characteristic compromise. M. Briand might go to France for his consecration, but secretly : nothing must be said about it before or after—and here, no doubt, ministers were thinking of the storm that would be created in Parliament and in the country if it were known that they were engaged in slipping round the Act of Supremacy. Once consecrated bishop, he must not use the title nor speak of his episcopate. He must be known as ' the Superintendent of the Roman Church in Canada '. Nor, of course, would he exercise any powers, prescribe any rules, make any appointments without the Governor's consent and approval. For thus only could the royal supremacy be maintained. Accordingly, in March 1766, the necessary instruments having been obtained from the Pope, M. Briand was privately consecrated at Suresnes by the Bishop of Blois; and in June he returned to Quebec.[1] It was an historic moment for the French-Canadians. Officially Monseigneur Briand might be known as Superintendent, but not to his flock. ' God has had pity on us,' they cried : ' we have got a bishop.' And they crowded into the cathedral to see him enthroned as of old, a pledge incarnate of the freedom of their faith, of the continuity of their Church, and of British toleration. Ministers might be criticized for acting behind the back of Parliament and the public : the formal subordination of the Bishop's jurisdiction to the Governor's might be hard to enforce and become in time a dead letter : but no other concession could have given to the French-Canadians so dramatic and convincing a proof of the conciliatory intentions of the British Government or have confirmed so decisively the allegiance of the French-Canadian Church. Nor could a better choice have been made than that of Monseigneur Briand. He lived a quiet and simple life ; he dispensed with most of the usual episcopal pageantry ; he strove to work in harmony with the civil authorities ; and, when, in the day of reckoning, the Government needed his help, he gave it, as will be seen, without stint.[2]

[1] Masères, *Occasional Essays* (London, 1809), pp. 364 ff. ; *Letters*, pp. 53–54 ; Chapais, *Cours d'Histoire*, vol. i, pp. 45–60 ; Kingsford, vol. v, pp. 174–175 ; C. D., p. 191. Masères describes the appointment as made ' privately, almost clandestinely, by mere connivance of ministers '. For Burke's influence see Masères, *Occasional Essays*, p. 369, cited in Chapais, p. 51, note. See also the subsequent Board of Trade Report, July 10, 1769, C. D., pp. 389–390.

[2] Chapais, *op. cit.*, p. 53, citing the *Quebec Gazette*. Charges against Mgr. Briand of maintaining all the usual pomp are combated by Kingsford, vol. v, p. 175, n. 2. Masères, something of a bigot in religion (see p. 84, below), describes in one of his letters a ' great procession ' at Quebec on

In the matter of law, likewise, the Rockingham Government was inclined to do—and very nearly did—all that
Murray could have wished. In April, 1766, Attorney-
General Yorke and Solicitor-General De Grey presented their
report on the civil government of Quebec. The disorders
in the province were due, they declared, to two causes—
first, ' the attempt to carry on the administration of justice
without the aid of the natives, not merely in new forms, but
totally in an unknown tongue, by which means the parties
understood nothing of what was pleaded or determined ',
and, secondly, the false interpretation put upon the King's
Proclamation of 1763 ' as if it were his royal intention . . . to
abolish all the usages and customs of Canada with the
rough hand of a conqueror rather than with the true spirit
of a lawful sovereign '. The first of these mistakes, they
continued, could be remedied by the admission of Canadians
to sit on juries and to plead, as recommended by the Lords
of Trade : the second by restoring the main body of French-
Canadian civil law. ' To change at once the laws and manners
of a settled country must be attended with hardship and
violence ; and therefore wise conquerors, having provided
for the security of their dominion, proceed gently and
indulge their conquered subjects in all local customs which
are in their own nature indifferent and which have been
received as rules of property or have obtained the force of
laws.' With regard, therefore, to titles of land and other
real property, to customs of bequest and inheritance and
to modes of assigning and conveying, judgements should be
made in accordance with the existing French-Canadian law.

Corpus Christi day in 1766, in which the bishop walked beneath a canopy,
dressed in purple and wearing his golden cross ; and suggests that in so
doing he was unfaithful to promises given in England (*Letters*, p. 54). As
will be seen (p. 84, below), Masères thought that, if Protestantism had been
encouraged and no concessions made to Romanism, the French-Canadians
could have been rapidly converted. For the appointment and consecration
of a coadjutor in 1772, see Coffin, *op. cit.*, pp. 436–437, Chapais, *op. cit.*,
p. 141.

As to ' personal actions grounded upon debts, promises, contracts, and agreements, whether of a mercantile or other nature, and upon wrongs proper to be compensated in damages ', the judges should remember that ' the substantial maxims of law and justice are everywhere the same ' and they will not ' materially err, either against the laws of England or the ancient customs of Canada, if in such cases they look to those substantial maxims '. In criminal cases, on the other hand, the English law should be adopted in the interests of the Canadians themselves because of its ' certainty ' and ' lenity '.[1]

The admission of French-Canadians to the courts had already been decided on. It was prescribed, as has been seen, by the Ordinance of July 1, 1766. But this was a relatively small point compared. with the proposals of the Crown Lawyers with regard to the retention of the French-Canadian civil law. Yorke and De Grey were eminent and influential men. Yorke was appointed Lord Chancellor in 1770, but died before he actually took office. In the same year De Grey became Attorney-General. And these leading lawyers had no sooner examined the facts of the controversy created by the Proclamation of 1763 than they had declared in favour of the main French-Canadian case. In the field of property and bequest, in which every French-Canadian was personally interested, they had pronounced for the Custom of Paris : and even in the field of debts and contracts in which the British mercantile community was primarily concerned, if their advice was somewhat evasive and unsatisfying, at least they had not recommended the adoption of English law. They had set the lines, in fact, along which the tedious controversy of the next eight years was to move ; and the decision taken at the end of those eight years was to be nearly the same decision as theirs. As it

---

[1] Report of Attorney and Solicitor-General regarding the Civil Government of Quebec, April 14, 1766. C. D., pp. 251–257 [K., pp. 44–47].

was, the issue was all but settled at once. Lord Chancellor Northington was the only member of the Government that objected to the adoption of the Yorke-De Grey report; and his opposition would certainly have been overcome or overridden if the Rockingham Ministry had not suddenly fallen.[1]

The policy of conciliation for which Murray had fought was thus evidently the policy of his masters in Whitehall; but, illogically enough, it did not follow that they were satisfied with their servant. No doubt the personal animosities that centred round him at Quebec were unpleasant and disquieting. No doubt, too, his enemies could make themselves heard in London.[2] But the fatal point against Murray was the fact that he had tried, as loyally as he could and much as he disliked it, to carry out the orders given him three years before. It seems, indeed, as if official opinion had found in him the necessary scapegoat for the blunders of 1763. In the autumn of 1765, the Board of Trade, of which Lord Dartmouth was now President, recommended that he should return to England to give an explanation in person of the complaints received from Quebec.[3] On April 1, 1766, he was formally recalled. In the Cabinet meetings of the following June, at which the Yorke-De Grey report was discussed, the one point at which Northington agreed with his colleagues was when he admitted that ' the method in which Murray had executed his instructions

---

[1] The Cabinet discussions are recorded in Lord Albemarle's *Memoirs of the Marquis of Rockingham and his Contemporaries* (London, 1852), pp. 350–357, giving the text of the Duke of Richmond's journal and letters by Hardwick and Rockingham. Masères (*Letters*, p. 68) was told by Yorke that the report ' would actually have passed, notwithstanding the difficulties it met with from Lord Northington's opposition, if the ministry had not suddenly changed '. For the reconsideration of the Yorke-De Grey report by the new Government and Northington's continued opposition, see p. 67, n. 6, below.

[2] For Walker's activities in London, see Mahon's *Life of Murray*, pp. 341–343.　　　　　　　　　　　　　　[3] C. D., p. 248.

was disapproved by everybody '.[1] It was under a cloud, therefore, that Murray, in midsummer, 1766, left Quebec. ' I glory ', he wrote when he was back in England, ' in having been accused of warmth and firmness in protecting the King's Canadian subjects and of doing the utmost in my power to gain to my royal master the affections of that brave, hardy people, whose emigration, if ever it shall happen, will be an irreparable loss to the Empire.'

3

Guy Carleton, who landed at Quebec in September, 1766, to take Murray's place, is one of the great figures in the history of the British Commonwealth ; and his influence on the shaping of the future destinies of Canada was stronger than that of any other man of his time. In him, on a much bigger scale than in Murray, the statesman was yoked with the soldier. His judgements were the quick, half-instinctive judgements of the practical man, but they were shrewd, far-sighted, and admirably clear and firm. He could choose a straight course and also keep to it ; and his earlier dispatches from Canada present in all its main principles the policy which he continued to preach and to practise for thirty years.

[1] *Rockingham Memoirs*, vol. i, p. 354.

[2] Murray to Shelburne, August 20, 1766, Kingsford, vol. v, p. 190. The charges brought against Murray were dismissed as ' groundless ' by an Order-in-Council of April 13, 1767 ; and though he did not return to Canada, he retained the Governor's office till Carleton succeeded him in 1768. Masères took the side of his opponents and wrote of his acquittal by the Privy Council as ' ridiculous and shameless ' (*Letters*, pp. 48–49, &c.). Murray's own letters (calendared in R. C. A., 1912, Appendix I) are over-much concerned with personal enmities and suspicions of intrigue (especially with regard to his quarrel with Gage and Burton over his military status, see p. 35, n. 1, above), but they put beyond doubt his genuine sympathy with the French-Canadians. In 1764, for example, he begs Lord Eglinton to secure his recall if he is expected to apply the Penal Laws in Canada (p. 98 ; cf. p. 120). For an instance of rudeness to a *seigneur*, for which he apologized (' it was only irritability '), see Memorial of Chevalier de Léry, 1767, R. C. A., 1888, pp. 29–31. His gallant defence of Minorca in 1781 is described in Mahon's *Life*, chap. xviii.

' Were not his decisions a little hasty, a little too clean-cut and sweeping ? ' the critic may ask. Better such errors on the right side—it may be answered—than the fatal political vices of vagueness and indecision. The difficulties of the Canadian problem had already been unnecessarily increased by confused and contradictory measures : the supreme need now was a policy so clear and so consistent that its meaning should be unmistakable and its sincerity beyond suspicion. By the end of this book it will be evident what would have happened to Canada if British statesmen had hesitated or delayed too long to meet this need ; and it is Carleton's claim to the high place he holds in history that he met it, and met it in time.

He saw, to begin with, more clearly than his contemporaries, more clearly even than his great successor, Durham, sixty years later, that the population of Quebec would remain predominantly French in race. Life in the St. Lawrence valley, he points out, is too hard and poor at present to attract a large supply of new European settlers ; and while the severity of the climate discourages immigration, its healthfulness fosters the increase of the stock which for a century past has been established there. ' Barring a catastrophe shocking to think of ', he writes, ' this country must, to the end of time, be peopled by the Canadian race, who already have taken such firm root and got to so great a height that any new stock transplanted will be totally hid and imperceptible amongst them except in the towns of Quebec and Montreal.' [1] Yet more striking in the light of events seven years later and the part he was himself to play in them is Carleton's recognition of the bearing of this fact on the external aspects of the Canadian problem. He weighs the probability of a renewal of war with France and the possibility of disaffection in the British colonies to the South, and he perceives in Quebec the strategic key to

[1] Carleton to Shelburne, November 25, 1767, C. D., p. 284.

North America.[1] ' When I consider that the King's dominion here is maintained but by a few troops, necessarily disposed . . . amidst a numerous military people . . . I can have no doubt that France, as soon as determined to begin a war, will attempt to regain Canada, should it be intended only to make a diversion. . . . But should France begin a war in hopes the British colonies will push matters to extremities, and she adopts the project of supporting them in their independent notions, Canada probably will then become the principal scene where the fate of America may be determined. Affairs in this situation, Canada in the hands of France would no longer present itself as an enemy to the British colonies, but as an ally, a friend, a protector of their independency. Your lordship must immediately perceive the many disadvantages Great Britain would labour under in a war of this nature ; and on the other hand how greatly Canada might for ever support the British interests on this continent (for it is not united in any common principle, interest or wish with the other provinces in opposition to the supreme seat of government) was the King's dominion over it only strengthened by a citadel, which a few national troops might secure, and the natives attached by making it their interest to remain his subjects.' [2]

This dispatch deserves attention quite apart from the remarkable foresight it displays ; for, later on, as will be seen, some of Carleton's opponents maintained that his policy was wholly inspired by the idea of using French-Canada to overawe and, if need be, to suppress the disaffected British colonies in the South. That this was one of his reasons for desiring to conciliate the French-Canadians

[1] In the dispatch cited in the preceding note he writes : ' Time must bring forth events that will render it essentially necessary for the British interests on this continent to secure this port of communication with the mother country.' An accurate forecast, as will be seen.

[2] Carleton to Hillsborough, November 20, 1768, C. D., p. 326. On the strategic position of Canada, see also Carleton to Gage, February 15, 1767, C. D., p. 280 ; Carleton to Shelburne, November 25, 1767, C. D., p. 281.

is clear. It would occur to any soldier's mind on the morrow of the Stamp Act troubles. It had occurred to Murray, who spoke of Quebec as ' a guarantee for the good behaviour of its neighbouring colonies '. But the first enemy to be feared was the French-Canadians' mother country ; and, in any case, to suggest that antagonism to the British colonies was the mainspring of Carleton's policy or Murray's is to reverse the true order of ideas. To conciliate the ' new subjects ' was obvious wisdom. Danger on the North American horizon merely made it more obvious.[1]

Anxious days were to come when ministers would wish that Carleton's advice to fortify Quebec had been accepted : but at the moment they were more interested in the major problem of winning the loyalty of the French-Canadians. While discounting the rumours which had reached Whitehall of an intended rising against British rule, Carleton had ' not the least doubt of their secret attachments to France ', and confessed that ' the interests of many would be greatly promoted by a revolution '.[2] To transform this state of affairs was his chief concern : and he had quickly framed a policy as frankly conciliatory as the Government's and far more clearly defined. Religious toleration he accepted as a matter of course. He denounced the introduction of English law as ' a sort of severity never before practised by any conqueror, even when the people, without capitulation, submitted to his will and discretion ' : and to remove the prevalent confusion and discontent he recommended Government as an immediate provisional measure to repeal the ordinance of September 17, 1764, and for the present to ' leave the Canadian laws almost entire '.[3] Some months later he had made up his mind as to the permanent solution of the problem. ' The only way of doing justice and giving satisfaction to the Canadians . . . is to continue the laws

[1] See pp. 94–97, 117, 137, below. Mahon, *Life of Murray*, p. 199.
[2] Carleton to Hillsborough, November 20, 1768, C. D., p. 325.
[3] Carleton to Shelburne, Dec. 24, 1767, C. D., pp. 289–290 [K., p. 56].

of England with respect to criminal matters and to revive
the whole body of the French laws that were in use there
before the conquest with respect to civil matters.'¹ Meantime, soon after his arrival, he had given instructions for the
compilation of a summary of French-Canadian law, which
then lay buried in a mass of royal edicts, judgements by the
parlements of Paris, and provincial ordinances :² and by
1769 an invaluable abstract of all the laws held to be in
force in Canada at the time of the conquest had been
prepared.³

The removal of 'those causes of complaint which affect
the bulk of the people and come home almost to every man ',
the maintenance of the Canadians 'in the quiet possession
of their property according to their own customs ', the
lessening of the expense and delay involved in the existing
system—these measures were in Carleton's view essential.
' But besides these points of justice,' he writes, ' as long as
the Canadians are deprived of all places of trust and profit,
they never can forget they no longer are under the dominion
of their natural sovereign.' ⁴ With the old aristocracy of the
province Carleton, like Murray before him, found himself
instinctively in sympathy ; ⁵ and this was the class which

---

¹ Masères's statement of Carleton's opinion, February 27, 1769, C. D.,
p. 370 [K., p. 57].
² Carleton to Shelburne, December 24, 1767, C. D., p. 289. Murray
had recommended the preparation of a short and well-digested code
in his Report on Quebec in 1762 (C. D., p. 53).
³ Carleton to Shelburne, April 12, 1768, C. D., p. 300 and n. 3 ; cf. p. 438.
The abstract was published in London in 1772 and 1773 in five parts.
M. Cugnet and several other French-Canadian jurists were its authors
(Chapais, *op. cit.*, p. 126, n.). For the difficulty of the work, see Masères's
letter to Richard Sutton, Under-Secretary of State, August 14, 1768
(*Letters*, p. 101).
⁴ Carleton to Shelburne, January 20, 1768, C. D., p. 294.
⁵ Murray's first opinion of the *seigneurs* was unfavourable. In his
Report in 1762 he wrote : ' They are extremely vain and have an utter
contempt for the trading part of the colony, though they made no scruple
to engage in it, pretty deeply too, whenever a convenient opportunity
served. They were great tyrants to their vassals who seldom met with
redress, let their grievances be ever so just. This class will not relish the

had suffered most palpably in its 'interests' by the conquest. Ill cultivated as they were and continually decreasing both in size and in economic value by their division and sub-division at each owner's death among the members of his family under the old French law,[1] the landed estates of the *seigneurs* could not suffice to maintain them as a class in the social position they claimed by right of birth. They had always depended, therefore, for their livelihood at least as much on employment in the King's service, military and civil, as on the rents and produce of their land. But now they found themselves completely excluded from the profession which, except for the Frenchmen sent direct from Europe, they had once monopolized. The militia had been disbanded on the establishment of civil government in 1763 ; the regular troops in the province were officered of course by Englishmen ; the doors of the provincial civil service were closed to them. ' To be excluded by the state from partici-pating in it ', they declared in a moderately phrased petition

British Government from which they can neither expect the same employ-ments or the same *douceurs* they enjoyed under the French ' (C. D., p. 79). But he seems to have revised his opinion and reprobated the insulting attitude of the British business community towards them. Murray to Shelburne, August 20, 1766 (Kingsford, vol. v, p. 198).
  [1] See Munro, *The Seigniorial System in Canada*, pp. 82–83. The division inevitably led to the shrinkage of individual tenures into long and ever narrower strips, since a frontage on the St. Lawrence was essential—a process which the French Government had tried to check (see the edict of Louis XIV, cited in C. D., p. 345, note, and referred to by Masères, *ibid.*, p. 533). South Africa provides a close analogy. Under the old Roman-Dutch law, not altered in the Transvaal till 1902, subdivision of land at the owner's death among all his children was compulsory, with the result that in course of time properties were sliced up into narrow strips as in Canada, and individuals became entitled to minute fractions of an acre. One farm in the Transvaal in 1908 was three miles long and sixty yards broad ; theoretically it was divided among several owners. See the lucid account in the *Transvaal Indigency Commission Report, 1906–1908* (T. G., 13, 1908), which points out that the custom of subdivision had outlasted the law and was the chief cause of the existence of the ' poor white ' class in rural districts. Indian agriculture has similarly suffered from sub-division : see L. C. A. Knowles, *The Economic Development of the British Overseas Empire* (London, 1924), p. 432.

to the King, asking for admission to office, 'is not to be a member of the state'.[1] Carleton may have overestimated their influence over the *habitants*,[2] but it was none the less obviously just and wise to try to win for the King of England the good service they had given to the King of France. And the effect of such a policy, he argued, would extend beyond the seigniorial class : for the exclusion of a class from office 'affects the minds of all from a national spirit'. His immediate proposals were moderate enough. ' Three or four of their principal gentlemen with the rank of Councillors, was it little more than honorary, though on many occasions they might prove useful ; a few companies of Canadian Foot, judiciously officered, with three or four trifling employments in the Civil Department ', these small concessions would go far in the minds of the French-Canadians to induce them, in part at any rate, in the event of war with France, to 'emulate the zeal of the King's national troops ' ; and to the *seigneurs* they would hold out hopes that ' their children . . . might support their families in the service of the King their master, and by their employments preserve them from sinking into the lower class of people by the division and sub-division of lands every generation '.[3]

4

Such was the positive side of Carleton's policy : on its negative side he was strongly opposed to the establishment of representative government. Just as his natural sympathies were with the old landed gentry of the province, so they were against the immigrant traders. If the quarrel

---

[1] Petition of the Seigneurs of Montreal, February 3, 1767, C. D., p. 272. Masères stated that 120 *seigneurs* had been turned out of office by the conquest (Coffin, *op. cit.*, p. 298, n. 2).

[2] ' The common people are greatly to be influenced by their *seigneurs* ' : see the dispatch cited in the following note. For the weakening of this influence, see pp. 116–118, below.

[3] Carleton to Shelburne, January 20, 1768, C. D., p. 295.

was not so violent in his time, if the language on both sides was more restrained, his opinion of the British malcontents was much the same as Murray's.[1] But his opposition to an Assembly was not only based on the character of the British or the incapacity of the French. Like most men of his class and time Carleton was an oligarch ; he brushed aside newfangled notions of democracy as peremptorily a he brushed aside such individuals as ventured to question his authority or oppose his will ; and the passage in a dispatch of 1768 in which he discusses the question of an Assembly may well be given at length, revealing as it does, together with some sound common sense, the limitations of his political outlook—limitations which, shared by a multitude of lesser men, had made it so difficult for the governing class in eighteenth-century England to work in harmony with their kinsmen in the American colonies. After describing the presentation of a petition for an Assembly ' by three or four of the old subjects about a year ago ', and his unfavourable reply to it, he continues :

I imagined they had laid aside all thoughts of the kind till lately one John McCord, who wants neither sense nor honesty and formerly kept a small ale house in the poor suburbs of a little country town in the North of Ireland, appearing zealous for the Presbyterian faith and having made a little money, has gained some credit among people of his sort. This person purchased some spots of ground, and procured grants of more, close to the barracks, where he ran up sheds and placed poor people to sell his spirits to the soldiers. Finding that his lucrative trade has lately

[1] See Carleton to Shelburne, October 25, 1766, C. D., p. 276, a characteristic account of a dispute with some members of his Council. ' The great leader of the intended opposition is Mr. Mabane, who followed the army as surgeon's mate into this country.' Another member ' has acted as a strolling player in other colonies '. Carleton expects the opposition to die down, except that of ' a few self-interested individuals '. See also his stringent reply to his opponents' remonstrance (ibid., p. 279). The other side of the picture is given by A. L. Burt (C. H. R., vol. iv, p. 321), who in this controversy as in that of Livius (C. H. R., vol. v, p. 196) forms a much lower estimate of Carleton's character than his general record or the opinions of his friends and supporters suggest.

been checked, by inclosing the barracks to prevent the soldiers getting drunk all hours of the day and night, he has commenced patriot, and with the assistance of the late Attorney General [he] and three or four more, egged on by letters from home, are at work again for an Assembly, and purpose having it signed by all they can influence. On the other hand the better sort of Canadians fear nothing more than popular Assemblies, which, they conceive, tend only to render the people refractory and insolent. Enquiring what they thought of them, they said, they understood some of our colonies had fallen under the King's displeasure owing to the misconduct of their Assemblies, and that they should think themselves unhappy if a like misfortune befell them. It may not be improper here to observe that the British form of government, transplanted into this continent, never will produce the same fruits as at home, chiefly because it is impossible for the dignity of the throne or peerage to be represented in the American forests. Besides, the Governor, having little or nothing to give away, can have but little influence. . . . It therefore follows, where the executive power is lodged with a person of no influence, but coldly assisted by the rest in office, and where the two first branches of the Legislature have neither influence nor dignity, except it be from the extraordinary characters of the men, that a popular Assembly, which preserves it's full vigour and in a country where all men appear nearly upon a level, must give a strong bias to republican principles. Whether the independent spirit of a Democracy is well adapted to a subordinate Government of the British Monarchy, or their uncontrollable notions ought to be encouraged in a province, so lately conquered and circumstanced as this is, I with great humility submit to the superior wisdom of His Majesty's Councils : for my own part, I shall think myself fortunate if I have succeeded in rendering clear objects not allways distinctly discernable at so great a distance.[1]

5

At the date of this dispatch His Majesty's Councils had definitely begun the task of acquiring, if not a very superior wisdom, at least a little knowledge of the facts. The Government inquiry into the condition of Canada was

[1] Carleton to Shelburne, January 20, 1768, C. D., pp. 295–296. (Original spelling retained, but punctuation modernized.) McCord, pp. 77, 182, below.

already afoot. Masères, the new Attorney-General of Quebec, had stated plainly that no permanent settlement could be made without an Act of Parliament. How, he asked, except by Act of Parliament could the toleration of Roman Catholics, contrary to laws in force in England, be given an authority which ' neither the new English inhabitants of the province can contest nor the French Catholics suspect to be inadequate'? How otherwise can the question of an Assembly be determined? How, especially, can the provincial revenue be provided? Since the Governor-in-Council was expressly debarred from any powers of taxation,[1] the only existing sources of revenue were those which the British Crown had inherited from the French,[2] consisting mainly of the rental of Crown lands, certain feudal dues of no great value, and customs duties, chiefly on wine and spirits, the yield of which had fallen steadily.[3] So low, in fact, had the revenue sunk that the greater part of the annual cost of the provincial government, estimated at £10,000, was borne by the British Treasury.[4] Evidently new taxes were needed in Quebec, and as long as it possessed no representative Assembly, only the British Parliament could impose them.[5]

Convinced by these arguments and unwilling to commit themselves to legislation without a closer knowledge of the facts,[6] ministers had launched an official investigation

---

[1] See Murray's Commission, p. 36, above.

[2] According to Lord Mansfield's judgement in Campbell v. Hall, interpreting the Proclamation of October 7, 1763, as it applied to Grenada (C. D., p. 522 [K., p. 79]).

[3] The decline, as Masères explains, was mainly due to the cessation of the import of wines and spirits from France. For a further reason see p. 79, below. The French had drawn most of their revenue from the monopoly of the fur-trade in the north, but the British Government had leased this for only £400 a year (Coffin, op. cit., p. 362).

[4] Masères's estimate. In 1768, £6,722 figures in the British budget for the civil establishment of Quebec (Coffin, op. cit., p. 364).

[5] *Considerations on the expediency of procuring an Act of Parliament, &c.*, by Masères (C. D., p. 267 [K., p. 49]).

[6] The proposals of the Yorke-De Grey report were reconsidered by the

into the conditions of the province. The provincial Government was instructed to prepare reports, and in August 1768 Mr. Maurice Morgan, a member of the Home Civil Service and a friend and adviser of Shelburne's, was sent out to Quebec to discuss these reports with Carleton and his colleagues and to bring them back to London.[1] But Carleton, feeling that no amount of discussion with a subordinate official nor of correspondence at so great a distance with his chiefs could adequately explain the gravity of the issues at stake or the strong opinions he had formed on them, asked leave to return himself to England. ' I really believe ', he wrote, ' I could more effectually promote and advance (the King's interests in Canada) by a residence of a few months in London than of so many years in this country.'[2] His request was granted : and in the autumn of 1770, leaving Mr. H. F. Cramahé, member of Council, in charge of the government,[3] he sailed for home. So indispensable did ministers find him that he remained there not for a few months only but till the passing of the Quebec Act in 1774.

Chatham Government ; but Lord Northington, who was again Lord Chancellor, still opposed their adoption on the ground of insufficient information. *Autobiography of the Duke of Grafton* (ed. Sir William Anson ; London, 1898), p. 170.

[1] On August 28, 1767, a resolution of the Privy Council was passed to obtain ' precise, solemn, and authentic information ' as to the condition of the laws in Quebec and the reforms needed, and to send out ' a fit and proper person ' for the purpose stated above (C. D., p. 285). Morgan arrived in Canada in August 1768 (note the delay) and remained there till January 1770. He reported home from time to time, but Carleton's return naturally left him in the background. Masères writes amusingly of ' Mr. Morgan the legislator, as we use to call him ' and his ' pompous way of talking ' (August 31, 1768, *Letters*, p. 118). It is clear from his letter to Shelburne (August 30, 1769, printed as Appendix E in the *Masères Letters*, p. 130) that Morgan fell completely under Carleton's influence and adopted his opinions rather than those of Masères. See also the paper in the *Lansdowne MSS.*, vol. lxiv, quoted by Alvord (*The Mississippi Valley in British Politics*, vol. ii, p. 220) and identified by him as a reprint of Morgan's report to Shelburne.

[2] Carleton to Hillsborough, March 15, 1769, C. D., p. 392, note.

[3] Cramahé was appointed Lieutenant-Governor in 1771 (C. D., p. 423).

III

THE QUEBEC ACT

I

NEVER was good advice more needed : for the ministers who carried the Quebec Act were the men whose only resource for dealing at that same time with the rising disaffection in the thirteen older colonies in North America was the three penal measures which precipitated the great rebellion. Chatham's last ministry had only lasted two short years ; its leader's protracted illness had fatally impaired its strength and its coherence ; but, if it had been unable to prevent Townshend's wild and unauthorized adventure in colonial policy, it had at least contained a number of Chatham's disciples who shared in some degree their master's interest in the colonies and his understanding of the colonial problem. Camden, the Lord Chancellor, Conway and Shelburne, Secretaries of State for the Northern and Southern Departments, had all stood with Chatham against direct American taxation. But in 1768 Conway, Shelburne, and lastly Chatham himself, resigned, and if Camden remained for a time on the woolsack, he took no further part in politics. When Carleton returned to London he found Lord North at the head of the Government, and Lord Hillsborough in the newly created office of Secretary of State for the American Department, in which he was succeeded in 1772 by Lord Dartmouth.

The mass of material which was presented to North and his colleagues between 1770 and 1774, the petitions and counter-petitions from Canada, the voluminous reports of

departmental officials and legal advisers in London, and
finally the evidence given before the House of Commons in
committee on the Quebec Bill, all centred in the division of
nationality which the first decade of British government had
shown to be the dominant factor in the Canadian problem.
Stripped of its complex of legal technicalities, the controversy
over the Quebec Act was a square fight between the claims
of the ' new ' subjects of the British Crown in Canada and
those of the ' old '.

During the three years and more of delay, while Carleton was
in London and the framework of the Quebec Bill was being
slowly built up in ministers' minds, a cloud of uncertainty
and suspense hung over Canada. Of the two parties the
French-Canadians on the whole had less reason for anxiety.
The ordinance of 1766 had 'contributed very much to quiet
their minds '.[1] ' The signal favour of possessing a bishop ',
so they themselves declared in 1767, had ' roused in the hearts
of all the new subjects the liveliest sentiments of gratitude '.[2]
The alarm excited by Murray's recall had been stilled by the
discovery that yet another British Governor could understand and sympathize with their national aspirations.[3]
And Carleton was expressly instructed by Hillsborough to
explain to them the difficulties of framing a permanent
settlement and ' to prevail upon them to suffer patiently '
the unavoidable delay.[4] Further steps, meantime, were
taken to alleviate provisionally their legal grievances. Great
hardships had been caused by the rigorous judgements of
the local magistrates, appointed from the British Protestant

[1] Acting-Governor Irving to the Lords of Trade, August 20, 1766,
C. D., p. 269. For the ordinance of July 1, 1766, see p. 51, above.
[2] Petition of the Seigneurs of Montreal, February 3, 1767, C. D., p. 272.
[3] The petition, cited in the preceding note, had expressed a hope that
Murray would continue in office: this does not support Masères's suggestion
(*Letters*, p. 49) that Murray was unpopular with the French-Canadians
because of his ordinance of September 17, 1764.
[4] Hillsborough to Carleton March 6, 1768, C. D., p. 298.

community, and especially by their severe enforcement
of the British system of seizure of lands and goods and
personal imprisonment for debt. Carleton himself ordered
the release from gaol of sixteen debtors whose total debts
had amounted to less than £40 ; [1] and early in 1770 he passed
an ordinance transferring the power of dealing with cases
affecting property from the magistrates to the Court of
Common Pleas and regulating the process for recovery of
debt so as to enforce the plaintiff's responsibility, to protect the defendant against the seizure of his ' beasts of the
plough ' and agricultural implements, and, where the debt
did not exceed £12, of his house and land, and to give him
reasonable time and opportunity for paying the debt before
execution.[2] In the next year, moreover, Carleton was
empowered to make grants of land henceforth ' in fief or
seigneurie' in accordance with French custom before the conquest instead of in the English forms of ' free and common
soccage ' as hitherto [3]—the most definite departure so far
made from the policy of 1763 and admittedly a 'fresh proof'
of the Governor's conciliatory intentions.[4] But these concessions notwithstanding, the anxiety of the French-
Canadians was by no means allayed. No provisional
regulations could dissipate the fog which hung so thickly
and confusingly round the legal system ; and who could
say what its final form would be ? The seigneurs' principal
grievance—exclusion from all office on religious grounds—
remained unredressed. And if religious toleration in its
narrower sense might seem assured, especially since the
appointment of Bishop Briand, yet the legal status of the
Church was still uncertain. Under the French régime
the priesthood had been supported by the tithes of their

[1] Kingsford, vol. v, p. 214.
[2] Ordinance of February 1, 1770, C. D., p. 401 [K., p. 63].
[3] Additional Instructions to Governor Carleton, July 2, 1771, C. D.,
p. 423—doubtless inspired by Carleton, now in England.
[4] Cramahé to Hillsborough, May 5, 1772, Coffin, op. cit., p. 459.

parishioners ; and, though, since the conquest, the tithes had generally still been paid,[1] how long could the Church afford to dispense with the legal obligation for their payment among a people to whom any voluntary system of Church maintenance was quite unknown ? Inevitably their fears increased with the increasing agitation of the British minority. These antagonists of theirs, however unjust their claims might seem, were brothers in blood with British ministers : they could pull a hundred wires in London : their outcry, it seemed, had led to Murray's fall. And if the new Governor was no less broad-minded and conciliatory, the new Attorney-General made no concealment of his anti-Papist prejudices. What if the British traders should prove in the end as powerful as they were noisy ? What if Carleton shared Murray's fate ? What if distant and preoccupied ministers were prevailed on, if only for peace and quiet, to yield to the men of their own race, to revoke their concessions, and to deliver them into the power of an alien and tyrannical faction ?

Spurred on by these misgivings, the French-Canadians did what they could to counter the British agitation. When Carleton left for England, they confided to ' this worthy representative of your Majesty, who perfectly comprehends the condition of this colony and the customs of the people ', a petition for the restoration of their law, ' the basis and foundation of their possessions and the rule of their family life ', and for admission to the service of ' our King and our country ', their humiliating exclusion from which ' seems to

[1] In evidence before the House of Commons Committee on the Quebec Bill, Carleton said that very few of the clergy had not received the tithes and parochial dues as formerly. Protestant landowners had probably not been asked to pay. The clergy had acted ' with great moderation and discretion . . . hoping in a short time that the laws would be ascertained. . . .' (Cavendish, *Debates in the House of Commons on the Quebec Bill* (London, 1839), pp. 103–104 [K., p. 106; E. & G., pp. 52–53]). See also Masères's evidence: ' It has often happened that they have not paid tithe ; much oftener that they did, from their regard for their religion.' Cavendish, p. 130 [K., p. 116; E. & G., pp. 71, 72].

have made of us a reprobate nation '.[1] Three years later
they refused to be enticed by the organizers of the British
party into joining in its demand for an Assembly,[2] and the
British petition and memorials were pursued to London by
a counter-petition and memorial of their own. Once more,
on the eve of the great decision, they proclaimed with all the
fervour of their race the allegiance of a conquered people
to their conquerors. They recalled the generous policy of
Amherst in the period of military government—the retention
of their own laws, their own civil judges, their own militia,
and the toleration of their faith confirmed by the treaty
of peace. *Nous n'oublirons jamais cet excès de bonté.* But
with civil government an unhappy change had come. Their
judges were dismissed ; their militia disbanded ; all office
closed to them ; and the laws of England introduced, laws
' infinitely wise and useful for the mother country ' but not
to be blended with Canadian customs without the utter
destruction of their property. They had just cause, therefore, to be uneasy and afraid : and only the restoration of
their ancient laws and of the civic privileges they had once
enjoyed could dissipate these fears and this uneasiness.
This, then, was the boon they humbly asked of their ' most
illustrious and generous sovereign '. ' Vouchsafe to bestow
your favours upon all your subjects equally and without
distinction ! Preserve the glorious title of sovereign of a
free people ! Grant us in common with your other subjects
the rights and privileges of English citizens ! ' [3]

[1] *Une nation réprouvée,* C. D., pp. 419–420.
[2] See p. 77, below.
[3] Petition of French Subjects, December 1773. Sixty-five signatures
(C. D., p. 504 [B. K., pp. 31–34]).

2

These impassioned appeals by themselves might have
proved an inadequate presentment of the French-Canadian
case : but at the ears of King and ministers was also Carleton's quiet and persistent voice. In conversation and in
writing he continued for three years to urge the opinions
he had so quickly formed in Canada. Nor was his influence
on the framing of the Quebec Bill confined to Government
circles. He was the chief and the most closely questioned
witness before the House of Commons Committee on the Bill,
and the trenchant statements of the man who had fought
with Wolfe for Canada and had been for four years its
actual Governor were bound to impress the politicians at
Westminster.[1] His picture of the 150,000 Canadians,[2]
almost wholly French and almost wholly Roman Catholic,
whose claims must in common justice rank superior to those
of the 600 British immigrants, stood out clearly from a long
and detailed examination which left all the main points of
his policy unshaken. He stood firmly by the suggestion he
had urged in his dispatches that the Canadian gentry should
be admitted to the military and civil service of the Crown.
' I have often told them ', he said, ' that I believed it would
be the case in time.'[3] As to the legal system his principal
statements were as follows :

The Canadians are very anxious to have Canadian law to

[1] For a modern instance of the importance of local experience in
determining forms of government for oversea countries of the British
Commonwealth, note the part played by officials and ex-officials of the
Government of India in the preparation of the India Bill of 1919, in the
discussion of it by the Joint Committee of both Houses of Parliament, and
in its passage through the House of Lords (Letter from the Government of
India, 1919 [Cmd. 123] ; Report of Joint Committee, Evidence, 1919, p. 203 ;
Hansard, House of Lords, vol. xxxvii, no. 109).

[2] Carleton admitted that his figure for the French-Canadian population
was a very rough estimate. Masères, in his evidence, speaks of 90,000.
Thurlow, in 1773, puts it at 80,000 or 100,000 (C. D., p. 442).

[3] Cavendish, op. cit., pp. 113, 118–119 [K., pp. 110–112 ; E. & G.,
pp. 62–64].

decide in matters of property. I believe they are pretty indifferent in regard to criminal law.

The partiality and attachment which they have to the laws and customs they possess is well known ; and they apprehend that laws unknown to them may introduce something terrible to them—they know not what. With regard to any portion of their [civil] law, one custom separate from another, I believe they would be extremely hurt to have *any part* of their customs taken from them, except when the commercial interest of the country may require a reasonable preference. . . . I believe they would make no objection to any such commercial laws if they may know what those laws are.[1]

Of his examination on the question of an Assembly, the following was the chief part :

Are the Canadian inhabitants desirous of having an Assembly ?—Certainly not.

Have they not thought with horror of an Assembly in the country, if it should be composed of the old British inhabitants now resident there ?—No doubt it would give them great offence.

Would they not greatly prefer a government by the Governor and Legislative Council to such an Assembly ?— No doubt they would.

Is that the only idea of the Assembly that you ever knew suggested to the Canadians . . . ?—I put the question to several of the Canadians. They told me Assemblies had drawn upon the other colonies so much distress, had occasioned such riots and confusion, that they wished never to have one of any kind whatever.

Have they such objections to the form of an Assembly as [not] to wish to make their ideas prevalent in such an Assembly ?—They do not wish for Assemblies : but if Assemblies there must be, no doubt they would wish them to be a free representation of the people. If that should be the case, they would compose a great part of that Assembly.

Would they have an objection to a seat in such an Assembly in which they might have an opportunity of delivering their opinions ?—They never had an Assembly

---

[1] Cavendish, *op. cit.*, pp. 106, 117 [K., pp. 106, 111 ; E. & G., pp. 55, 62]. Lieut.-Governor Cramahé, now acting for Carleton at Quebec, shared his chief's opinions : see his dispatch to Dartmouth, December 13, 1773, C. D., p. 492.

or anything like an Assembly, nor have they the least desire to have one ; but if there should be one, they ought to have a share in it.[1]

A clear case clearly put. Unquestionably the French-Canadians were fortunate in their advocate.[2]

3

The British community in Canada, meanwhile, were well aware that the current of official opinion was running against them. Their vociferous indignation at the Government's initial concessions to French sentiment and at Murray's acts and attitude had given place to a more sober and anxious frame of mind when they found that Carleton's sympathies were akin to Murray's : and when the news that a permanent settlement was being considered in London roused them to a last vigorous effort to vindicate their claims before the issue was finally decided by the authority of Parliament, in method and manner their agitation was better calculated than heretofore to attain its ends. Their demands were far more moderate, their language far more restrained than that of the Grand Jury of 1764, when in 1770 they presented to the Crown their petition for an Assembly. In this short and temperate document the emphasis is laid as before on the need of promoting the commercial prosperity of the province and on the predominant share of British merchants in its trade : but ' the

---

[1] Cavendish, *op. cit.*, pp. 105–106, 119 [K., pp. 106, 112 ; E. & G., pp. 54–55, 64].

[2] Murray did not give evidence. The Opposition, hearing that he was in the House and opposed to the Bill, demanded that he should be heard ; and the Government, who claimed that he supported the Bill, agreed : but finding that he had left the House, North refused to delay the progress of the Bill for his attendance (Cavendish, pp. 176–188). Presumably Murray would have backed the French case as a whole rather than the British ; but he was not on good terms with the man who had supplanted him at Quebec, and he might have favoured Masères's opinion on the question of law rather than Carleton's.

extreme poverty and misery' of the French population, who ' have hitherto proved rather a burden than any benefit to themselves or advantage to the community ', are now put forward as an argument for an Assembly on the ground that it alone can prompt them to improve the natural advantages of the province by making and enforcing due obedience to laws for encouraging agriculture and regulating trade. ' There are now ', the petitioners declare, ' a sufficient number of your Majesty's Protestant subjects residing in and possessed of real property in this province and who are otherwise qualified to be members of a General Assembly.'[1] Three years later, when preparations for the Quebec Bill were already far advanced, a committee was formed at Quebec under the auspices of John McCord, and an unsuccessful attempt was made to enlist the co-operation of some of the local French-Canadians.[2] A second committee was formed at Montreal, and in the ensuing months both were busily engaged in drafting a series of petitions and memorials and obtaining the signatures of the British residents, outside official circles, in the province.[3] Throughout these documents the stress is laid on the Home Government's promise

[1] C. D., p. 417. The petition carries thirty-one names. Its claim that three-fourths of the trade is in British hands was contested. Carleton in his evidence stated that he heard about two-thirds of the trade was in French-Canadian hands. He also pointed out that the cultivation of the land was almost entirely in their hands and that since the conquest they had grown wheat ' in great abundance ' and that ' large quantities ' of wheat had been exported (Cavendish, *op. cit.*, pp. 104–105 [K., pp. 105–106 ; E. & G., pp. 53–54]). Masères said that perhaps seven-eighths of the *export* trade was British (Cavendish, p. 141).

[2] Minutes of the Quebec Committee, C. D., pp. 487–490. For the leading part played by ' a Mr. McCord from the North of Ireland, who settled here soon after the conquest where he has picked up a very comfortable livelihood by the retailing business, in which he is a considerable dealer, the article of spirituous liquors especially ', see Cramahé to Dartmouth, December 13, 1773, C. D., p. 491 ; and cf. Carleton's reference to him, p. 65, above.

[3] Petition to the Lieutenant-Governor, November 29, 1773, C. D., p. 493 ; Petition to the King, December 31, 1773, p. 495 ; Memorial to Lord Dartmouth from Quebec, December 31, 1773, p. 498 ; from Montreal, January 15, 1774, p. 501.

that British immigrants into Canada should enjoy the benefit of the laws of England and, as an essential part of those laws, of representative institutions. Anything that might be construed as offensive to French-Canadian sentiment is now carefully avoided. The establishment of an Assembly and of English law is represented as a means of harmony between the two races. The question of religious toleration is not raised ; and there is no trace of antagonism to the Roman Church except in connexion with a reasonable plea for the provision of Protestant colleges and schools where alarm is expressed at the exposure of Protestant children to 'the known assiduity of the Roman Catholic clergy' and at the creation of exclusively Catholic seminaries from the 'immense funds' of their Church.[1] Even as to the constitution of an Assembly no demand is advanced for a religious qualification for membership. 'Your memorialists', writes the Quebec Committee to Dartmouth, 'conscious of their own inability, will not presume to point out how this Assembly should be composed and constituted. That is a matter in their opinion fitting only for the wisdom and consideration of his Majesty and his learned Councils.'[2] But the underlying assumption throughout is, rightly enough, that British ministers are not prepared to admit Roman Catholics to a colonial legislature ; and in order to forestall the conclusion that, the great mass of the population being Roman Catholic, no Assembly can therefore be established, the Committee reminds the Home authorities once more of the importance of the British community in

[1] Quebec Memorial to Dartmouth, C. D., p. 500 ; Montreal Memorial, p. 502. The establishment of the seminary is 'the more alarming as it excludes all Protestant teachers of any science whatever' (p. 502).

[2] Quebec Memorial to Dartmouth, C. D., p. 499. Cf. Quebec Committee to Masères, November 8, 1773, C. D., p. 490 : 'They wish for an Assembly, as they know that to be the only means of conciliating the new subjects to the British Government. . . . They would not presume to dictate. How the Assembly is to be composed is a matter of the most serious consideration. They submit that to the wisdom of His Majesty's Councils.'

numbers, in property, and in commercial activity. From such a body, it is clearly hinted, an excellent Assembly could be chosen.[1]

Unreasonable as it may seem in the light of the conditions then obtaining in Quebec, it was only to be expected that the British immigrants would agitate for an Assembly. It must once more be remembered that many of their leading spirits had recently come from the colonies in the South ; and the little community had soon become indoctrinated with the democratic principles which had been generally accepted there for generations past and were now being upheld with a special zest because they seemed to be in danger of repudiation by the British Government. And in Quebec, as in Massachusetts, the cardinal issue of taxation had been forced to the front. It has been seen above that the only taxes which could be levied in Canada after the conquest without new legislation were the import duties previously imposed by France ; but these the British traders held to be illegal, and when on their refusal to pay them they were prosecuted by the Government, British jurymen acquitted them.[2] Those of them at least who hailed from the other colonies had protested, moreover, against the Stamp Act which during the winter of 1765–1766 had been in force in Canada as elsewhere, and had vainly attempted to persuade the French-Canadians to dispute it.[3] They

---

[1] ' The number and real property of his Majesty's ancient subjects are not so trifling as may have been represented, for several of them possess the largest and best cultivated seigniories in the province (the lands of the religious societies excepted), and most of them are proprietors of freehold estates. Their personal estates by far exceed those of the new subjects ' (Quebec Memorial, C. D., p. 500).

[2] Coffin, op. cit., p. 314. After several such verdicts Government seems to have given up the attempt to collect the duties. Masères, who prosecuted for the Government, was himself doubtful as to their validity. See Masères Letters, pp. 49–50, 56, 88–91.

[3] Murray stated (August 20, 1766) that the Canadians had ' cheerfully obeyed the Stamp Act ', and an address to Carleton on his arrival in the autumn of 1766, from both British and French residents in Quebec district, claimed that the province had lately given a signal proof of its respect for

were little likely, then, to tolerate the imposition by Parliament of new taxes to replace the French : and Lieutenant-Governor Cramahé rightly perceived in the claim that they should only be taxed by their own representatives, the mainspring of their agitation for an Assembly. Commenting on their petitions to the Secretary of State, he observes that the ' old subjects ' in the province, however diverse their origin, have generally ' adopted American ideas in regard to taxation ', and declares that the news that ' a duty upon spirits was intended to be raised here by authority of Parliament was a principal cause of setting them upon petitioning for an Assembly '.[1]

As on previous occasions the appeals of the British traders in Canada were echoed by their commercial associates in London. While the Quebec Bill was being debated in Parliament, a protest against its provisions was drawn up by a group of firms in the Canadian trade and copies of it distributed among members of both Houses. They claim a personal interest in the controversy on the ground that quantities of goods and extensive credits had been provided by them for their clients in Canada on the confident assumption that English law, especially as regards commerce and property, would be maintained in accordance with the promise of 1763. Had French law been supposed to be still in force or likely to be revived, ' we would not ', they declare, ' have had any commercial connexions with the inhabitants of the province '. No objection is raised to the continuance of French law concerning the tenure or inheritance of land for the existing generation or concerning marriage agreements and similar family contracts. As to the form of government, venturing into greater detail than

Parliament's authority ' by an immediate and universal obedience to the Stamp Act ' (Coffin, *op. cit.*, pp. 316–317).

[1] Cramahé to Dartmouth, July 15, 1774, C. D., p. 503. Masères desired the imposition of new duties by Parliament, a point on which his attitude was fundamentally different from that of the British colonial element in Canada. See p. 86, n. 1, below.

their clients in Quebec, they state their preferences in a descending sequence of priority : first, a purely Protestant Assembly ; second, if there is no hope of an Assembly, a purely Protestant Council with powers of legislation ; third, if in the worst event the Council is not to be exclusively Protestant, the maintenance of a Protestant majority in it and the admission of ' only a few of the most moderate sort of Roman Catholics '. Finally they urge that, if a legislative Council is established, its members may be removable only by the King-in-Council, so that they may ' both act with a spirit of freedom and independence becoming their high offices of legislators, and be thought to do so by the people of the same, instead of being considered as dependent creatures and tools of the will and pleasure of the Governor for the time being '.[1]

4

That the merchants of Quebec and Montreal had stated their case in a somewhat less didactic strain than their *confrères* in the City of London had been largely due to the influence of the Attorney-General of the province. Francis Masères [2] was a capable lawyer and a clear-headed and indefatigable writer. For the first two years of his residence in Canada he seems to have worked smoothly with

[1] Case of the British Merchants trading to Quebec, C. D., pp. 512–521 [K., pp. 72–79]. Special stress is laid on trial by jury and the writ of *habeas corpus* as essentials of British law (p. 517). If French law *is* to be restored, they ask for a delay of three years to allow of the withdrawal of their goods and the recovery of their debts under English law (p. 515). Acquiescence in the French law as to inheritance of land is limited to land ' belonging to Canadians born, or to be born, of marriages already contracted ' (p. 517). Independence of Council (p. 520).

[2] Masères (1731–1824) was born and spent most of his life in England. He had had a successful career as a mathematician at Cambridge ; he was ' fourth wrangler ' in 1752 and became a Fellow of Clare College in 1756. For a good account of the man and his work, see W. S. Wallace's introduction to *The Masères Letters*.

Carleton and, though he could never agree with his tolerant attitude towards the Roman Church, to have more or less shared his views on the legal question. But in the course of 1769 their opinions diverged ; and when Masères tendered his resignation in the autumn of that year, Carleton, never very patient with those who differed from him, gladly accepted it. Masères had thus preceded Carleton to London, and from no other quarter, not even from the Law Officers or the Board of Trade, were ministers and legislators bombarded with such profuse and persistent exposition and argument. And on one vital point, at any rate, on the question of law, the case of the British minority as he handled it was undeniably attractive. For Masères was pleading for just such a compromise as is supposed to be peculiarly tempting to the British mind. ' The French-Canadians ', he argued in effect, ' are a peasant people. On its material side their life is concentrated on their land, on the money they earn from it, and on the little stock of household treasures they hand down from generation to generation. To the legal customs that concern these things, cumbrous as they are, they have become devoted by a century and more of use and wont. Their replacement by an alien system, itself by no means perfect—the language in which it is presented, the principles on which it is based, alike strange and unintelligible—would not only involve these simple peasants in confusion and expense but would seem to them to shake and undermine the very foundations of their lives. Leave them, then, their ancient mode of holding, buying, selling, bequeathing land. Leave them, too, for a time at any rate, their marriage customs, their rules of dowry and the like. Let all that part of their law be codified and given authority by Parliament. But do not go on to cripple the commercial prospects of the country and ruin the British traders you have encouraged to settle in it by retaining, together with these customs, the whole body of the French-Canadian civil law. Such a course would not only be uneconomical and unjust : it would be dangerous. It would be French, not English, law in that case that Canadians would be called upon to venerate and obey. The constant reference to French edicts, to French judgements, to French law-books, would perpetuate the historic tie between New France and Old. Generation after generation of *habitants* would learn as of yore to look with pride to France and not to England as the original source of justice. And how does that accord with your desire to make Canada a British province, to assimilate it in course of time with the rest of your colonial system ? ' [1]

While he thus skilfully argued their case for the retention

[1] The main points of Masères's case may be found in three documents : Considerations on the expediency of providing an Act of Parliament for the settlement of Quebec, C. D., p. 257 [K., p. 49; B. K., p. 12] ; Draft of an intended report of the Governor-in-Council, p. 327 ; and Criticism of Carleton's report on the laws p. 370 [K., p. 58]—and also in his evidence before the House of Commons in Committee on the Quebec Bill (Cavendish, pp. 123–141 [K., pp. 112–118; E. & G., pp. 65–74]). For his further writings, see *A collection of Several Commissions . . . and other papers relating to the state of the Province of Quebec* (London, 1772) ; *An Account of the Proceedings of the British and other Inhabitants of Quebec* (London, 1775) ; *Additional Papers concerning Quebec* (London, 1776); *The Canadian Freeholder* (London, 1776–1779, 3 vols., containing rather ponderous dialogues between a British and a French-Canadian and arguing for the repeal of the Quebec Act). For his life and opinions while in Canada, see *The Masères Letters*, from which it appears that in 1768, after two years' residence in Canada, he was not averse to Carleton's plan—the restoration of the whole French civil law. His ' Draft of a report ' (February 1769) simply states the four possible methods of settling the question with their respective merits and demerits, with a recommendation that the French law as to land-tenure, inheritance, &c., should be restored for the time being (C. D., pp. 361–363, 369). It is not till his ' Criticism of Carleton's Report ' (September 1769) that he definitely rejects Carleton's plan and advocates the compromise described above (see Wallace's Introduction to the *Letters*, pp. 20–21). A brief statement of his final position is given in a letter to the Lord Chancellor (Lord Apsley) April 30, 1774 (C. D., p. 531). He supported the view that the Government was bound by Article XXXVII of the Capitulation of Montreal and by the Treaty of Paris to maintain the French law as regards land-tenure (p. 374) ; cf. p. 33, above. For his resignation and Carleton's report to Hillsborough as to his anti-Roman prejudices and antipathy towards the French-Canadians, see Chapais, *op. cit.*, p. 116, n. 2.

of the greater part of the English law, Masères parted company with the British community on the question of an Assembly. It was not that he was any more kindly disposed than they were to Roman Catholicism. If his descent was French, it was also Huguenot : and it is one of the multitudinous proofs of the folly of the persecution of their Protestant subjects by the autocrats of France that in such a man as Masères a rooted prejudice against Roman Catholics should overmaster a natural sympathy with Frenchmen.[1] Nor did he dissent from the British view that, now Canada was a British province, French-Canadian nationality must gradually die out. He looked forward—as who would not ?—to a ' coalition of the two nations ' ; but, like Durham at a later day, he conceived this happy event as ' the melting down the French nation into the English in point of language, affections, religion and laws '.[2] So superficial in his eyes were the strongest elements in the traditional life of French Canada that he even believed (at least he professed the belief) that the supersession of Catholic by Protestant clergy after the conquest would not only have been accepted without dissatisfaction by their parishioners but would have led in many cases to actual conversion. ' They are a submissive quiet people ', he told the House of Commons : ' I believe in many places, if a Protestant minister had been put in upon the vacancy of a priest, a very little pains taken by the Protestant minister would have brought over many to the Protestant religion.' ' It is a mere conjecture ', he added : and doubtless ' a mere conjecture ', too, was his statement that, had they not been united and stiffened in the performance of their duties by the appointment of a bishop, the Canadian priesthood themselves ' would probably have forsaken first one doctrine, then

---

[1] Masères's grandfather had left France on the revocation of the Edict of Nantes and settled in England, where he obtained an appointment in the English civil service.

[2] Considerations on the Expediency, &c., C. D., p. 267 [K., p. 51].

another, of their own religion '.[1] To such hopes as these he regarded the ' establishment ' of the Roman Church in Canada by the legalization of tithes as a fatal blow ; [2] and in the same spirit he vigorously opposed the annexation of the *hinterland* to Quebec province as ' fortifying the Popish religion when there is no necessity for so doing '.[3] But, while on these points Masères shared the prejudices of the British minority in Canada, and while he had no more wish than they to see Roman Catholics admitted into a Canadian Assembly, he could not swallow their doctrine of race ascendancy and support their plea for a purely Protestant legislature. ' An Assembly so constituted ', he said, ' might pretend to be a representative of the people there, but in truth it would be a representative of only the 600 new English settlers and an instrument in their hands of domineering over the 90,000 French. Can such an Assembly be thought just or expedient or likely to produce harmony and friendship between the two nations ? '[4] He was therefore opposed to the creation of any Assembly at all ;

[1] Cavendish, pp. 131, 137–138 [E. & G., pp. 72–74] ; cf. Masères's letters to Mr. Fowler Walker (London agent for the British traders in Canada) of July 17 and November 19, 1767, where he condemns the appointment of a bishop as ' a most pernicious measure ', especially because it hinders the process of conversion. The Protestant ministers with whom he proposes to replace the Catholic priests are of course to be *French* Protestants. He seems to have been impressed by a single instance of a French-Canadian Recollet monk who had become Protestant. Carleton had a poor opinion of this individual ; and after his appointment as rector at Trois Rivières he was described as ' a most dissolute character ' who ' never does any duty at all ' (*The Masères Letters*, pp. 53–57, and footnotes).

[2] Cavendish, p. 130 [K., p. 116 ; E. & G., p. 71].

[3] Cavendish, p. 134.

[4] Considerations on the Expediency, &c., C. D., p. 267 [K., p. 51]. This was written before Masères went to Quebec ; and, being dependent on official papers, largely Murray's, it was coloured by some prejudice against the British settlers. He refers to them as ' English adventurers ' and ascribes their desire for an Assembly to the ambition of ' displaying their parts and eloquence in the characters of leading Assemblymen ' (p. 268). His attitude to the British was somewhat modified by his two years' residence at Quebec, but he maintained his opposition to a Protestant Assembly.

for he had other arguments, besides that of the religious bar, against an Assembly constituted of *both* races. Bigoted in their faith, prejudiced against English ways, the French members would inevitably quarrel with their British colleagues and with the provincial Government over any measures introduced with a view to ' anglicizing ' Canada. Their ignorance of the English language, moreover, would lead to the conduct of debates in French—a serious obstacle this, to the fusion of the nations. He disliked, too, like Carleton, the democratic tendencies which the possession of Assemblies had fostered in the older American colonies : anything which might tend to weaken the supreme authority of Parliament in Canada was in his view to be strictly avoided.[1] And his final argument was also Carleton's— that the French-Canadians do not want an Assembly.[2] In its place he proposed an enlarged Legislative Council which, unlike an Assembly it would seem, might justly be composed of Protestants alone : its members, he agreed with the London merchants, should be independent of the Governor.[3]

Thus, for a large part of their case but not for the whole of it, the British also possessed an advocate of official standing and local experience ; and Masères spoke out for them as sincerely and as positively as Carleton for the French.

[1] He held that, since the levy of the old French customs dues was of questionable legality, Parliament should have imposed new duties in 1766. ' I think it would have been particularly seasonable to do so at that time, as it would have been a beneficial exertion of that taxative authority which the Parliament claimed over the colonies and which they made an Act of Parliament on purpose to declare [i.e. the Declaratory Act of 1765]. Such an exertion would have shown the Americans that the Parliament was really in earnest in their assertion of the right of taxing them, and did not mean to assert it only in words and on parchment, which is what all the Americans now conceive ' (Masères to Charles Yorke, May 27, 1768, *Letters*, pp. 90–91).

[2] Considerations on the Expediency, &c., C. D., p. 267 [K., p. 52].

[3] Masères to Dartmouth, January 4, 1774, C. D., p. 486. In his evidence he recommended the admission of some Roman Catholics to the Council ' with a large quorum consisting of Protestants only '. Cavendish, p. 132 [K., p. 117].

5

To the information and the arguments set forth by the
protagonists there was little to be added by the other leading
figures in the case. Chief Justice Hey had always believed
with Carleton that conciliatory treatment would induce the
French-Canadians to ' withdraw from every idea of return-
ing to their old government and become good British
subjects ' : but he had left Carleton and followed Masères
in proposing that only part of the old civil law should be
retained. He admitted, however, in his evidence, that this
compromise might not now satisfy the French-Canadians.
' They have risen in their demands of late ', he said, ' and
hope to be gratified to the utmost extent of their desires.'
He admitted, too, that trial by jury was not appreciated by
the French-Canadians : the *seigneurs* regard it as degrading,
' the lower orders look upon it (as in truth it is) as a burden
to them '—a burden that might be lightened by payment
for their ' time and trouble '. Hey was more inclined than
Masères, moreover, to discount the claims of the British
minority : and in the House of Commons Committee he
made one telling point against them. ' They are wonderfully
zealous ', he said, ' for the trial by jury : and the misfortune
is they do not act up to it : for *I can never get them to attend.'* [1]

Only one French-Canadian personally represented the
opinions of his countrymen, M. Chartier de Lotbinière,
a *seigneur* of high standing and wide estates and on that
account an imperfect representative of his countrymen as
a whole. His main objection to the Bill was its retention of
the English criminal law, partly because its procedure was
strange to the French-Canadians but chiefly because it was
to his mind inconceivable that a jury could be as just,

[1] Cavendish, pp. 151–152, 156–157 [K., pp. 118–119, 121–122 ; E. & G.,
pp. 75–76, 80–81].

impartial, and enlightened as judges chosen from the ' most honourable men in the province, all thoroughly acquainted with the law '. He was ready to admit that Council government as established by the Bill was ' despotism ', and declared that his countrymen would wish to choose their Council for themselves, but in any case its members should be taken, irrespective of course of their religion, ' only from the class of the principal and larger proprietors in the matter of land '. But in the main and especially on the crucial point of the civil law, M. de Lotbinière's case supported Carleton's. ' Do you not think ', he was asked, ' the English laws best for the Canadians ? ' ' I make no doubt but your laws are wise and good ', he courteously replied, ' and make you a happy people, but my countrymen prefer their old laws and customs.' [1]

There remained the official legal advisers of the Government, whose views, as might be expected, took their colour for the most part from Carleton's views as before they had from Murray's. The Board of Trade, it is true, bent upon freeing the British exchequer from the cost of the Canadian administration, at one time favoured a small Assembly in which the Protestant members were to be secured a narrow majority over the Roman Catholics, while in the Council five out of fifteen members should be Catholic French-Canadians.[2] But this proposal was made before

[1] Evidence in the Commons Committee, Cavendish, pp. 161–163; Memorandum on the Quebec Bill, C. D., pp. 564–567.

[2] Report of the Lords of Trade, July 10, 1769, C. D., pp. 383–384. Roman Catholics were also, of course, to be admitted to the Courts and to Government offices. The Assembly was to consist of twenty-seven members ; and the seven members for Quebec City, the four for Montreal City, and the three for Trois Rivières Town were all to subscribe the test against transubstantiation, i.e. they would be Protestants. The remaining thirteen representatives of the rural districts were expected to be Catholics. As to taxation, the Board declared that ' it is neither just nor reasonable that the expense of the establishments in Quebec should any longer continue a burthen on this country ' (p. 391).

Carleton came to London, and the reports of Solicitor-General Wedderburn and Attorney-General Thurlow, completed three years later, followed Carleton practically all along the line.[1] Both accepted Carleton's conception of Quebec as a province that was and would be French. So far, indeed, had ministerial opinion swung away from the ideas of 1763 under the influence of increasing knowledge of the real conditions in Canada that Wedderburn could calmly declare it not to ' the interest of Britain that many of her natives should settle there ', and Thurlow could sneer at ' the unprincipled and impracticable expectations of those few among your Majesty's subjects who may *accidentally* resort thither '.[2]   Both were agreed on the inadvisability of creating an Assembly for the present.   A purely British body they ruled out at once, and a house composed of both races, said Wedderburn, would not only be ' a dangerous experiment with new subjects ' but also ' an inexhaustible source of dissension and opposition between them and the British subjects '.[3]   Both argued that in civilized times, ' when subjects, not slaves, are the fruits of victory ', a conqueror violates the *jus gentium* if he deprives the conquered of their property ; and both declared for the restoration of the French-Canadian civil code entire, provided that holders of land be allowed to change at will from the French to the British form of tenure : but they laid more stress than Carleton on the *seigneurs'* antipathy to trial by jury and urged

---

[1] The greater part of these Reports dated December 6, 1772, and January 22, 1773, is printed in C. D., pp. 424–437, 437–445. Probably the time taken to prepare these official Reports was the chief cause of the delay in drafting the Bill ; see Coffin, *op. cit.*, pp. 393–394.

[2] C. D., pp. 430 and 445. In the debate on the Bill, Wedderburn was still more emphatic, ' I do not wish to see Canada draw from this country any considerable number of her inhabitants. I think there ought to be no temptation held out to the subjects of England to quit their native soil, to increase colonies at the expense of this country.' British traders might come and go, but ' it is one object of this measure that these persons should not settle in Canada '. Very different ideas of colonial policy from those of 1763 !   [3] C. D., p. 426.

that the old French criminal law should also be restored.[1] As to religion Wedderburn maintained that, while the Roman Church in Canada must exercise no temporal authority nor any ecclesiastical powers derived from the see of Rome, it followed as a matter of course from the grant of freedom of worship that 'the ministers of that worship should be protected and a maintenance secured for them '.[2]

This general harmony of opinion in official circles was broken by one somewhat ponderous note. The massive ' plan of a code of laws for the province of Quebec ', presented by Advocate-General Marriott, differed from the proposals of Masères as to the legal system and religion only in the prolixity of its argument and the wealth of legal learning it displayed. He favoured the compromise between English and French civil law : he condemned the maintenance of the Romish religion as ' an established religion of the state ' in any British province. The legislature he desired to be representative, within limits, of the whole colony—not necessarily an Assembly, possibly an elective Council. But if his opinions were thus at variance with those of his colleagues, he was not prepared to press them ; and when he appeared before the Committee of the Commons, he made a clever but rather frivolous attempt, at once irritating and amusing to his audience, to conceal his dislike of the Bill by insisting on applying the rules of evidence as enforced in a court of law and evading a frank answer on any question of opinion or even as to facts of which he had no direct and personal knowledge.[3]

[1] Wedderburn, C. D., p. 431 ; Thurlow, C. D., pp. 442–444.
[2] C. D., p. 427.
[3] For ' The Plan &c.', see C. D., pp. 445–483 (the exposition of Roman Catholic doctrines at the close and the arguments drawn therefrom are omitted). For Marriott's evidence before the Commons Committee, see Cavendish, pp. 163–176.

6

Out of this complex of opinions the Bill at last took shape. In January 1774 a first draft of it was ready, a second in March, a third in April ; and on May 2 the Colonial Secretary, Lord Dartmouth, introduced the fourth draft in the House of Lords.[1]

The Bill dealt first with the boundaries of Quebec Province, which were extended to include the western *hinterland* between the Ohio and the Mississippi, the northern country up to the frontiers of the Hudson's Bay territory, and eastwards the coast of Labrador and the islands in the mouth of the St. Lawrence, which had been entrusted since 1763 to the Government of Newfoundland.

Secondly, the Proclamation of 1763 as far as it applied to Canada, together with all commissions and ordinances relative to the civil government and administration of justice issued in pursuance of its terms, was revoked.

Thirdly, it was declared that Roman Catholics in the province were to enjoy the free exercise of their religion subject to the supremacy of the King and that their clergy were to receive their accustomed dues and rights, but from members of their own faith only.

Fourthly, *all* disputes as to property and civil rights were in future to be determined in accordance with the laws and customs of Canada, ' until they shall be varied or altered ' by ordinance of the Governor and Council. But this clause was not to deprive existing owners of property of their present rights of alienation and bequest ; nor to apply to lands already granted or in future to be granted by the Crown in free and common socage.

---

[1] The drafts are printed in C. D., pp. 535–548. The final text of the Bill is given in Appendix B, p. 208, below. The clause annexing the *hinterland* is not inserted till the third draft. Only part of the English criminal law is prescribed in the second draft ; all of it in the third. In general the changes show an increasing desire to make the policy of conciliation as full and clear as possible.

Fifthly, the criminal law of England was to be retained.

Sixthly, it being 'at present inexpedient to call an Assembly ', a Council was to be appointed by the King, ' with the advice of the Privy Council', consisting of not more than twenty-three nor less than seventeen residents.   This Council, or the major part thereof, would have powers of legislating by ordinance for the peace, order, and good government of the province but not of levying any taxes or duties therein.   (Revenue was provided ' for defraying the charge of the administration of justice and the support of civil government ' by a separate measure, the Quebec Revenue Bill, which imposed fresh import duties on spirits and molasses in lieu of the old French duties but maintained the minor ' territorial or casual revenues ' which had passed from the French to the British Crown.[1])   Every ordinance of the Council was to be submitted to the Crown for approval or disallowance ;   and   no   ordinance   touching   religion   or inflicting a new punishment more serious than a fine or short imprisonment was to take effect until the Crown approved it.   No religious test for membership of Council was mentioned :   and Lord North stated in the House of Commons that the Government intended a minority of the Council to be Roman Catholic French-Canadians.[2]

7

Such was the Quebec Bill.   From beginning to end, with two or three minor exceptions only, it embodied Carleton's policy.   The exceptions were first, the extension of the provincial boundary westwards without any provision to

---

[1] The Quebec Revenue Act (14 George III, c. 88) is printed in C. D., p. 576 [K., p. 136].   It does not seem to have been contested, and no mention of it is made in the *Parliamentary History* or the *Annual Register*. For the subsequent Act, amending it, see p. 120, below.

[2] Cavendish, p. 241.

discourage or prevent the French-Canadians or other Roman
Catholics from migrating into this predominantly Indian
area ; and second, the clause permitting the continued grant
of land by the Crown in the English form of tenure. On
the first point, at any rate, Carleton was reassured. He was
told by Dartmouth that the Cabinet did not construe the
boundary clause as by any means implying an intention to
promote further settlement in the *hinterland*.[1]   But the
tenure clause remained in the Bill, and on one further point
the Government had not accepted Carleton's views.   Supported in this both by Hey and by Masères, he had recommended that the provisions of the *Habeas Corpus* Act should
be extended to Canada : but Wedderburn had argued that
the Canadians as British subjects were in any case entitled
to the old Common Law right to the writ and that before
allowing them the additional safeguards of the Act, requisite
as these had been found in seventeenth-century England for
the exercise of the Common Law right without evasion or
delay, it would be wise ' to be better assured of their fidelity
and attachment '.[2]   Carleton had not pressed this point,
and there was nothing else with which he could quarrel.
To a leading question in the House of Commons Committee
on the merits of the form of government prescribed by the
Bill, he answered : ' I should think it the best form advisable to give in the present state of the colony.'   It was
a natural answer.   The Quebec Bill was practically Carleton's Bill.

Nobody questioned Carleton's sincerity, nobody doubted

[1] Carleton's objections in which he was supported by Hillsborough
are stated in Hillsborough's memorandum, C. D., p. 551 ; Dartmouth's
reply, *ibid.*, p. 554. The third draft of the Bill contained a second tenure
provision enabling existing occupiers to change their tenures from French
to English. Carleton also objected to this, and it was struck out.

[2] Wedderburn's Report, C. D., p. 431.   See p. 128, n. 2, below.   The
author of *The Justice and Policy of the late Act of Parliament, &c.*
(probably Under-Secretary Knox, see p. 117, n. 3, below) points-out (p. 63)
that the position as regards *habeas corpus* was the same in the other colonies
as in Quebec.

his good intentions,[1] but the mere fact that the Bill was backed by his authority could not be expected to silence criticism or to disarm the opposition of the minority in Parliament which hated North's administration and distrusted all its works. It was impossible for Chatham in the Lords, for Burke and Fox and Barré in the Commons, to dissociate the Quebec Bill from the critical events which had occurred so recently in other colonies so close to Canada. The news of the ' Boston tea-party ' had reached London at the end of January ; in the following months the Bills for coercing Massachusetts were forced through Parliament ; and the third reading of the second of them was carried in the Commons on the very day that the Quebec Bill was introduced in the Lords. It was known, moreover, that the American colonists resented this measure scarcely less than its predecessors.[2] It mattered little that the policy of the Bill had gradually developed during the previous years ; or that the kernel of it had been shaped as long ago as 1766 in the Yorke-De Grey report ; or that its general principles had been agreed on by ministers before relations with New England, which had seemed for some time past to be entering on a friendlier phase, had been so suddenly and sharply strained ; or that in the series of Cabinet meetings which decided on the penal measures the Quebec Bill was not discussed at all.[3] In vain North and Thurlow

[1] Thomas Townsend, one of the most vigorous opponents of the Bill, said in the course of the debate : ' With regard to the Governor, as a military man, I entertain for him great respect; as a gentleman, everybody respects him : and if despotic government is to be trusted to any hands—I will not say it will be safe in those of General Carleton—but I am persuaded it will be as safe in his as in anybody's. This is only doing justice to his character. When I recollect the complexion of his evidence, I am convinced that he is determined to do right ; and I wish to throw as few obstacles in his way as possible.' Cavendish, p. 280.

[2] Thomas Penn presented a petition to the House of Commons on behalf of the proprietaries of Pennsylvania against the boundary provisions of the Bill on May 31 (Cavendish, p. 72). Burke and other members alluded in the debates to the complaints of the colonists.

[3] See Alvord, *op. cit.*, vol. ii, p. 235 and n. 436, citing the minutes of the

repudiated any intention of encroaching upon other colonies
or barring their established claims, and proved their sincerity
by remodelling the boundary clause in consultation with the
Whig leaders and by inserting a proviso to safeguard the
existing boundaries of the colonies.[1] In vain they urged
the real motives for the annexation of the *hinterland* to
Quebec—the necessity for regulating settlement and trade
in the Indian territories, the need of giving its scattered
European residents some civil government, and, since the
great majority of them were French, the expediency of
grouping them with their kinsmen under the Government of
Canada, as stated in the preamble of the Bill.[2] A cool un-
prejudiced judgement was not to be expected at the close of
that historic session ; and the little company of Whigs, who
day after day sat impotent while the measures which made
civil war in America inevitable were carried over their heads,
were almost bound to regard the Quebec Bill as one of the
same series, to prejudge it as yet another act of hostility
towards the ' rebels ' in America, and, when its text was in

Cabinet meetings preserved in the Dartmouth MSS. As a matter of fact
some of the Opposition leaders had been themselves in some degree committed to the policy of the Quebec Bill. Carleton left England to take up
his governorship just *after* the formation of the Chatham ministry in 1766.
In 1767 he had determined on the policy which was afterwards embodied
in the Bill ; he communicated his opinions to Shelburne and was continued
in office.

[1] Cavendish, pp. 25–26, 73, 188–197, 253. North said : ' It was never
intended that the Bill should entrench upon other colonies. Whenever any
proposal is made to us, whatever can tend to secure Pennsylvania and the
other proprietaries shall meet with no opposition from me.'

[2] Cavendish, pp. 25, 58, 195. The only other conceivable policies were
(i) to leave the territory separate under military government—a great
hardship to the European residents who were growing in numbers (Advocate-
General Marriott estimated them at 7,000, C. D., p. 467) and asking for
civil government (Petition from Illinois district in 1773, Coffin, *op. cit.*,
p. 473) ; (ii) to annex it to one of the other colonies—which was obviously
barred by the impossibility of deciding between their jealously conflicting
claims. See Coffin (*op. cit.*, pp. 398–431), who clearly shows that the
policy of the boundary clause was an old and consistent policy and had
nothing to do with the Boston troubles. For further discussion, see p. 106,
n. 1, below.

their hands, to find what they sought in almost every line. On the rest of the Government's colonial policy they had shown, with Chatham on their side, a better appreciation of the principles at issue than North and his colleagues : but now, though Chatham was still with them, the roles were reversed. Their whole minds intent upon the rights of their fellow citizens in the British colonies, the Whigs did not perceive that in Canada the new problem of nationality had cut across the old problem of self-government. Their policy was in essence the ignorant policy of 1763. They had escaped the course of study which had been imposed since then upon the Government. They did not know the facts ; and when in Committee they listened to the evidence of the men who knew them, it was mainly those facts which told in favour of the claims of the British colonists in Canada and elsewhere that they seized upon and quoted in debate. And so it happened that, on this occasion, the real champion of freedom was North, not Fox, nor Chatham.

The Bill passed rapidly through the Lords, and in the Commons the debate, which was thinly attended throughout, opened on May 26 and continued for nine days.[1] From first to last the attitude of the Opposition was uncompromisingly hostile.[2] The language of the Bill was ' the language of despotism '. It was framed on ' the principles which prevailed in the days of Charles II '. It was ' Popish from beginning to end '. There was not a ' spark or semblance of liberty ' in it. Could ' an English Parliament disgrace

[1] The number of members who voted on the various stages of the Bill averaged from 120 to 130. At one point the attendance sank to 45.

[2] Sir Thomas Mills, Receiver-General of Quebec, was in London at the time and wrote to Haldimand : ' We have had as hard fighting and many more battles to establish government for Canada as there were to conquer it. You would be astonished at the opposition made to the Bill ; ten nights the House of Commons was kept till one o'clock in the morning successively. Every inch of the ground was argued and every word disputed ' (June 14, 1774 ; quoted by Coffin, *op. cit.*, p. 395).

itself' by enacting so tyrannical a measure?[1] That the
critics were reading the Bill through Boston spectacles was
most evident perhaps in Barré's speeches. The Bill, as he
oddly phrased it, 'carries in its breast something that
squints and looks dangerous to the inhabitants of our other
colonies in that country'; and in a somewhat melodramatic
passage, reminiscent of the days when Strafford's Irish
army cast its shadow over English politics, he went so far as
to discover in the Bill a deliberate design to concentrate in
Canada a great Roman Catholic force for the reduction of the
disaffected colonies. 'I know what you mean!' he cried.
'*Liberavi animam meam* : I have foretold the thing!'[2]

Fox and Burke were greater men than Barré. They lent
no support to such extravagant suspicions, to so ruthless
an appeal to the old religious fears and prejudices of Englishmen. Much as they desired to destroy the Bill, they said
nothing to enhance the uneasiness which the religious clauses
of the Bill must have awakened in strictly Protestant con-
sciences on both sides of the House. In a fine passage Burke
extolled the principle of toleration,[3] and Fox rejoiced that
the penal laws were not to be applied to Canada.[4] But
they were at one with Barré in regarding the Bill as part of
a sinister policy of reaction in colonial government. In
the retention of the French-Canadian civil law and the
postponement of an Assembly they saw nothing but a refusal
to set up in a British colony the foundations on which alone
British freedom could be built—trial by jury, the right of
habeas corpus, representative institutions; nothing but
a deliberate preference for absolutist methods which was
part and parcel with the coercion of Massachusetts and
boded ill for the cause of liberty throughout America. They

---

[1] Phipps, Cavendish, p. 79 ; Glynn, p. 49 ; Barré, p. 238 ; Fox, p. 61
[K., p. 100 ; E. & G., p. 44] ; Barré, p. 81.
[2] Cavendish, pp. 43, 228 [K., p. 97].
[3] See p. 115, below.
[4] Cavendish, p. 62 [K., p. 101 ; E. & G., p. 45].

brushed impatiently aside the undisputed evidence that the French-Canadians wanted their own laws and did not want an Assembly : it was the business of the British Parliament to make them free despite themselves. The Bill, Burke argued, restores the French-Canadians to Bourbon absolutism ; ' the only difference is they will have George III for Louis XVI '. ' Instead of making them free subjects of England, you sentence them to French government for ages. . . . They are condemned slaves by the British Parliament : you only give them new masters. There is an end of Canada !' Nor would the evil thing be confined to Canada. ' No free country can keep another country in slavery. The price they pay for it will be their own servitude. . . . When we are sowing the seeds of despotism in Canada, let us bear in mind that it is a growth which may afterwards extend to other countries. . . . At some time or other it will come home to England.' Suppose, moreover, that the French-Canadians would tolerate tyranny, what of the British immigrants ? ' I do not know that one Englishman can beat two Frenchmen ; but I do know that in this case he ought to be more valuable than twenty Frenchmen if you estimate him as a freeman and the Frenchmen as slaves. . . . Do you propose to take away liberty from the Englishman because you will not give it to the French ? I would give it to the Englishman though ten thousand Frenchmen should take it against their will. . . . I claim protection for the three hundred and sixty English families whom I do know against the prejudices of the *noblesse* of Canada whom I do not know ' And progress, after all, has always warred with prejudice. ' Was all England pleased with the Revolution ? No. The wishes of the majority were sacrificed to the reason of the better part and the interests of the whole.' By the same rule liberty must be imposed on both races in Canada. ' Give them English liberty, give them an English constitution, and then, whether they speak French or English, whether they go to mass or attend our own communion, you will render them valuable and useful subjects of Great Britain '.[1] In a similar strain Fox urged the application to Canada of his doctrine of constitutional ' assimilation '. Of this doctrine the refusal to give the Canadians a representative legislature seemed on the face of it an obvious violation ; more cautious, however, on this point than Burke, he only suggested, he did not positively affirm, that the establishment of an Assembly was immediately expedient. But in any case, he argued, better now than never : and the creation of a Council, appointed by the Crown, so far from being, as ministers had intimated, a step towards assimilation, was bound to prove a permanent obstacle to an Assembly. ' Is it likely ', he asked, ' this Legislative Council would go on, from day to day, considering how they would abridge their own power ? . . . I never wish to see the liberties of a country dependent on such extraordinary virtue.' And with his usual debating skill Fox dragged to light the special motive for postponing an Assembly which in North's mind at any rate transcended any other. ' No one has urged ', he said, ' the circumstance of the people of Canada being Roman Catholics as an objection to an Assembly, and I trust I shall never hear such an objection stated.' [2] The challenge was unmistakable and North did not evade it, ' Is it safe ', he asked, ' for this country—for we must consider this country—to put the principal power into the hands of an Assembly of Roman Catholic new subjects ? ' But on the wider question of assimilation North's

[1] Cavendish, pp. 89, 288–290 [K., pp. 103, 131–132 ; E. & G., pp. 50, 93–95]. Before the evidence was taken, Burke declared that he desired to treat the French-Canadians kindly, that he was unaware of any complaint on their part against English law, and that, if it should be forthcoming, he would give it a fair hearing. After the evidence, however, he maintained his previous opinion as above.

[2] Cavendish, pp. 246–247 [K., p. 125 ; E. & G., pp. 88–89]. Fox devoted the greater part of his speeches on the Bill to a futile attempt to quash it outright by arguing that the clause legalizing tithes made it a money Bill which could not be initiated in the House of Lords.

attitude was less candid. ' That it is desirable to give the
Canadians a constitution in every respect like the constitution of Great Britain, I will not say ; but I earnestly hope
that they will, in the course of time, enjoy as much of our
laws and as much of our constitution as may be beneficial
for that country and safe for this. But that time is not yet
come.' [1] A good example this of the parliamentary art of
saying much and meaning nothing ; but from George III's
favourite minister, with truculent Massachusetts on his
hands, a genuine conversion to the doctrine of assimilation
could scarcely be expected. Thurlow, at any rate, more
outspoken than his chief, repudiated it outright. Did they
intend, he inquired, to vest the sovereignty of Canada
ultimately in a Governor, a Council, and an Assembly as
the sovereignty of Britain is vested in King, Lords, and
Commons ? Yet that is what must happen ' if you follow
your assimilating idea '. And in that case, ' is their money,
are their forces, to be applied to support the British Empire ?
Are they content that the King, Lords, and Commons of
Great Britain shall be judges of the drawing forth of those
forces and the applying of that money to the protection of
the British Empire ? ' ' To be sure ', he exclaimed, ' it is
a grossness—it is making two allied·kingdoms, totally out
of our power, to act as a federal union if they please, and
if they do not please, to act as independent countries.' [2]
Events were already showing, and, long years ahead, events
were again to show how pertinent these questions were, how
near the mark this mocking logic : but Thurlow and his
colleagues were readier to state dilemmas than to face and
master them, and—such was the irony of circumstance—it
was the failure both in England and America to solve

---

[1] Cavendish, pp. 247-248 [K., p. 126 ; E. & G., p. 90].

[2] Cavendish, p. 36 [K., p. 95 ; E. & G., pp. 40-41]. The text reads ' as
an independent country '. Thurlow goes on to describe this hypothetical
relation between the United Kingdom and Canada as ' a federal condition
pretty near the condition of the states of Germany '. The looseness of the
federal tie in Germany before the days of Bismarck was of course notorious.

precisely that problem of fairly distributing between the mother country and the colonies their common burden of defence which at that very moment had brought the British Empire to the brink of disruption.

8

It was of small consequence which side of the House secured the honours of the debate. North was as sure of a majority on the Quebec Bill as on the Bills for punishing Boston ; and the third reading was carried on June 13 by 56 votes to 20.[1]

It returned to the House of Lords unaltered in all its main provisions but improved by certain minor changes and additions. The amendment of the boundary clause so as not to encroach on existing colonial frontiers has been mentioned. A further concession, inspired by Lord Mansfield,[2] to the principle of toleration was made by the insertion in the Bill of a new oath of allegiance for Roman Catholics in the province, which, unlike the customary form prescribed in England for more than two centuries past and for more than seventy years to come, contained nothing offensive to their religion. To the clause dealing with tithes an equitable provision was added enabling tithes paid by Protestants to be applied to ' the encouragement of the Protestant religion and the maintenance and support of a Protestant clergy '. And an exception was made to the Council's inability to levy taxes : it might authorize the inhabitants of any town or district to levy rates for roads, public buildings, or other local services.[3]

[1] Cavendish, p. 296.
[2] See the correspondence between Mansfield and Dartmouth given in C. D., p. 551, n. 1. Mansfield also supported the legalization of tithes : see the memorandum, probably by him, on the ' clause concerning religion ' (C. D., pp. 549–551).
[3] For these uncontested amendments, see Cavendish, pp. 226, 244, 250, 254, 282.

The Lords accepted the Commons' amendments and on June 16 the Bill was quickly carried through its final stage, but not without one last dramatic scene. The bitter antagonism of the American colonists to almost every letter of the Bill had found an echo in the heart of their greatest champion. Throughout those fateful months of 1774 Chatham's sick mind was tortured by the tragic prospect of rebellion : his one thought was how to avert the impending rupture. And because the passage of the Quebec Bill would unquestionably weigh down the scale against the hope of peace, he could not judge it on its merits. In Chatham, moreover, the memory of the 'Forty-five, when England, at grips with France, had been brought within an ace of disaster by Jacobite treason, had bitten so deep that he could never bring himself to extend to Roman Catholics the toleration which he always urged for Protestant dissenters. A Bill which would at once buttress Popery and undermine the Empire could not be suffered to pass without at least one desperate protest, one word of warning, as solemn and impressive as only he could make it. So the ghost of the great war minister appeared in the House of Lords to denounce the use to which his victories had been turned. From the imperfect record which survives, his speech appears to have been a vigorous but indiscriminate attack upon the Bill. It would involve a great country in a thousand difficulties. It was the worst of despotism, a most cruel, oppressive, and odious measure, tearing up justice and every good principle by the roots. Rather than lose trial by jury and the writ of *habeas corpus*—the two bulwarks of personal security, but seemingly regarded as mere moonshine by the framers of the Bill—every true Englishman was ready to lay down his life : and the idea that the French-Canadians could not benefit from law and liberty because they had been used to arbitrary power was as ridiculous as it was false. Turning to the bench of bishops, he told them that the Bill made Roman Catholicism the established religion of a vast continent. ' The Bill ', he said, ' is the child of inordinate power. I desire to know if any one on that bench will hold it out for baptism.' The power given to the Governor to admit Roman Catholics to the Council ; the substitution of a common oath of allegiance for the oath of supremacy which Parliament had no more right to do away with than the Great Charter or the Bill of Rights ; the establishment of Popery and arbitrary government over the vast and fertile region now annexed to the province of Quebec and capable of containing, if fully peopled, not less than thirty million souls ; the conversion of the fisheries of Labrador into a nursery of French-Canadian seamen to man the fleets of France in the event of war—he condemned all these provisions as fatal mischiefs and dangerous innovations at variance with all the safeguards so wisely provided in the constitution against the return of Popery and Popish influence. . . . So far the speech had been one long tirade, broken only by citations from the legal record of Anglican intolerance : but at the close the orator changed his note. In moving words he laid bare before the House the sovereign reason for his hatred of the Bill. ' He pathetically expressed his fears ', so ends the record, ' that the Bill might finally lose the hearts of all his Majesty's American subjects.' [1]

Of the handful of peers who voted only six took Chatham's side. Carried by twenty-six votes to seven, the Bill now only waited for George III's assent. Could the King, who

[1] *Chatham Correspondence*, vol. iv, pp. 351–353 [E. & G., pp. 95–97]; cf. Williams, *Life of William Pitt*, vol. ii, pp. 299–301. The question of the Labrador fisheries was not forgotten by Government. The Instructions issued to Governor Carleton after the passing of the Act described the fisheries as ' nurseries of seamen, on whom the strength and security of our kingdoms depend '. The French-Canadian claims were to be respected, but they were declared to ' extend to but a small district of the coast ' and that mostly unsuitable for cod-fishing. In all other parts the Governor was to attend carefully to the interests of British fishermen from the mother country (Instructions to Governor Carleton, 1775, Articles 33 to 36, C. D., pp. 607–608 [K., p. 157]).

in after years was to prove himself so hard an enemy of his Catholic subjects in Ireland, approve a measure so friendly to his Catholic subjects in Canada ? Such a decision would run counter to his deepest feelings ; nor would it by any means enhance his popularity with the great mass of Englishmen. Chatham's invective had been wasted on the peers ; but his voice had carried beyond the precincts of Parliament and in every coffee-house and tavern it stirred up the old unsleeping hatred of the Popish faith. Feeling ran high in the City, where commercial interest was linked with religious prejudice : and on the morning of June 22, the very day fixed for the prorogation of Parliament, a deputation, headed by the Lord Mayor, arrived at St. James's to present a strongly-worded address against the Bill. It recalled the stipulations under which the reigning House had superseded the Catholic branch of Stuarts and bluntly reminded the King of his coronation oath to maintain the Protestant religion.[1] It was a telling appeal to the Hanoverian, but it came too late. Not without a struggle with his conscience, George III had made up his mind, and he could be as obstinate in a good cause as a bad. Refusing to answer the address he came down to Westminster amid cries of ' No Popery ' from an angry mob and in a short speech assented to the Bill. ' It is founded ', he said, ' on the clearest principles of justice and humanity, and will, I doubt not, have the best effect in quieting the minds and promoting the happiness of my Canadian subjects.'[2] The

[1] The petition is printed in Kingsford, vol. v, pp. 230–231.

[2] *Annual Register*, 1774, p. 78. The groans and hisses of the mob are described by Horace Walpole (*Last Journals* (London, 1910), vol. i, pp. 357–358). Some of the bystanders shouted ' Remember Charles I ! Remember James II ! ' Walpole himself swallowed the Whig judgement of the Bill whole. He speaks of ' the Court preparing a Catholic army ' (p. 353), and deplores the indulgence shown by the bishops towards the Catholics in Canada (pp. 346, 354). He likens the pro-Popish policy of George III to that of the Stuarts. ' The thought is so shocking, the prospect so gloomy, I am almost tempted to burn my pen and discontinue my journal.' Fortunately he decides to ' continue it in hopes of better days ' (p. 358).

thirteenth British Parliament was forthwith prorogued and
shortly afterwards dissolved.   Its one good action in
colonial policy had been its last.

9

The controversy over the Quebec Act long outlived its
passing : it was an important factor in the American
Revolution : and Chatham's indictment of it lingered on in
the Whig tradition of the history of that disastrous time.[1]
Even in the calmer atmosphere of our own day it has sometimes been condemned as a measure which solidified French
nationality and doomed Canada to a permanent racial
division.[2]   It may be worth while, therefore, briefly to
restate the main points in the controversy and to attempt
a fair judgement on them.

The boundary clause, it is true, however reasonable and
candid its motives, was not a practical solution of the problem of the *hinterland*.   The steady westward movement of the
Atlantic colonists could never have been held up by a line
drawn on a map in London and strategically indefensible
in peace or war.   The problem of the West could only
be solved by the Americans themselves ; and as long as they
could not unite to frame a consistent and equitable policy
and also to enforce it, they had no right to blame the
statesmen of the mother country if they wrestled with the
impossible and tried as best they could to discharge their
responsibilities for preventing or at least mitigating the
friction and the danger which had inevitably resulted from

---

[1] The most eloquent modern exponent of the Whig tradition of the
Revolution breaks frankly away from it over the Quebec Act.   ' From
among the truculently impolitic laws by which it is surrounded in the
statute-book, it stands out as the work of statesmen and not of policemen '
(Sir G. O. Trevelyan, *The American Revolution*, vol. ii, p. 75).
[2] e.g. Goldwin Smith, *Canada and the Canadian Question* (London,
1891), pp. 80–81 ; Coffin, *op. cit.*, pp. 534–543.

the contact of the white man with the red. With still less justice could the Whigs complain : for the boundary clause in its cardinal principle was but the culmination of a long-considered policy in the framing of which their own leaders had played an important part—a policy, too, which was not inspired by commercial interests only but foreshadowed, like Burke's own great speeches on British rule in India, the slow awakening of the British conscience to the true nature of the task imposed upon the Commonwealth by the inclusion in it of the backward races of mankind.[1] But the boundary

[1] See p. 95, n. 2, above. Full treatment of this important aspect of Anglo-American relations lies beyond the scope of this book : students will find a wealth of material in the recent researches of American historians (especially Alvord and Coffin, *op. cit.*, C. E. Carter, *Great Britain and the Illinois Country*, Washington, 1910, and F. J. Turner, *The Frontier in American History*, New York, 1921 : for a clear and authoritative summary of the question, see S. E. Morison, *Sources and Documents illustrating the American Revolution and the Formation of the Federal Constitution*, Oxford, 1923, pp. xvii–xxxii). The main points are these : (1) The Indian reservation was only in the North-west; it afforded no obstacle to the expansion of the colonies along the Ohio and down the Mississippi. Shelburne and Grenville seem to have contemplated in 1767 that settlements should also be allowed within the reservation if the land was regularly purchased through British officials (Alvord, vol. i, pp. 175, 179, 219–225). Continued ' unofficial ' settlement may have made the North Government anxious to discourage this (*ibid.*, p. 239). The boundary clause was certainly meant to prevent the extension of New York or Pennsylvania into the reserved area. (See Knox and Hillsborough, cited C. D., p. 552, n. 1.) (2) No doubt can be raised as to the sincerity of British ministers' desire to protect the Indians from exploitation. All parties were agreed on this point. Thus the same regulations for control of British officials which were drawn up in 1764 were sent to Carleton in 1775 to guide his administration after the Quebec Act. (These regulations, printed in C. D., pp. 614–619, are an interesting example of the best traditions of British rule over backward races.) (3) Commercial motives for conciliating the Indians were, as Coffin fairly points out (pp. 406–408), closely bound up with philanthropic. It was good business to make the Indians peaceful and friendly ; but provided it was effectually controlled by an enlightened Government, trade in North America, as elsewhere, was not necessarily incompatible with humanity (No. 38 of the above-mentioned regulations forbade the sale of alcohol or rifles to Indians). For the importance attached to the fur-trade by Government, see Shelburne's speech in the House of Lords in 1775, P. H., vol. xviii, p. 651 ; and the Board of Trade Reports in C. D. (4) The colonists resented the mother country's control of this trade as much as its interference with free occupation of the land ; and

clause and the policy it stood for in America southward of the Great Lakes were not to be tested by time. A few years later the colonists had enforced their claim to the *hinterland* by war and taken the fate of its Indian inhabitants for better and for worse out of the hands of the British Commonwealth.

It may safely be said that the criticism of the other clauses of the Act would never have been so violent if the problem of governing French Canada on the morrow of its conquest could have been considered on its merits and quite apart from the disparate and confusing issues at stake in the old-established British colonies. As it was, the analogy was superficial and misleading. There was reason, for example, in charging North's ministry with tyrannical conduct in its attempt to coerce Massachusetts ; but it was ridiculous to attribute the same ideas and objects to the constitutional provisions of the Quebec Act and to denounce it as a calculated act of despotism, a deliberate substitution of autocracy for self-government. It is true that the constitutional system established by the Act in Canada was a backward system ; that it was only natural for the British immigrants to boggle at it ; that Englishmen in the mother country would have had to think themselves back in the Middle Ages before they could have tolerated such a system for a moment in eighteenth-century England. For Canadians government by a Governor and a nominated Council, in which legislative, executive, and judicial functions were

they regarded the annexation of the reserved area to Quebec as practically excluding them from the trade which, in their view, would be monopolized by the British and French-Canadian merchants at Montreal. This was Shelburne's chief argument against the Quebec Act : see speech cited above. The trade was to be open to British subjects from any colony under the regulations to be framed by the Quebec legislature (Instructions to Carleton, 1775, Article 32, C. D. i, p. 428) ; but doubtless traders in Canada, British as well as French, would benefit from their easier access to the provincial Government. See Dartmouth's suggestion to Carleton as to new advantages for British traders, p. 126, below.

combined, was akin to what government by the King and his Council had been for Englishmen before the days of Edward I and Parliament ; and for Canadians it made no substantial difference that the Government of Canada was controlled in the last resort by the elected representatives of the British people. It is true, again, that the system of the Quebec Act was only defensible if it was regarded as a transitional system. The inclusion of the French-Canadians in the British Commonwealth implied that sooner or later they should share equally with their fellow members of British race the rights and responsibilities of membership. But the process of assimilation had at any rate begun. The military rule of a Commander-in-Chief had been replaced by the civil rule of a Governor and Council. The next stage would clearly be the introduction of representative government and the establishment of an Assembly in Canada corresponding to the House of Commons in Great Britain. Further than this there was for the moment no practical need to look ; and North and his colleagues, much as they distrusted the doctrine of assimilation, much as they disliked the aggressive democratic temper which representative government seemed to have fostered in New England, were prepared at any rate to look as far. ' As soon as the Canadians shall be in a condition to receive an Assembly ', said North, ' it will be right they should have one.' [1] But the Whigs were almost as impatient with such procrastination as the British minority in Canada. An Assembly, they insisted, must be established at once or at any rate within a very brief period to be stated in the Act.

The soundest doctrine is apt to be misapplied when its exponents become *doctrinaires* : and the policy of assimilation would have suffered as much from undue haste in its development at this stage as it suffered later from undue

[1] Cavendish, p. 290. Wedderburn declared the Bill to be ' essentially a temporary one ' (*ibid.*, p. 57).

delay. The rule that all members of a commonwealth are
equally entitled to self-government is conditional upon
their being fit for it ; and without considering the reasons
which most influenced North—their recent change of
allegiance and their religion—the French-Canadians were
manifestly not yet fit. They had had no experience, even
in local affairs, of the methods of representative government.
They had never gleaned from books or newspapers a vestige
of the meaning or the purpose of political responsibility.
The vast majority were totally illiterate. There was not
even a substantial minority of educated or politically-
minded men to guide the great body of their countrymen
along a path so strange to them and so difficult. Neither
their priests nor their *seigneurs* desired an Assembly : there
was no one of their race to play the educative role of agitator,
to preach the merits of self-government, to proclaim their
right to it, to stir them a hair's breadth from their comfortable apathy. To suppose them capable of appreciating
the doctrine of assimilation was patently absurd. ' Do they
understand ', was the simple-minded question put to Hey
in the Committee, ' that there is a resemblance between the
House of Assembly and the House of Commons ? ' And of
course he answered : ' They do not understand the principles
of either.' Something, it is true, was stirring beneath the
crust of ignorance and indifference which had grown so
thick and hard beneath the rule of France. The *habitants*
were beginning to lose something of their old docility, to
acquire some new sense of personal independence. The
reality of this change of temper was soon to be proved by
events ;[1] but the movement was essentially a peasant

[1] The new attitude of the *habitants* is more fully described, pp. 153–157,
below. The appointment by the Governor of the parish bailiff with minor
local duties from a list of six names drawn up annually by the householders
of each parish is the only trace of local self-government in this period
(see Coffin, *op. cit.*, p. 293). As to illiteracy, M. de Lotbinière doubted
' whether there are more than four or five persons, in general, in a parish
who can read ' (Marriott, C. D., p. 455).

movement, it was as yet only social or agrarian, not political. The *habitant's* whole heart was in the land—the one thing he really knew and understood : he knew nothing, cared nothing, about the liberties of British subjects or the ' rights of man ' for which his neighbours over the border were prepared to fight and die. His incipient revolt was against the tyranny of landlords, not of kings. Only in so far as his feudal connexion with the landlord involved service through the landlord to the state were his personal interests in any sense political. His right to the land with the obligations it entailed was an intelligible and exciting question : his right to the vote was an almost meaningless and quite uninteresting theme. To impose on such a people, at one sudden stroke, the responsibilities of a parliamentary electorate was obviously unwise. ' I shall never be induced ', said Burke, in the debate on the Quebec Bill, ' to consider government in the abstract ' ; [1] but on what other considerations could he urge the entrusting of ' the machine of a free constitution '—which, as he reminded the electors of Bristol a few months later, is ' no simple thing but as intricate and delicate as it is valuable ' [2]—to a people who knew nothing of its working or its purpose ?

But if the authors of the Quebec Act were justified in withholding representative government from a people unqualified to exercise it, they may justly be criticized for taking no steps to qualify them. If the French-Canadians were uneducated, it was the business of British statesmen to educate them ; if inexperienced in the duties of citizenship, to give them experience. Except for the work of the old religious communities, which was mainly directed to preparation for the priesthood, there was practically no provision for education in Canada whether for Catholics or for Protestants. It seems reasonable to ask why British

[1] Cavendish, p. 86 [K.. p. 102 ; E. & G., p. 47].
[2] Speech to the Electors of Bristol, November 3, 1774, *Works* (*World's Classics* edition), vol. ii, p. 166.

ministers did not at least begin in 1774 to lay the foundations
of a system of public schools : the very difficulties of the
task—the size of the province and the lack of good and
rapid means of communication, especially in winter, the
primitive conditions of the *habitant's* life, the depth of his
illiteracy—were surely themselves strong arguments for
taking it in hand without delay. The question is easily
answered. The idea that it was a function of the state to
assist and even in some measure to control the education
of its citizens had not yet entered the mind of the English
governing class ; and even when it became widely prevalent
in continental Europe, Englishmen were slow to adopt it,
some for fear lest state education would unduly foster
individual liberty, some for fear lest it would cramp and
stifle it. It was not till 1833 that the House of Commons
first voted a grant ' in aid of private subscriptions ' to
provide facilities for the education of the poor : it was
not till 1870 that any serious effort was made to establish
a national system of education. Lord North, then, would
have shown himself unexpectedly in advance of his time
if he had included in the Quebec Bill a clause providing
for the state establishment and maintenance of Canadian
schools. None the less, he might well have realized how
much more difficult it was in a colony than in England to
provide any education at all without state aid. Only ten
years after the passing of the Quebec Act, one of the ablest
British officials at Quebec was already convinced that an
essential preliminary to any further constitutional development was ' a free school in every parish '.[1]

In another respect Lord North had no excuse. In politics
an inch of experience is better than an ell of book learning :
and though the Canadians could not yet be given the

[1] Postmaster-General Finlay to Nepean, October 22, 1784, C. D., p. 739
[K., p. 170]. For the unsuccessful efforts of the Quebec Assembly, established
in 1791, to provide public education, see Arthur Buller's Report, Appendix D
to the *Durham Report* (Lucas's edition, Oxford, 1912, vol. iii, p. 240).

machinery of representative government on the full provincial scale, they might at once have been given the means
of learning the habits and the temper it required in the same
' preparatory school ' in which Englishmen themselves had
learned them long before the growth of a national Parliament.   The Quebec Act ought certainly to have made provision for a simple form of local self-government in each of
the three towns and in small-scale rural areas, by means of
which the Canadians could have obtained an invaluable
training in practical politics before entering on the wider field
of a provincial legislature.   It was not arguable that the new
rulers of Canada had no call to change the civic system of
the country.   It was not indeed their business to interfere
with the personal and social habits of the French-Canadians,
to violate their national tradition of speech and faith and
legal custom : but it was their business to interfere with
their political habits ; to put before them a new ideal of
political responsibility, to help them to understand and to
value political liberty and to fit themselves for its exercise,
and in due course, when the desire and the capacity alike
had grown in them, to offer them, since they had developed
no such institutions of their own, the forms of self-government which Englishmen had fashioned, ' not without dust
and heat ', from the lessons of their long experience.   Only
by this gift of freedom and of such preliminary training as
might be needed for its use could the expansion of the
British Commonwealth by war, whether defensive in its
character or not, be ultimately justified to the conscience of
a later age.   So only could the conquerors compensate the
conquered for the severance of their political connexion
with the old home of their race.   For the ties which had
united them with France had also bound them to the steps
of the Bourbon throne.

On the merits of the legal provisions of the Quebec Act

as a whole no certain judgement can be passed.   The retention of the English criminal law was little disputed at the
time or since, in England or in Canada.   But would it have
been wiser to follow Masères and Hey rather than Carleton,
and establish a mixed code of French and English civil law ?
The language of the Act made it possible for such a mixed
code to be developed in course of time in so far as the French
law might be ' varied or altered ' by ordinances of the
Legislative Council ; and very soon after the passing of the
Act, as will be seen, ministers were contemplating somewhat
drastic alterations by this means.   But such changes were
only prospective.   What Parliament had done, what the
Act in itself did, was to restore the French civil law entire ;
and unquestionably this severely penalized the British
immigrants, some of whom may have been intolerant and
self-interested, but whose commercial energy and experience
were of no slight value for the future welfare of the province.
There was much, again, in the French law which was too
old-fashioned to last—a drawback that applied, however,
to the parts which the proposed compromise would have
left French almost as much as to the parts it would have
made English.[1] If a mixed code, moreover, had been carefully drafted and published, it might have proved more
effective than the provisions of the Act in clearing up the
confusion which continued for several years to clog the wheels
of justice.   But the only valid test must be the effect on
the French-Canadians.   Would they, as Carleton contended,
have been extremely hurt at losing *any* part of the Custom
of Paris—or at any rate so hurt as just to make all the difference to their attitude to British rule ? To that question
there is not evidence enough to give a certain answer.[2] It

---

[1] For the ultimate conversion of the feudal forms of land-tenure and the
friction it entailed see Munro, *The Seigniorial System in Canada*.

[2] Carleton had said that he believed they would not object to the introduction of some English law in matters of commerce (see p. 75, above).
For the Government's policy on this point, after the passing of the Act,
see pp. 126–127, below.

can only be said that, if the rejection of the compromise on the civil law in favour of conceding all the French-Canadians asked was a mistake, it was a mistake on the right side. Only by generosity can conquerors ever hope to conciliate the conquered. Generosity was wise in South Africa in 1906; it was probably wise in Canada in 1774.

On the religious question, on the other hand, there can be no doubt whatever. 'Are we to establish the Roman Catholic religion in Canada', an indignant Whig had asked in the House of Commons, 'and tolerate the Protestant religion?'[1] And the legalization of tithes meant, it was true, that the state recognized and supported the Roman Church as the national church of Canada.[2] Nor could it be denied that in this the Act went beyond the promise given in the Capitulations and the Treaty of Paris. But if the promise had been kept only in the strict letter of its terms, it would have been broken in spirit and presently in substance also. Voluntary religious organization was one day to become common, but in 1774 to have withheld the sanction of the law for the collection of tithes would have struck a serious blow at the material basis of the Church; and unless it had been supported by Roman Catholic funds in Europe, the extent and efficiency of its parochial work must have been increasingly curtailed. And certainly this was not what British generals and statesmen had intended when they pledged their country's honour that the French-Canadians should be free to practise their religion. Very pertinent was the question put to Chatham by a contemporary publicist—'Would you now construe the free exercise of religion to be less than the Canadians thought it when they threw themselves upon our faith?'[3] But

[1] Dunning, Cavendish, p. 19.

[2] Ministers continued to deny that this was tantamount to 'establishment': see p. 130, below.

[3] *A Letter to the Earl of Chatham on the Quebec Bill* (London, 1774), p. 29. Cf. p. 34: 'Would you wish, my Lord, to spoil the fruits of your own

the American colonists, of whose angry protests Chatham's
invective was the anxious echo, were not overmuch concerned with the interpretation of the treaty pledge : they
resented the whole policy of toleration which had begun
with the conquest and only reached its logical culmination
in the Quebec Act. And will any one nowadays contend
that George III and his ministers are not to be commended
for rising for once above the common prejudices of their
day and suffering in Canada the freedom of conscience they
would not suffer nearer home ? Will any one nowadays
dissent from Burke's unequivocal approval of this aspect of
the Act ?   ' There is ', he said, ' but one healing, catholic
principle of toleration which ought to find favour in this
House. It is wanted not only in our colonies but here.
The thirsty earth of our own country is gasping and gaping
and crying out for that healing shower from heaven. The
noble lord has told you of the right of those people by the
treaty ; but I consider the right of conquest so little, and
the right of human nature so much, that the former has very
little consideration with me. I look upon the people of
Canada as coming by the dispensation of God under the
British Government. I would have us govern it in the same
manner as the all-wise disposition of Providence would
govern it. We know that He suffers the sun to shine upon
the righteous and the unrighteous ; and we ought to suffer
all classes, without distinction, to enjoy equally the right
of worshipping God according to the light He has been
pleased to give them.' [1]

conquest in the worst manner possible—which would be to keep the hearts
of the Canadians devoted to France whenever she might call them to arms ?'
This pamphlet was ascribed by the colonists to Lord Lyttelton, whose
name appears on the copies printed in Boston ; but the author was
Sir William Meredith, a member of the Privy Council from 1774 to 1777.

[1] Cavendish, pp. 222–223 [K., p. 124]. Burke argued that the ' protection ' of the clergy by the legalization of tithes merely ' confirmed '
a religion already ' established '. ' The establishment was not made by
you : it existed before the treaty . . . no legislature has a right to take it
away, no governor has a right to suspend it.'

10

The truth is that the party quarrel over the Quebec Bill
was not a real conflict of principle. The leaders of the
Opposition were inspired throughout by external considerations : they were attacking not so much the Government's
Canadian policy as its American policy. If the problem of
Canada could have been considered quite apart from the
greater and graver problem of the older colonies, and if it
had fallen to Whig ministers to deal with it, they would
inevitably, after studying the facts, have drafted a very
similar measure. As it was, the Whigs for the most part
denounced the Bill without thinking twice about its principles, because they distrusted its motives towards the
American colonists and dreaded its effects on them.

They were wrong in distrusting its motives. Apart from
principles and treaty obligations, the one obvious motive
of the Bill was to reconcile the Canadians to their conquerors. And the one obvious reason for trying to attain
this end without delay was the possibility, or rather the
probability, of a renewal of war with France. Even Chatham,
though no one better understood how closely the destinies
of the New World and the Old were linked together, made no
allowance for this paramount factor in the Government's
case. Yet, as he knew and as Shelburne knew, from the
moment the Treaty of Paris was signed, the French Government, in close concert with Spain, had been busily engaged
in striving to repair its weakened resources with the fixed
purpose of renewing at its chosen time the old struggle with
England and reversing, if it might be, the decision of the
Seven Years' War.[1] Under these circumstances, to wean the

[1] For the network of intrigue spun by France and Spain in those years,
see Lord Fitzmaurice, *Life of Shelburne* (London, 1912), vol. i, chap. viii.
Probably Chatham felt that in the event of war in North America the
loyalty of the British colonists would be more important than that of the
Canadians. But, if he had been in power, would he have estranged
the Canadians, perhaps irretrievably, in order to placate the British ?

Canadians as far and as soon as possible from their old
attachment to France was naturally and necessarily the
primary purpose of Carleton's policy, and the Government's
policy was simply Carleton's. It is true that Carleton and
the Government recognized also from the outset that the
active allegiance of the Canadians, could it be secured,
might be of no little service to the Crown if the old colonies
should carry their chronic discontent to the point of open
rebellion.[1] And when, as it happened, the sudden aggrava-
tion of the quarrel in New England coincided with the final
embodiment of the conciliation policy in the Quebec Bill,
Lord Lyttelton, less tactful than his silent colleagues in the
Commons, candidly admitted that, ' if British America was
determined to resist the lawful power and pre-eminence of
Great Britain, he saw no reason why the loyal inhabitants
of Canada should not co-operate with the rest of the Empire
in subduing them and bringing them to a right sense of their
duty '.[2] But at the time when the provisions of the Bill
were being determined, the prospect of an American
rebellion was regarded as a less immediate and a far less
serious matter than the prospect of war with France. The
purpose of the Bill was to forestall the greater danger :
it was an additional but quite secondary advantage in its
authors' eyes that it carried with it an insurance policy,
so to speak, against the lesser.[3]

[1] See p. 60, above.   [2] P. H., vol. xvii, p. 1402.
[3] See p. 94, n. 3, above. It is sometimes suggested that William Knox,
Under-Secretary of State for the American Department (1770–1782) and
thus closely concerned with the Quebec Act, was mainly inspired by the
idea of using the French-Canadians against the colonists. There is no
evidence of this. What did influence Knox was the prior consideration that
generous treatment of the French-Canadians might induce them to resist
the appeal to join in a colonial rebellion if it should occur. In the pamphlet
entitled *The Justice and Policy of the late Act of Parliament for making more
effectual provision for the government of the Province of Quebec, &c.* (London,
1774), of which Knox was almost certainly the author (see his reference to
such a pamphlet in his *Extra-Official State Papers, addressed to the Rt. Hon.
Lord Rawdon, &c.*, London, 1789, vol. i, part ii, p. 6), the following passage
occurs (p. 28) : ' The inducement to adopt a plan of lenity and indulgence

But while they misjudged the motives of the Bill, the
Whigs were right in their forecast of its effects on American
opinion. If the Whigs had been prejudiced against the Bill
by the company in which it came, their feelings were but
a pale reflection of the anger of New England. To the
victims of the programme of coercion the Quebec Act was
bound to be regarded as one in purpose with its fellows and
perhaps the most odious of them all. It was not to be
expected that they should give a thought to the diplomatic
situation in far-off Europe, to the possible recrudescence
of the old danger to themselves from France, or even to the
conditions imposed on British policy in Canada as the terms
on which that danger had been for the time removed.
Inevitably they jumped straight to the conclusion that the
only object of the Act was to make Canada, deliberately
kept for the purpose under arbitrary government, an instrument for the destruction of freedom throughout the continent. There is no reason to doubt their sincerity. Intent
on their own injuries, knowing nothing of the real problem
in Canada except the grievances of their British friends,
they would naturally have looked in any Canadian measure
North's Government might have passed for further proof
of its hostility to them : and they naturally found it in
an Act which so openly flouted their sentiments and their

. . . was greatly heightened by a consideration of the avowed purpose of the
old colonies to oppose the execution of the laws of England and to deny the
authority of the supreme legislature : for, however different the views and
purposes of the leaders of this opposition might be from the wishes of the
Canadians, yet, it was not to be doubted, they would take advantage of
any discontent which a harsh proceeding might excite among them, and,
by fair promises of redress, endeavour to lead them to take part in their
undertaking.' This is scarcely tantamount to advocating the revival and
perpetuation under British rule of the old menace of French Canada to the
American colonies, with which aim Knox and the Government are sometimes, more or less vaguely, charged : and except those few sentences
there is nothing else on this point either in the pamphlet or in the *Extra-
Official State Papers* which disclose much of Knox's attitude to the American
question. In another and slighter pamphlet, *Thoughts on the Quebec Act*
(London, 1774), the Act is similarly represented (p. 37) as a means of
deterring the French-Canadians from rising against British rule.

convictions. To them the French-Canadians were still their old relentless enemies of the border warfare rather than fellow subjects. Why then, except with a sinister design, should British ministers strive to conciliate these aliens at the very moment they were bent on antagonizing their own kinsmen ? For what other reason, again, should British ministers cosset and suborn a Church which Puritan New England hated ? To the narrower-minded colonists the religious policy of the Act seemed positively wicked. It ' must have caused ', they said, ' a jubilee in Hell '.[1]

It was mainly, of course, among the extremists and principally in Massachusetts that the Act was so instantly and sweepingly condemned. There were ' loyalists ' in every district prepared to support the Government in this as in its other measures ; and the temper of those who ultimately joined in the rebellion was not yet anywhere so much inflamed as it was in Boston. The petition presented to Parliament by the New York Assembly as late as March 1775 was couched in moderate and deferential terms.[2] It disclaimed ' the most distant desire of independence from the parent kingdom '. It made only a passing reference to ' the jealousies which have been excited in the colonies ' by the extension of the limits of a province in which the Roman Catholic religion had received ' such ample supports '. Its main concern was with the commercial results of the extension. By a sheer oversight, it seems, the Quebec Revenue Act [3] had prohibited the entry of any goods on which it laid duties into any part of the province except by way of the St. Lawrence or, if carried overland or by other waterways, except through the frontier post of St. John's between Lake Champlain and Montreal. This meant that

---

[1] Max Farrand, *The Development of the United States* (London, 1919), p. 38.
[2] Representation and Remonstrance of the General Assembly of New York, March 25, 1775, P. H., vol. xviii, pp. 650–655.
[3] The text is given in C. D., p. 576 : for its passing, see p. 92, above.

trade in dutiable goods between New York and the contiguous Indian territory now included in the province of Quebec must travel by so circuitous a route as to drive it altogether out of competition with the trade of Quebec itself. By its response to the petition the Government showed that at any rate in its annexation of the *hinterland* to Quebec it had not been deliberately trying to injure the other colonists. North confessed that the duties ' were not laid exactly as they ought to be ',[1] and a short amending Bill was rapidly passed into law, annulling the restrictions of the previous Act as regards direct imports into the annexed area on the ground that they would ' operate to the prejudice and disadvantage of the commerce carried on with the Indians '.[2]

But this little proof that the Government's intentions were not quite so black as they were painted was too slight and too late to check the current of antagonism. The first impulsive condemnation of the Act had quickly settled into a fixed and ineradicable opinion. Already, in the autumn of 1774, Congress had given it full public confirmation in its manifesto to the People of Great Britain.[3] In this document the Quebec Act is denounced at least as violently as the Coercion Acts. It is described as part of ' the ministerial plan for enslaving us '. The Canadians, it is declared, detached from the other colonies by civil as well as religious prejudices, swollen in numbers by Catholic emigrants from Europe, are to be used ' to reduce the ancient Protestant colonies to the same state of slavery with themselves '. The unhappy condition of the British settlers in Canada, robbed of their heritage of freedom, is deplored. ' Nor can we suppress our astonishment that a British Parliament

---

[1] P. H., vol. xviii, p. 644.
[2] 15 George III, c. 40. Text in C. D., p. 580.
[3] September 5, 1774. *Annual Register*, 1774, pp. 207–214. The Quebec Act is similarly coupled with the other Acts in the Declaration and Resolves of Congress, October 14, 1774 (Morison, *Sources and Documents*, pp. 119, 122).

should ever consent to establish in that country a religion that has deluged your island in blood, and dispersed impiety, bigotry, persecution, murder and rebellion through every part of the world.' As the quarrel grew, these reckless charges became an essential part of the orthodox revolutionist creed. In the summer of 1775, Alexander Hamilton, then a youth of eighteen, repeated them in a more sober but no less unfair strain in a pamphlet entitled *Remarks upon the Quebec Bill*.[1] And when at last the day came for the solemn declaration of their schism from the British Empire, the colonists denounced the Act once more in that historic document as a plan ' for abolishing the free system of English laws in a neighbouring province, establishing therein an arbitrary government, and enlarging its boundaries, so as to render it at once an example and fit instrument for introducing the same absolute rule into these colonies '.[2] Thus the effect of the Quebec Act was even as Chatham had foretold. The finishing touch, as the indignant colonists conceived it, in the scheme for their punishment and intimidation, it ' finally lost their hearts '.

Yet, for all that, Chatham's invective was unjustified. The Quebec Act was not the decisive factor in the outbreak of the American Revolution. It aggravated the quarrel, but it had not made it, nor did it determine its issue. If it had never been drafted, the result of the Government's other measures would have been the same. And if North's ill-fated Government had done the wrong thing in Canada as well as in Massachusetts, if it had made such a settle-

[1] *Works* (New York, 1904), vol. i, pp. 181–196. Cf. F. S. Oliver, *Alexander Hamilton* (London, 1912), pp. 29–31. The pamphlet is in two parts : (1) deals with the arbitrary form of government and the retention of the French law ; (2) deplores the establishment of the Roman Church, pictures ' droves of emigrants from all the Roman Catholic states in Europe ' flocking into Canada, and making it, in accordance with Government's ' dark design ', a hostile and dangerous neighbour.

[2] Declaration of Independence, Morison, *Sources and Documents*, p. 159.

ment as the British minority in the province and their friends outside desired, it would not have altered a hair's breadth nor delayed a moment the inexorable outcome of its policy of coercion in the South. Nay, rather, it would have made matters worse in the end. The alternative policy to the Quebec Act meant a repudiation in spirit of treaty-faith, a negation in a greater or less degree of nationality : and if British statesmen had treated Canada as Ireland had been treated, torn up the Treaty of Paris like the Treaty of Limerick, and cynically applied the familiar doctrines of religious intolerance and race ascendancy, the British government of Canada would surely not have lasted long. No one can be certain about the might-have-beens of history ; but in this case the probability is very strong. The incorporation of the Canadians in the British Empire was very recent ; they were still uncertain what the change would mean for them ; and if once they had been convinced that it meant the restriction or suppression of their national life and, above all, of their religion, surely they would not passively have acquiesced in such a fate, but, when the time came, they would have risen, *seigneur* and priest and peasant together, joined forces with the ' rebel ' colonists, and for better or worse escaped with them from British tyranny. It was fortunate indeed, then, for the destinies of the British Empire that North and his colleagues made no such fruitless sacrifice of honour and justice, that they did not add that crowning folly to the rest. Without the Quebec Act they would still have lost the thirteen colonies. With it Canada at least was saved.

No more for its effects, therefore, than for its motives as they bore upon the other colonies can the Quebec Act be condemned. As it was framed, so it must be judged, as a measure primarily concerned with Canada alone.

IV

THE CRISIS

I

THE Quebec Act had not been passed a day too soon. Before a year was out the practical merits of the policy it defined and confirmed were put to the sternest of proofs. The Act came into force on May 1, 1775. Twelve days earlier the first blood in the American War of Independence had been shed at Lexington.

There was time, therefore, before the crisis came, for the provisions of the Act, though unfortunately not its actual effect in operation, to become known in Canada. Carleton, the task he had set himself in England so triumphantly achieved, was back at Quebec on September 18, 1774, and he lost no time in imparting the good tidings to his French-Canadian friends. Within a few days he was writing to Dartmouth to report his satisfaction at the first impressions which ' the King's great goodness towards them ' had created. ' All ranks of people amongst them ', he wrote, ' vied with each other in testifying their gratitude and respect, and the desire they have by every mark of duty and submission to prove themselves not undeserving of the treatment they have met with.' [1] From *seigneur* to *seigneur*, from priest to priest, the news spread quickly through the educated class of French-Canadians ; and Carleton reported in November that letters and addresses from the ' more remote ' parts of the province echoed the sentiments

[1] Carleton to Dartmouth, September 23, 1774, C. D., p. 583. See also Carleton to Gage, September 20, 1774, quoted p. 139, below.

of Quebec.[1] So far, so good : but to what extent these enthusiastic documents represented the opinions of the great majority of the population, the scattered and uneducated *habitants*, there was as yet no certain evidence.

Of the reception of the news by the British section Carleton reported nothing ; but its general character could scarcely be in doubt. That the ' old subjects ' would regard the passing of the Act with disappointment and dismay was a foregone conclusion. The supreme authority of Parliament, beyond which lay no appeal, had closed the long controversy with a clear judgement against them: in almost every clause the Act went dead athwart their wishes. And, however weak their case had been on the point of religious toleration or representative institutions, it was undeniable that by its restoration of the French-Canadian civil law the Act would seriously injure their commercial interests.[2] Yet the prospect was not so dark as they imagined. The Government had not simply ignored their case, especially when it was backed in influential quarters in the City of London. ' The English merchants trading to Canada ', North had said in the course of the debates, ' have an undoubted claim to the protection of Parliament. They are a most respectable body, and much of the flourishing condition of the colony is owing to their exertions. In compliance with their interests and desires I would go as far as the honourable gentleman [Mr. Mackworth] in granting them everything that can be granted without producing inconvenience and embarrassment.' Ministers, moreover, while they had insisted on the restoration of the whole French-Canadian civil law in the Act, had made it clear that they expected it to be modified, in course of time, by the local legislature to

---

[1] Carleton to Dartmouth, November 11, 1774, C. D., p. 586.

[2] Carleton stated in his evidence that some of the British immigrants had left Canada since 1770. ' I am afraid their circumstances have been so reduced as to compel them to quit the province ' (Cavendish, p. 103 [K., p. 104 ; E. & G., pp. 51–52]).

meet the interests of the British community. The French law, North had explained, was to be ' the basis upon which the Governor and the Legislative Council are to set out '. ' All that the Parliament of Great Britain can do is to lay down general rules ; to say, you shall proceed according to Canadian customs or according to the English law. Every alteration which the circumstances of the country can admit of—every variation which the interests of the old subjects may require—all those circumstances will be more properly considered upon the other side of the water.' [1] Similarly, with regard to the jury-system, Wedderburn had held out hopes that the French-Canadians would presently lose their prejudice against it, and that it would ultimately form part of the judicature to be established by the Quebec Administration. He had only deprecated ' sudden or violent alteration '. ' To make the Canadians competent judges in civil matters must be the work of time.' [2]

Cold comfort for the British minority, had that been all : but the idea of some less vague and less prospective concession was already shaping in ministers' minds. There is a plain hint of it in Dartmouth's reply to Carleton's dispatch. After opening with a brief reference to his report of the French-Canadian attitude, ' As you are silent ', it continues, ' as to the sentiments of his Majesty's natural-born subjects in Canada respecting the late Act, I am not at liberty to conclude that they entertain the same opinion of it, but the King trusts that, when the provisions of it have taken place and his Majesty's gracious intentions with respect to the plan of judicature that is to be established are well known, prejudices which popular clamour has excited will cease, and that his Majesty's subjects of every description will see and be convinced of the equity and good policy of the Bill.' And Dartmouth goes on to

[1] Cavendish, pp. 11, 235, 256–257 [K., pp. 86, 127].
[2] *Ibid.*, pp. 56, 273–275, 278 [K., p. 99].

urge Carleton to persuade the British minority that their interests have not been neglected ' as far as it was consistent with what was due to the just claims and moderate wishes of the Canadians ', and especially to point out the advantages bestowed upon their trade by the extension of the province.[1] It appears, then, that during those anxious autumn months, while the clouds were banking up in Massachusetts, the Government was thinking as much of conciliating the little British minority in Canada as it had previously thought of conciliating the great French majority. The plan of judicature, or, in other words, the draft ordinance for the reorganization of the Canadian courts in the light of the Quebec Act, was mainly the work of Chief Justice Hey, who, as has been seen, had followed Masères rather than Carleton on the question of civil law. Being only an instrument for setting up new law courts, it was not concerned with the nature of the law ; on that point it merely repeated the phraseology of the Act : but it was concerned with the method of administering the law ; and on that point it conceded what the champions of the British minority had demanded with greater vehemence than anything else. It provided for the summoning of a jury, at the instance of either party in a case, to determine questions of fact and to assess damages for personal wrongs.[2] Nor was that all. The twelfth article in the new Instructions which were drafted in December 1774, and dispatched to Carleton on January 7, 1775, reminded him of the great ' care and circumspection ' required in the establishment of the legal system of the province under the recent Act.[3] ' For, as, on the one hand, it is our gracious purpose, conformable to the spirit and intention of the said Act of Parliament, that our Canadian subjects should have the benefit and use

[1] Dartmouth to Carleton, December 10, 1774, C. D., p. 585.

[2] C. D., pp. 637–660, and p. 584, n. 2.

[3] Instructions to Governor Carleton, 1775, Article 12, C. D., p. 599 [K., p. 152]. Italics not in the original.

of their own laws, usages, and customs in all controversies respecting titles of land and the tenure, descent, alienation, incumbrances and settlement of real estates [1] and the distribution of the personal property of persons dying intestate ; so, on the other hand, it will be the duty of the Legislative Council to consider well in framing such ordinances as may be necessary . . . for the better administration of justice whether the laws of England may not be, *if not altogether, at least in part the rule* for the decision in all cases or personal actions grounded upon debts, promises, contracts, and agreements, whether of a mercantile *or other* nature ; and also of wrongs proper to be compensated in damages ; and more especially where our natural-born subjects . . . may happen to be either plaintiff or defendant in any civil suit of such a nature.' Clearly these Instructions and the Draft Ordinance taken together went very far to meet the British claim. There is no vague promise now of future modifications of the French law when circumstances may require it. There is no talk now of a period of preparation for the jury-system. The Draft Ordinance provides at any rate optional juries at once ; and it is the plain suggestion of the Instructions that Carleton and his Council should proceed to legislate for the application of English law, at least in part, to all civil actions other than those concerned with the ownership of land or the property of persons dying intestate—a drastic departure from the ' basis ' of French law established by the Quebec Act. The difference between this policy and the language held by ministers in Parliament is unmistakable. Ultimate concessions to the British minority they had always contemplated ; but now, because they were growing more uneasy about British sentiment in the other colonies or because

---

[1] That ministers sincerely meant to maintain the French law as regards land is clear from Article 38 of the Instructions which prescribed that all future grants of Crown lands were to be made ' in fief or *seigneurie* ' (C. D., p. 429 [K., p. 158]).

they were feeling the effect of pressure from the City or because Carleton had left England, they were bent on speeding up the process of concession.[1]

Similarly as regards the statutory right of *habeas corpus* ministers were ready, it seems, in January to concede to the British minority what they had refused in June. They had sat silent then while Burke and Chatham scolded them for withholding from British subjects such an essential element of British liberty ; but now, behind the scenes, they spoke the language of the Opposition as if it had always been their own. ' Security to personal liberty ', ran the Instructions, ' is a fundamental principle of justice in all free governments, and the making due provision for that purpose is an object the legislature of Quebec ought never to lose sight of ; nor can they follow a better example than that which the Common Law of this Kingdom hath set in the provision made for a writ of *habeas corpus*, which is the right of every British subject in this Kingdom.' In other words the Legislative Council was recommended to provide by ordinance in Canada a written guarantee for the full exercise of the Common Law right such as had been provided in England by the famous statute of 1679.[2]

With this latter concession to British feeling the French-Canadians could scarcely quarrel : and, however anxious they might be to conciliate the Opposition, ministers were wise enough to refrain from tampering with the most vital part of the Act, its wise and seemingly decisive settlement of the

---

[1] The author of *The Justice and Policy of the late Act, &c.* (probably W. Knox, see p. 117, n. 3, above) significantly emphasizes the clause ' Until they shall be varied, &c.', which he prints in big capitals (p. 58).

[2] The protests of the British minority in Canada and of the Opposition in Parliament suggested that the right of *habeas corpus* was completely withheld under the provisions of the Quebec Bill. But, as Wedderburn, in his official capacity as Solicitor-General, had admitted, the Common Law right had existed in Canada since the conquest and was unaffected by the Bill. It might indeed have been argued that in criminal cases the introduction of the English criminal law under the Bill would imply the introduction of the *Habeas Corpus* Act. See Lucas, *History of Canada, 1763–1812* (Oxford, 1909), p. 88, note. The proposed ordinance was passed in 1784.

religious question.   North and his colleagues had not
enjoyed the task of defending in Parliament so unpopular
a cause as that of the Roman Catholic Church in Canada ;
and, shaken by Chatham's thunder and the groans of the
London mob, they were doubtless willing to do what they
could, within the terms of the Act, to placate Protestant
prejudices and favour Protestant interests.   But to the main
policy of toleration as embodied in the Act they were
bound to adhere.   Eight of the twenty-three persons
nominated by the Government to form the new Council
were French-Canadians, and it may be presumed that most,
if not all, of these were Catholics, to whom the Governor
was instructed to tender the new form of oath.[1]   In ' matters
of ecclesiastical concern ' Carleton was to regard it as his
' indispensable duty to lose no time in making such arrangements . . . as may give full satisfaction to our new subjects
in every point in which they have a right to any indulgence '.
Of this tolerant spirit the instructions with regard to the
religious communities were a specific example.   Their fate
had been left unsettled at the conquest, when the French
request for their continued maintenance had been refused,
except in the case of the communities of nuns, ' till the King's
pleasure be known' ;[2] and the Quebec Act had not touched
the question.   It was now decided that the Seminaries of
Quebec and Montreal should continue to enjoy their
property, to maintain their numbers, and to carry on their
work of education for the priesthood as of old ; and all other
religious communities were to be allowed to remain pro-

[1] Instructions, Articles 1 and 3, C. D., pp. 595–596.   There were only two
or three Protestant French-Canadian families in the province.   One such
Protestant, François Mounier, had been included in the first Legislative
Council in 1764 and served till his death in 1769.   He had also been
appointed (1764) a judge in the Court of Common Pleas.   Masères describes
him (April 4, 1768) as ' a Frenchman who can't speak three words of
English, who was bred a merchant and still continues so.   He is a man of
good plain sense and I believe a very honest man ' (*Masères Letters*, p. 83
and n. 3).

[2] Capitulation of Montreal, Articles XXXII and XXXIII, see Appendix
A, pp. 200–201, below.

visionally ' in their present establishment ', with the single exception of the Society of Jesuits, which was at once to be ' suppressed and dissolved ', all its property passing to the Crown but its present members in Quebec being allowed ' sufficient stipends and provisions during their natural lives '.[1] Thus far ministers were prepared to observe both the letter and the spirit of the Act. Thus far, but no farther ; for the Instructions made it clear that religious toleration was not meant to imply religious equality. Carleton was bidden always to remember that the Catholics in Canada are entitled only to the free exercise of the faith of the Roman Church and ' not to the powers and privileges of it as an established Church ; for that is a preference which belongs to the Protestant Church of England '.[2] And on one minor point the spirit, though not the letter, of the Act was clearly violated. Should any benefice become vacant, all its rents and profits during the vacancy were to be reserved for the support of the Protestant clergy.[3]

[1] Instructions, Article 21, pars. 11 and 12, C. D., pp. 604–605 [K., pp. 155–156]. The British Government's treatment of the Jesuits in Canada was not less generous than that of Catholic Governments on the Continent. In 1764 all Jesuits in France had been ordered to leave the country within a month (cf. Wedderburn, C. D., p. 449). In 1773 Pope Clement XIV had officially suppressed the Society. The income of the Jesuits' estates in Canada was estimated in 1767 as only 22,658 livres (Coffin, *op. cit.*, p. 450).

[2] Instructions, Article 20, C. D., p. 602 [K., p. 154].

[3] Instructions, Article 21, pars. 4 and 5, C. D., pp. 603–604 [K., p. 155]. More excusable, perhaps, but no less repugnant to modern ideas of toleration are the provisions that all Catholic missionaries should be withdrawn by degrees from the Indian *hinterland* and replaced by Protestant missionaries (*ibid.*, par. 12, p. 605 [K., p. 156]). It is also prescribed (*ibid.*, par. 4, p. 603) that in a parish containing a Protestant majority, the incumbent shall be a Protestant and ' entitled to *all tithes payable* within such parish '. Coffin (*op. cit.*, p. 440) takes this to include Catholic tithes; but ministers surely did not intend to commit towards Catholics the very injustice from which the Act protected Protestants.

2

It was as well, perhaps, that nothing came of this dubious attempt to take the sting from the antagonism, at home and in Canada, to the Quebec Act. Carleton was determined to say or do nothing that could raise the faintest suspicion in the minds of the French-Canadians as to the completeness and sincerity of the policy of conciliation. Thus, though the first version of the Quebec Act, published in the *Quebec Gazette* in August, was incorrect, being an abstract of one of the discarded drafts of the Bill which had specifically ruled out the English civil law and had contained no suggestion that the laws should be ' varied or altered ' by the Legislative Council, Carleton did not put the matter right : he left the disquieted British merchants to learn the truth from the text of the Act as published in the *Gazette* of December 8.[1] But it was soon far more difficult for him to keep silent. In January 1775, he received Dartmouth's letter, revealing the ministers' anxiety as to the attitude of the British community and their hopes of conciliating it as soon as their ' intentions with respect to the plan of judicature are well-known '. A few weeks later Carleton was informed of the new turn in the Government's policy to its full extent. His new Instructions and the Draft Ordinance arrived : and in the seventh instruction he found himself ordered ' forthwith to communicate such and so many of these Our Instructions to Our said Council wherein their advice and consent are mentioned to be requisite '. Such, obviously, was the twelfth instruction, which betrayed so unmistakably the Government's desire for a compromise on the question of the civil law. Obviously, too, the Government wished that, as soon as the Council was in being, Carleton should call on it, in the light of this instruction, to enact the draft Ordinance.

[1] W. Smith, *The Struggle over the Laws of Canada*, C. H. R., vol. i, pp. 174-175.

Nor was there any thought of official secrecy in the matter. The sooner the disgruntled British merchants heard the good news, the better. So Carleton was faced with a dilemma. He had built all his policy on the hope of maintaining and confirming the confidence of the French-Canadians. Now he must either risk the loss of it or risk his reputation and even perhaps his career. He had admitted, it is true, in his evidence before the House of Commons, that the French-Canadians might not object to the introduction of new ' commercial laws ' if they knew what they were ; [1] but he can scarcely have contemplated the immediate transference of the whole field covered in the twelfth instruction from French to English law. He was bound to feel that such a drastic and hasty course, however strictly in accord with the letter of the Act, would seem very like a violation of its spirit ; and to weaken the trust of the French-Canadians in the British Government's good faith in order to placate the British minority was to defeat the main purpose of the Act and to return to the confused thinking and mixed motives of 1763. For the moment, at any rate, Carleton could still conceal the Government's new move without positive disobedience ; for the Council could not be created until the Act came into force on May 1. And after the outbreak of war in the South in April, he was so fully occupied with organizing the military defence of the province that the Council did not meet till August. By then Carleton had made one of the most serious decisions in his life. The crisis was now upon him ; everything now depended—so at least it seemed to him—on the good effects of the Quebec Act policy on the attitude of the French-Canadians. And so, as officials confronted with an emergency and out of touch with their superiors have often felt obliged to do, though never without grave risk to themselves, he decided to disobey his orders. He read his

[1] See p. 75, above.

Commission to the Council but none of his Instructions. He seems, indeed, to have permitted a discussion on the question of new commercial laws ; and, had he communicated the twelfth instruction and himself pressed the measures it recommended, it is conceivable that the French-Canadian members of the Council might have yielded. As it was, they clung stubbornly to the whole body of their law. ' Inflexible to any arguments either of expediency or justice ', reported Hey, who, of course, advocated the policy he had incorporated in the draft Ordinance, 'they will admit no alteration in their ancient laws, particularly in the article of commerce'.[1] Thus the British Government's plan for conciliating the ' old subjects ' was not given a trial.[2]

It is difficult to blame Carleton. If the policy of the Quebec Act was right, he was surely wise not to weaken its effectiveness, at the critical moment, in the desperate hope of placating the disaffected element in the British minority. For already in the spring of 1775 their attitude towards the Home Government could no longer be determined by its Canadian policy. Boston was nearer to Montreal than Edinburgh to London ; and by what they did at Boston and nowhere else ministers were being judged by their kinsmen in the northern colony as in all its southern neighbours. The disaffected among them would be little influenced by compromise in Quebec as long as coercion was the rule in Massachusetts : the loyalists would subordinate their own provincial grievance to a quarrel which concerned all North America. And in the autumn, when the Revolution and the War had actually begun, still less could any question of Canadian law determine the sympathies of either section.[3]

[1] Hey to Lord Chancellor, August 28, 1775, C. D., p. 671.

[2] The Council did not meet again till 1777, and the Instructions were withheld from it until, after continual controversy, they were disclosed by Governor Haldimand in 1781. See W. Smith, *The Struggle over the Laws of Canada*, C. H. R., vol. i, pp. 166–186.

[3] For an adverse judgement on Carleton's conduct, see W. Smith's scholarly paper, cited in the preceding foot-note.

That a large proportion of the British minority—it is impossible to fix the actual numbers—were loyalists or 'Tories' (as their opponents called them), prepared at such a time of strain to suspend all public opposition to the Quebec Act, had already been discovered by Carleton before he was aware of the new tendency in the Government's Canadian policy. 'The most respectable part of the English residing in this place', he reported from Quebec in November 1774, 'notwithstanding many letters from home advising them to pursue a different course . . . presented an address expressive of their wish to see universal harmony and a dutiful submission to Government continue to be the characteristic of the inhabitants of this province, and assuring me that nothing should be wanting upon their parts to promote so desirable an end.' But not all were loyalists. 'I believe', continues Carleton, 'most of those who signed this address were disposed to act up to their declaration, which probably would have been followed by those who did not, if their brethren at Montreal had not adopted very different measures.' At Montreal, so it was said, 'letters of importance' had been received from the General Congress in the South :[1] the British residents had flocked to the coffee-house to hear the news, to air their grievances in public, and to discuss means of redress. A Committee had been appointed, had set out forthwith for Quebec, and had there issued an invitation to all British subjects to meet them at a tavern in the town. At this gathering, which 'several discreet people' declined to attend 'as soon as they discovered what they aimed at ', a committee had been chosen for Quebec. 'There have been several Town Meetings since, as they are pleased to style them, and meetings of the Joint Committees, at which, 'tis said, they have resolved to write letters of thanks to the

---

[1] Among these 'letters of importance' was the Address from Congress discussed below.

Lord Mayor and Corporation of London, to some of the
merchants in the City, and to Mr. Masères, for having taken
the province under their protection, and praying a continuance of their zealous endeavours in so good a cause. They
intend a handsome present in cash to Mr. Masères with
the promise of a larger sum in case he succeeds. Petitions
are likewise to be presented to the King, to the Lords, and
to the Commons. But of all this I speak doubtfully as they
have taken uncommon pains to keep their whole proceedings
from my knowledge.' [1]

3

Carleton had not been misinformed. In the middle of
January, 1775, the petitions for the repeal of the Quebec Act
reached Masères, whom the Joint Committees had formally
appointed as their agent ; and the first of them, the petition
to the Crown, was presented to Dartmouth on January 18—
only eleven days after his dispatch to Carleton of the
recommendations which conceded almost all the petitioners
asked. But in their ignorance of any change in the Government's attitude, they could but urge again the arguments
that had been urged before the passing of the Act.[2] The
King in his ' royal wisdom ', the Lords ' as the hereditary
guardians of the rights of the people ', were implored once
again to consider the unhappy state of British subjects
deprived of the rights of *habeas corpus* and trial by jury and
governed by strange laws, ' disgraceful to us as Britons and -
in their consequences ruinous to our properties '. And the

[1] Carleton to Dartmouth, November 11, 1774, C. D., pp. 586–588. Of
the agitation in Montreal Carleton says : ' Mr. Walker, whose warmth of
temper brought him . . . the very cruel and every way unjustifiable revenge
which made so much noise, now takes the lead, and is not unmindful of his
friend, Mr. Masères, upon this occasion.' The bitter touch in the last few
words shows how strained the personal relations of Carleton and Masères
must have become. For the Walker affair, see p. 46, n. 2, above.
[2] Petition to the King (186 signatures), C. D., p. 589; to the Lords, p. 591;
to the Commons, p. 592 [B. K., p. 66]. All dated November 12, 1774.

Commons were once again reminded how much of the Canadian trade—' four parts in five of all the imports and exports '—was in British hands.

For the Whigs in London, all the more anxious as the outlook in Massachusetts steadily darkened to prove to their exasperated fellow subjects that the Government's policy was not the policy of the mother country as a whole, these old arguments were good enough. The petitions to Parliament were presented and motions proposed for the introduction of a Bill to repeal the Act by Camden in the Lords on May 17 and by Savile in the Commons on the following day. The brief debates revealed that the Opposition were still quite incapable of regarding the Quebec Act with a cooler judgement than was to be expected of the angry colonists. The protests of Congress had stiffened them in their belief that the Act had been framed as an essential part of the Government's programme of coercion. Once more ministers were denounced for deliberately plotting ' to secure a Popish Canadian army to subdue and oppress the Protestant British colonists '.[1] And Fox went so far as to say that, ' if the disputes had not arisen with the old American colonies, the Act of last year would not have been thought of, but the colony would have been left without law or any political regulation whatever '.[2] Ministers, of course, stood firmly by the Act. They could not read out in Parliament the new instructions they had already sent to Carleton. They could not confess they were already trying to blunt the edges of the Act in the interests of the British minority in Canada. But the debate enabled the Government to make two important points. Dartmouth again exposed the popular illusion that the Act had deprived British subjects in Canada of even their Common Law right to the writ of *habeas corpus* as well as of trial by jury in all cases— ' the former of which it is evident ', he said, ' they are

---

[1] P. H., vol. xviii, p. 657.　　　　[2] *Ibid.*, p. 681.

entitled to by the laws of England, and the latter they now
enjoy in all criminal matters '.[1] Of graver purport was
North's frank declaration that ' if the refractory colonies
cannot be reduced to obedience by the present force, he
should think it a necessary measure to arm the Roman
Catholics of Canada and to employ them in that service '.[2]
No such threat had escaped North's lips in the debates of
the previous summer. But the hearts of George III and
his compliant advisers had been hardened since then by
the continued and aggravated opposition of the Boston
' rebels ' : and North saw no reason now for not confirming
the hint which Lyttelton had given, nearly a year ago, as
to the resources at the Government's command in Canada.
Let the Whigs acclaim it as a corrobation of their slanders
on the real motives of the Act. If indeed, as ought surely
to be assumed from Carleton's report, the Act had succeeded
in confirming the allegiance of the French-Canadians to
their new rulers, could any loyal Englishman, he asked himself, deny the Government's right to use that allegiance,
if the worst came to the worst, in order to suppress rebellion,
and prevent the disruption of the Empire ? The time might
come, in fact, for realizing the insurance policy which the
Act had carried with it. Let the position be openly stated
then. The threat might cool hot heads in Boston.

The time *had* come. While North was speaking, the news
of Lexington was on its way to England : a few weeks
later it was known in London that the sequel to this trivial
' skirmish ' had been the rising of the colonists in arms and
the investment of the British garrison in Boston : and on
July 1 Dartmouth wrote to inform Carleton that ' the King
relies upon the loyalty and fidelity of his Canadian subjects
for their assistance to suppress rebellion, and it is his
Majesty's pleasure that you do, if you see no objection,

---

[1] *Ibid.*, p. 662.   [2] *Ibid.*, p. 681.

immediately on the receipt of this letter take the proper
steps for raising a body of 3,000 Canadians . . . to act as
light infantry either in a separate corps or in conjunction
with his Majesty's other troops, as shall upon consulting
General Gage be thought most expedient '.[1] Worse news
from Boston increased the Government's call on the fighting
strength of Canada. On July 24 Dartmouth wrote authoriz-
ing Carleton to raise the number of his levy from 3,000 to
6,000.[2]

4

Before these letters reached him Carleton had learned
that the trust they showed in the active loyalty of the
French-Canadians as a whole—a trust he had himself tried
most to inspire—was an illusion. It was a bitter disappointment. He saw now what years ago he had foreseen—the
old colonies in rebellion ; Canada the strategic key to
the now inevitable struggle ; the fate of Canada, perhaps
the fate of North America, dependent on the attitude of the
Canadians. In view primarily of a renewal of war with
France, but secondly of just this very emergency, he had
worked unceasingly to make British policy in Canada so
liberal and so candid that, when the crisis came, a grateful
and contented people would rally whole-heartedly to defend

---

[1] Dartmouth to Carleton, July 1, 1775, C. D., p. 667, note. On June 7
Dartmouth had written complacently reporting the defeat of the Opposition's attack on the Quebec Act. ' How little impression it made within
doors will best appear from the great majority in both Houses ; and I have
the satisfaction to assure you that it met with no greater encouragement
without doors and that to all appearance the people of England in general
concur in the measures which have been adopted for America.' The short
dispatch closes with a brief reference to ' an account published here of
a skirmish between the King's troops and the provincials in the neighbourhood of Boston ' which has increased ' that just indignation which every
friend to Government feels for the insult offered to the constitution in the
rebellious resistance to the authority of Parliament by the people of
North America ' (C. D., p. 663).

[2] Dartmouth to Carleton, July 24, 1775, C. D., p. 667, note.

a Government which had understood their wishes and
freely granted them. Slowly—too slowly it seemed now—
he had secured the first part of his policy : and the highest
expectations he had cherished of its result had seemed
justified when first he returned to Canada with the Quebec
Act in his pocket. How sanguine were his hopes that
September is clear from other and more conclusive evidence
than his jubilant report to Downing Street. Within twenty-
four hours of his landing at Quebec an anxious letter arrived
from Gage asking him if he could send at once to Boston
two of the four British regiments then in Canada. ' The
present situation of affairs in this province ', Gage wrote,
' obliges me to collect all the force in my power.' At the
same time he submitted it to Carleton's judgement whether
' anything is to be dreaded from the absence of those corps
internally in the province of Quebec during the winter ',
at the end of which the regiments might be replaced. ' As
I must look forward to the worst ', he continued, ' from the
apparent disposition of the people here, I am to ask your
opinion whether a body of Canadians and Indians might
be collected and confided in for the service in this country,
should matters come to extremities.' [1]   Carleton's first
impressions of French-Canadian satisfaction at the Act were
fresh upon him and he did not hesitate over his reply.
The very next day he wrote to inform Gage that the two
regiments would be ' ready to embark at a moment's
notice '. As to the internal insecurity of Canada, left with
so scanty a garrison, he made no difficulty whatever. And,
most assuredly, he would raise a force of French-Canadians.
' The Canadians ', he said, ' have testified to me the strongest
marks of joy and gratitude and fidelity to the King and to
his Government for the late arrangements made at home
in their favour. A Canadian regiment would complete their

---

[1] Gage to Carleton, September 4, 1774, C. D., p. 583. The regiments
were the 10th and 52nd.

happiness, which in time of need might be augmented to two, three, or more battalions.'[1]

Gradually, as winter drew on, these bright hopes of the autumn began to fade. In November a new note of anxiety is already audible in Carleton's references to the attitude of the Canadians. In his dispatch reporting the activities of the disaffected British in Quebec and Montreal he mentions the ' uneasiness' their proceedings have created among the French-Canadians in the towns. ' They are surprised ', he writes, ' that such meetings and nocturnal cabals should be suffered to exert all their efforts to disturb the minds of the people by false and seditious reports : ' and they are ' not without their fears ' lest ' some weak and ignorant people ' among their countrymen may be unduly influenced by the malicious misrepresentations of the Quebec Act which are being spread abroad. ' I have assured the Canadians ', continues Carleton, ' that such proceedings could never affect the late measures taken in their favour . . . so that they might remain in perfect tranquillity upon that account : ' but he warns ministers that, trifling and transient though he believes the effects of this agitation will be, they ' cannot guard too much or too soon against the consequence of an infection imported daily, warmly recommended, and spread abroad by the colonists here, and indeed by some from Europe not less violent than the Americans '.[2]

Carleton's evident anxiety was well founded ; and by February the process of disillusionment has advanced a long step farther. Replying to another inquiry from Gage as to

[1] Carleton to Gage, September 20, 1774, C. D., p. 584. As to the Indians, Carleton wrote : ' The savages of this province, I hear, are in very good humour. A Canadian battalion would be a great motive and go far to influence them ; but you know what sort of people they are.' This last note of warning was justified. At the critical period of the war in Canada the Indians were canvassed by both sides but held aloof. As appeared in the later stages of the war, the moral effect on colonial opinion of their fighting for the British more than outweighed any military advantage. See Lucas, *History of Canada, 1763–1812*, p. 158.

[2] Carleton to Dartmouth, November 11, 1774, C. D., pp. 586–588.

the forces to be raised in Canada, Carleton repeats his old
assurances of the effect on the Canadians in general of the
Quebec Act. ' All that have spoke or wrote to me upon the
subject express the most grateful sense of what has been done
for them.' But they are proving, it seems, a little difficult
to handle. The new troops, for instance, as indeed he had
always contended, must enjoy the full status and pay of
regular regiments. ' The gentry, well-disposed and heartily
desirous as they are to serve the Crown and to serve it with
zeal when formed into regular corps, do not relish commanding a bare militia.' But the chief obstacle to calling out the
militia was the attitude of the *habitants*, on whom, of course,
since they formed the great majority of the population,
the whole situation depended. If Gage was familiar with
Carleton's previous opinions on this point, he must have been
startled and disquieted by the following admissions. ' As
to the *habitants* or peasantry, ever since the civil authority
has been introduced into the province, the government of
it has hung so loose and retained so little power, *they have
in a manner emancipated themselves* ; and it will require
time and discreet management likewise to recall them to
their ancient habits of obedience and discipline. Considering *all the new ideas they have been acquiring for these
ten years past*, can it be thought they will be pleased at being
suddenly and without preparation embodied into a militia
and marched from their families, lands, and habitations to
remote provinces and all the horrors of war which they
have already experienced. It would give an appearance
of truth to the language of our sons of sedition, at this very
moment busily employed instilling into their minds that
the Act was passed merely to serve the present purposes
of Government and in the full intention of ruling over them
with all the despotism of their ancient masters.' Here is
a change indeed from the accepted version of the *habitant* !
Emancipation ? New ideas ? What had such things to do

with those ' quiet and submissive people ', anxious only to be allowed to continue their old ways, liable to be ' extremely hurt to have any part of their customs taken from them ' ? Carleton, it is true, was only discussing their attitude to service in the militia : he still maintained that a regular regiment could be raised. But he knew well enough that willingness to serve in the militia, to accept as of old the universal obligation to defend the country, was the touchstone of the *habitant's* loyalty. If this test could not safely be applied, he must needs feel that his policy had failed ; and there is already a sense of failure in his expressions of regret that the settlement of the Quebec Act had not been made when first he recommended it. It would not then, he thinks, have ' roused the jealousy of the other colonies ', and it would have ' had the appearance of more disinterested favour to the Canadians '.[1]

A few more months of anxiety, and then, with the sudden breaking of the storm, the whole truth was out. On May 19 Carleton had news from Gage of the outbreak of hostilities in Massachusetts : the next day he learned that the insurgents had invaded Canada. Montreal was nearer the point of danger than Quebec, and hurrying thither, Carleton called upon the *seigneurs* of the district to collect the *habitants* for its protection. Now, if ever, was the moment for them to show themselves as ready to defend Canada in the service of the King of England as they once had been in the service of the King of France. But, as Carleton sadly reported on June 17, ' though the gentlemen testified great zeal, neither their entreaties nor their example could prevail upon the people '. ' The gentry and clergy ', he repeats, ' have been very useful upon this occasion and shown great fidelity and warmth for his Majesty's service, but both have lost much of their influence over the people.'

---

[1] Carleton to Gage, February 4, 1775, C. D., pp. 660–662. Italics not in the original.

He even questions now whether a regular battalion could be raised, ' so much have the minds of the people been tainted by the cabals and intrigues '.[1] Attempts to raise a force of volunteers proved almost wholly futile except among the *seigneurs* and the loyal British in the towns ; and as the position grew more critical with every day's delay, Carleton made one last effort to bring the *habitants* to a sense of duty. On June 9 he proclaimed martial law and called out the whole militia of the province under the old French regulations.[2] The *seigneurs* promptly undertook the task which thereby fell to them of gathering their tenants under their command ; but, though in many cases they plainly told them that the denial of the old feudal service would legally involve the loss of their rights of tenure, their summons was met almost everywhere with a stubborn and often angry refusal. One *seigneur* was actually seized and kept in confinement by his tenants. Another, who was so foolish as to draw his sword, was set upon and thrashed. Under such circumstances to enforce the obligation was palpably impossible. The whole idea of a French-Canadian army had melted into air at the first attempt to realize it.[3]

[1] Carleton to Dartmouth, June 7, 1775, C. D., pp. 660–666. Cf. Cramahé to Dartmouth, September 21, 1775 : ' No means have been left untried to bring the Canadian peasantry to a sense of their duty, and engage them to take up arms in defence of the province ; but all to no purpose ' (C. D., p. 667). The loyal French-Canadians were obliged to confess the truth. See Madam Benoist's letter of May 25 (Verreau, p. 305), and M. Baby's letter of September 23 : ' Nos habitants des compagnes corrumpus et persuadés par des lettres circulaires répandus de tems en tems par nos voisins, et soutenus par les propos factieux de plusieurs Anglais et colons étrangers établis dans cette colonie, ont résolu jusqu'à présent de conserver la neutralité ' (Verreau, p. 314 ; cf. M. Guy, p. 306).

[2] The text of the proclamation is given in Masères's *Additional Papers concerning the Province of Quebec*, p. 170.

[3] For the conduct of the *habitants* towards the *seigneurs*, see the interesting ' contemporary account' given in Masères's *Additional Papers*, pp. 71–78, and reprinted in *Documents relating to the Seigniorial Tenure in Canada* (ed. W. B. Munro, Publications of the Champlain Society, No. iii, Toronto, 1908). As to the general attitude of the *habitants* during the invasion, scattered evidence can be found in (1) the British and American official documents as cited below ; (2) the private journals kept by individuals in

5

At the moment of crisis a balanced judgement of the *habitants'* attitude was not to be expected ; and in after times it has often been misrepresented and misunderstood. It should be easier, now that a century and a half has passed, to see clearly what were the main influences working on them and to estimate fairly what was in reason to be expected of them.

Account must be taken, in the first place, of the vigorous efforts made by the recalcitrant colonists in the South to win them over to their cause. It has been seen that the British Government's policy of conciliation was construed in New England as a sinister attempt to make the French-Canadians the instruments of their suppression ; and soon after the passing of the Quebec Act an organized propaganda was set on foot with the object of neutralizing its effects. On October 26 the Congress at Philadelphia addressed a formal appeal to the 'inhabitants of the Province of Quebec' for co-operation in obtaining the redress of their 'afflicting grievances'.[1] This long, wordy, but vigorous document, composed in the same rhetorical strain as the address issued a few weeks earlier to the people of Great Britain, deserves careful study ; for it set the tone and listed the arguments for the whole subsequent campaign of propaganda.

When the fortune of war (it began), after a gallant and glorious resistance, had incorporated you with the body of English subjects, we rejoiced in the truly valuable addition, both on our own and your account ; expecting, as courage

the American forces : most of these are in print, and a full list, with references, is given in an appendix to J. Codman, *Arnold's Expedition to Quebec* (New York, 1902) ; (3) the French-Canadian journals of Sanguinet, Badeaux, and Berthelot, and the correspondence between French-Canadian residents at Montreal and Quebec, printed in L'Abbé Verreau, *Invasion du Canada* (Montreal, 1873).

[1] The full text is given in K., p. 139, and in Kingsford, vol. v, p. 262.

and generosity are naturally united, our brave enemies would become our hearty friends, and that the Divine Being would bless to you the dispensations of his over-ruling Providence by securing to you and your posterity the inestimable advantages of a free English constitution of government, which it is the privilege of all English subjects to enjoy.

These hopes were confirmed by the King's Proclamation, issued in the year 1763, plighting the public faith for your full enjoyment of those advantages.

Little did we imagine that any succeeding ministers would so audaciously and cruelly abuse the royal authority as to withhold from you the fruition of the irrevocable rights to which you were thus justly entitled.

But since we have lived to see the unexpected time, when ministers of this flagitious temper have dared to violate the most sacred compacts and obligations, and as you, educated under another form of government, have artfully been kept from discovering the unspeakable worth of that form you are now undoubtedly entitled to, we esteem it our duty . . . to explain to you some of its most important branches.

An elaborate exposition follows, introduced by a quotation from ' the celebrated Marquis Beccaria ', of the general principles of British liberty. The ' first grand right ' it bestows upon the people is representative government, ' a bulwark surrounding and defending their property, which by their honest cares and labours they have acquired, so that no portions of it can legally be taken from them but with their own full and free consent '. The next right is trial by jury; the third the writ of *habeas corpus*.[1] ' A fourth right is that of *holding lands by the tenure of easy rents and not by rigorous and oppressive services, frequently forcing the possessors from their families and their business, to perform what ought to be done, in all well regulated states, by men hired for the purpose.*' The last right mentioned is the freedom of the press.

These are the invaluable rights that form a considerable part of our mild system of government ; that, sending its

---

[1] The inference is that even the Common Law right to the writ is somehow cancelled by the Quebec Act. See p. 128, n. 2, above.

equitable energy through all ranks and classes of men, defends the poor from the rich, the weak from the powerful, the industrious from the rapacious, the peaceable from the violent, *the tenants from the lords,* and all from their superiors. These are the rights without which a people cannot be free and happy. . . . These are the rights you are entitled to, and ought at this moment in perfection to exercise. And what is offered you by the late Act of Parliament in their place ? Liberty of conscience in your religion ? No, God gave it you ; and'the temporal powers, with which you have been and are connected,[1] firmly stipulated for your enjoyment of it.

The rest of the Quebec Act is submitted to the same destructive analysis. ' Are the French laws in civil cases restored to you ? It seems so. But observe the cautious kindness of the ministers who pretend to be your benefactors.' Those laws may be varied or altered by the arbitrary decree of the Governor and Council—a shrewder thrust, in the light of Carleton's new instructions, than Congress realized. It is the same with the benefits of the English criminal law. ' Such is the precarious tenure of mere will by which you hold your lives and religion. The Crown and its ministers are empowered, as far as they could be by Parliament, to establish even the *inquisition* itself among you.'

An indignant paragraph follows on the refusal of an Assembly and of the power of self-taxation. While the Quebec Revenue Act imposes an excise duty, ' the horror of all free states ', the Quebec Act itself only permits the levy of rates ' for the inferior purposes of making roads and erecting and repairing public buildings '. ' Have not Canadians sense enough to attend to any other public affairs than gathering stones from one place and piling them up in another? Unhappy people! who are not only injured, but insulted. . . .' And then at last, the way thus carefully prepared, the Address comes to the gist of the matter.

---

[1] Note the suggestion that the tie with France still in some sort continues, a point which Congress was by no means anxious to emphasize later on when France joined the colonies in the war ; see p. 187, below.

Nay more ! With such a superlative contempt of your understanding and spirit has an insolent ministry presumed to think of you, our respectable fellow subjects . . . as firmly to persuade themselves that your gratitude, for the injuries and insults they have recently offered you, will engage you to take up arms, and render yourselves the ridicule and detestation of the world, by becoming tools in their hands to assist them in taking that freedom from *us*, which they have treacherously denied to *you* ; the unavoidable consequence of which attempt, if successful, would be the extinction of all hopes of you or your posterity being ever restored to freedom : for idiotcy itself cannot believe that, when their drudgery is performed, they will treat you with less cruelty than they have us, who are of the same blood with themselves.

From this impassioned rhetoric the Address reverts, with something of an anticlimax, to academic exposition. 'What', it asks, 'would your immortal countryman Montesquieu have said to such a plan of domination?' and then, citing his 'decisive maxims' on the danger to freedom when the legislative, executive, and judicial functions are not separate, it bids the Canadians apply them to their own state. Finally, it invites them to choose between remaining on the one hand under the form of government instituted by the Quebec Act, which, as they will see if they exert 'the natural sagacity of Frenchmen', is but 'a painted sepulchre for burying your lives, liberty, and property', and on the other hand 'an entire adoption into the union of these colonies'. The shade of Montesquieu is invoked to guide their choice. If he were still alive and knew that the Canadians were being asked by their 'numerous and powerful neighbours' to join them in their righteous contest and 'to take a noble chance of emerging from a humiliating subjection under governors, intendants, and military tyrants into the firm rank and condition of English freemen', would not this be the purport of his advice ?—

Seize the opportunity presented to you by Providence itself. You have been conquered into liberty if you act as you ought. This work is not of man. You are a small people, compared to those who with open arms invite you into fellowship. A moment's reflection should convince you which will be most for your interest and happiness, to have all the rest of North America your unalterable friends or your inveterate enemies. The injuries of Boston have roused and associated every colony from Nova Scotia to Georgia. Your province is the only link that is wanting to complete the bright and strong chain of union. Nature has joined your country to theirs. Do you join your political interests.

One more point was needed. Delicate and thorny as the subject was, the appeal could not go out without some reference to the greatest and most obvious obstacle to union. A paragraph, therefore, is devoted to the question of religion —a very brief paragraph and couched in very different terms from those of the denunciation of Popery in the Address to the British people, published by the same Congress only five weeks before.[1]

We are too well acquainted (it says) with the liberality of sentiment distinguishing your nation to imagine that difference of religion will prejudice you against a hearty unity with us. You know that the transcendant nature of freedom elevates those who unite in the cause above all such low-minded infirmities. The Swiss Cantons furnish a memorable proof of this truth. Their union is composed of Catholic and Protestant states, living in the utmost peace and concord with one another, and thereby enabled, ever since they bravely vindicated their freedom, to defy and defeat every tyrant that has invaded them.

With a final warning against sacrificing ' the liberty and happiness of the whole Canadian people ' to the avarice and ambition of selfish individuals among them the Address closes with a formal invitation to the Canadians not ' to commence hostilities against the government of our common sovereign '—the time had not yet come for this—but to elect deputies for their towns and districts who should meet in a provincial congress and in turn elect delegates to attend

¹ See p. 120, above.

the continental congress to be held at Philadelphia on
May 10. ' That Almighty God may incline your minds to
approve our equitable and necessary measures, to add yourselves to us, to put your fate, whenever you suffer injuries
which you are determined to oppose, not on the small
influence of your single province but on the consolidated
powers of North America . . . is the fervent prayer of us,
your sincere and affectionate friends and fellow subjects.' [1]

This remarkable document was dispatched forthwith to
the leaders of the British malcontents at Montreal—there
was no means of preventing seditious correspondence between
one colony and another—and copies of it, translated into
French, were presently being scattered broadcast over the
Canadian countryside.[2] Much of it was singularly ill-suited
to its purpose. It was obviously addressed not to the
educated class of Canadians, the *seigneurs* and the priests,
but to the peasantry ; and its authors seem scarcely to have
realized that the vast majority of the *habitants* could not
read and knew nothing of history or politics. On such an
audience those disquisitions on the principles of government,
garnished with quotations, redolent of the study, would
be thrown away. What could the *habitants* know or care
of Beccaria or Montesquieu ? How could their religious
prejudices be combated by precedents from the history of
Switzerland ? And, suppose them to be sympathetic, how
could the suggested scheme for their representation at the
Philadelphia Congress be put into effect without systematic
explanation, organization, and leadership entirely beyond
the scope of the few disaffected British in the province ?
But with much that was academic and unpractical the

[1] Other appeals were made during the invasion, e. g. the letter from
Congress, January 24, 1776, printed in Sanguinet's Journal (Verreau, p. 99).

[2] For the communications between Boston and Montreal and the
propaganda in Canada, see J. H. Smith, *Our Struggle for the Fourteenth
Colony* (New York and London, 1907), a full and well-documented account
of the Revolutionary attempt to secure Canada, mainly from contemporary
American sources and with marked American sympathies.

Congress draftsmen had blended material of the highest propagandist value. Throughout the Address they had represented the Quebec Act, not as a generous concession by the British Government to what it sincerely believed to be the wishes of the Canadian people as a whole, but as a deliberate attempt to serve the interests of one class only of Canadians at the expense of the great majority. In the above quotations from the document, certain passages have been printed in italics to show how cleverly this telling note is sounded. Not that there is any reason to suppose that the writers were consciously perverting the facts. Those accusations, after all, were but a *réchauffé* of the public statements of Chatham and Burke and Fox—a little more fiercely heated, a little more highly spiced, by closer contact with the actual quarrel. In any case they were the best of ammunition for a revolutionist campaign in a relatively backward agrarian country of the eighteenth century. Thus armed, it might be possible for the incendiaries to stir up in Canada something akin to the temper of a peasant revolt—that terrible, primitive force that from time to time and in every land has shaken the old-established fabric of society, and within twenty years from the events now under discussion was to bring it crashing to the ground in France.

Throughout the winter the malcontents in Montreal and Quebec were hard at work indoctrinating the *habitants* with these dangerous ideas. ' Many Englishmen in this province ', wrote a Government official in the autumn of 1775, ' have taken infinite pains to set the Quebec Act in a most horrid light to the Canadians.' [1] Nobody obstructed them,

---

[1] Postmaster-General Finlay, September 20, 1775. *Home Office Papers, 1773–5*, given in Winbolt & Bell's English History Source Books, *American Independence and the French Revolution*, p. 50. To what lengths some of the malcontents were prepared to go is shown by an incident recorded by Sanguinet. On the night before May 1, the date on which the Quebec Act came into force, a bust of George III, in one of the public places of Montreal, was daubed with black and decorated with a necklace formed of potatoes and a cross attached to it with the words, *Voilà le pape du Canada et le sot Anglais* (Kingsford, vol. v, p. 253).

despite all their talk of the tyrannies of Government : and
Carleton and his colleagues, though more or less aware
of their activities, made no systematic attempt at counter-
propaganda.[1] At the end of March, John Brown, an agent
sent from Boston to establish personal contact with the
Montreal Committee,[2] reported that ' through the industry
and exertions of our friends in Canada, our enemies '—it
is already the language of war—' are not at present able to
raise ten men ' for the Government's support.[3] In April
the Montreal Committee informed the Committee of Safety
of Massachusetts that the bulk, not of the English only,
but of the Canadians too, wished well to their cause.[4]
These estimates were somewhat more sanguine than was
justified by the facts ; but without question the propaganda
inaugurated by the manifesto from Congress had borne
substantial fruit.   An observant French-Canadian loyalist,
watching events day by day from his home at Three Rivers,
noted in his diary that the Canadians were influenced not
a little by the Address.[5]

6

It would, indeed, have been surprising if the campaign
had proved altogether ineffectual.   It was conducted
on favourable ground, far more favourable than Carleton

    [1] See Carleton's reference to ' our sons of sedition ' in his dispatch of
February 4, 1775, quoted p. 141, above.   In a letter of August 28, 1775,
Hey alludes to ' the subtilty and assiduity of some colony agents who were
very busy here last winter ' (C. D., p. 669).   There was considerable
unofficial counter-propaganda, as will appear later.
    [2] For the letter he carried from Samuel Adams and his arduous journey
through the snow and the broken ice on Lake Champlain, see J. H. Smith,
op. cit., vol. i, chap. iii.
    [3] John Brown at Montreal to the Committee of Correspondence at
Boston, March 29, 1775, iv A. A., vol. ii, pp. 243-245.
    [4] April 8, 1775. Signed by Walker and three others, iv A. A., vol. ii,
pp. 305-306.
    [5] J. H. Smith, op. cit., vol. i, p. 103. For Maître Badeaux and his diary,
see Kingsford, vol. v, p. 422, note, and the text in Verreau (p. 143, n. 3,
above) and in the Lit. and Hist. Society of Quebec's Documents, vol. iii.

had ever supposed. In the ten or twelve years since the British conquest the old familiar *habitant*, humble, inert, unchanging, had belied his reputation and had changed. He had changed, for instance, in his attitude to the Government. In the days of the French *régime* his habitual obedience to authority had been due partly to a sense of personal loyalty to the King of France, inculcated by Government' and Church, and more directly to a rigorous and systematic administration which was careful not to lose contact with the rural population and tireless in its paternal interference in the affairs of their daily life. With the conquest both these controlling forces had been greatly weakened. The *habitant* could not lightly transfer his personal allegiance from Louis XV to George III : and the new provincial authorities left him mostly to himself. Government, in fact, as Carleton regretfully confessed when the crisis came, ' hung loose '.[1] There was no Intendant now to harry the *habitant* with trivial regulations ; and the control of the few local officials was light and unobstrusive.[2] Above all, the final conquest had freed him from the burden of military service which during the long period of intermittent war had torn him away so constantly from his livelihood and robbed him so often of life itself. The forced labour, too, which he had submissively performed in time of peace as part of his militia duties could no longer be exacted under British civil government. And he was quick to mark the change when, for example, he found the officials requesting him to work at the river transport of troops or military stores and lacking authority to compel him as of old. Nor was it to be wondered at if in some parishes he indulged in the novel luxury of refusal.[3] The change

[1] See the dispatch of February 4, 1775, quoted p. 142, above.

[2] Except for the judicial tyranny of some of the magistrates, which was, however, stopped by Carleton ; see p. 70, above.

[3] In the autumn of 1765 Murray refrained from issuing the press-warrants which had been used for this purpose during the military *régime*, and his strongly-worded request was refused by half the parishes applied

in fact from French to British methods had instantly brought with it a new atmosphere of individual freedom. The *habitant* somehow counted more, it seemed, with these new rulers of his, he was somehow respected more by them. There is no evidence that he disliked them or wished to defy them ; but he no longer felt himself the creature of their will and power. Writing home in the autumn of 1775, an English clerk in the commissariat department at Quebec ascribed all the trouble with the French-Canadians to their familiarity with ' that damned absurd word, " liberty " '— an admirably true and succinct account (clerkly epithets apart) of the change in the *habitants'* outlook which had come so quickly on the heels of British conquest.[1]

Associated with the *habitants'* changed attitude to Government but far more conscious, definite, and purposeful was the change in his attitude to the *seigneur*. It was the policy of Murray and Carleton to maintain the *seigneurs* in their old social status as the hereditary aristocracy of Canada : they regarded them as the natural and traditional leaders of the Canadian people : to secure their friendship and support, together with that of the Church, seemed the surest means of consolidating the new *régime*. Up to a point they were right ; but they seem scarcely to have realized how much the *seigneurs'* position and authority had been impaired as a result of the conquest. It is probable that many of the more capable and energetic members of their class were among those who refused to change their allegiance and left Canada for France together with most of the few older families which represented the real *noblesse*.[2] Never a large

to. The officer in charge reported that ' the Canadians are now poisoned in their minds and instructed that they cannot be forced on such services '. Murray was therefore obliged to issue the press-warrants and excuse this departure from the methods of civil government by the plea of necessity (Coffin, *op. cit.*, p. 289).

[1] Thomas Gamble to the Deputy Q.M.G., September 6, 1775, iv A. A., vol. iii, p. 963.

[2] Munro, *The Seigniorial System in Canada*, p. 192. See the official lists

or distinguished body, the *seigneurs* in Canada were thus suddenly reduced both in numbers and in capacity. Never wealthy, they were then suddenly deprived of their main source of income by their removal from all office. Further, by the disbandment of the militia and the establishment of British administration they lost those military and judicial functions which for a century past had been the hallmark of their class and the mainstay of its power. Diminished, impoverished, divested of their old authority, they were bound to suffer also in prestige ; and the *habitants* soon recognized that they were no longer in any real sense the governing class, that they were, in fact, mere subjects like themselves. Doubtless, too, the news got about that these once proud lords of theirs were treated with open disrespect by British settlers of humble origin and common mercantile pursuits.[1] It was impossible under such circumstances for the old pretences of rank and dignity, the old unquestioned claim to deference and obedience, to be long maintained. And indeed, in any case, the new sense of personal freedom must have told as fatally against the old caste order of society as against the old authority of Government. The British system in the eighteenth century might still be far from democratic, British statesmen and administrators might still cherish their belief in oligarchy, but nowhere on British soil could sheer medieval feudalism survive unchanged or undisguised.

The fall of the *seigneurs* from their high estate would have mattered less if there had been any strong sense of mutual loyalty between them and their tenants. But the gulf between the classes, if not so deep, was of the same kind in New France as in Old. Social intercourse was practically barred. The *seigneurs* were 'absentee landlords' for the most part, living in towns. But in the old days they had at any

of the *seigneurs* who emigrated and remained, drawn up in 1767 (in the latter class 110 names are given) ; R. C. A., 1888, p. 44.
[1] See pp. 46–48, above.

rate been constantly associated with the tenants as their leaders in war and the judges of their minor disputes; whereas now they were little else than the recipients of the grain and the fowls they brought to the manor house every St. Martin's Day in payment of the rent. Disputes, moreover, about these and similar feudal obligations, which, trifling as they actually were, had constantly arisen before the conquest, had become still more frequent since. Many of the *seigneurs* seem to have taken an unwise advantage of British ignorance not only to increase their customary demands on the services of their tenants, for agricultural labour for example, but also to exceed their legal rights. The former Government, whatever its shortcomings, had been always on the watch to check such tyranny; but little attention was now paid to local grievances, and the increased cost of litigation and the unfamiliarity of English judges with feudal law made it difficult for the *habitant* to obtain redress from the Courts. In some districts, lastly, relations between *seigneur* and *habitant* had been further strained through the purchase of vacated *seigneuries* by British immigrants who, strangers to the soil and its tenants, treated their estates as nothing but pecuniary investments and thought only of exacting their full dues and of augmenting them by planting new alien settlers among the old French peasantry. Thus, for a double reason, the seigniorial system had begun to gall the *habitants* as it has never done before. To their growing disrespect for the *seigneurs* as a class was added a growing suspicion and dislike of the obligations they demanded of them.[1]

Into this unfavourable atmosphere of resentment and

[1] Munro, *Documents relating to the Seigniorial Tenure in Canada*, Introduction, pp. lxxxviii–lxxxix, c–ci; and *The Seigniorial System in Canada*, pp. 192, 205–207. The British judges made the mistake of regarding the Custom of Paris as customary, not written, law; hence they tended to allow exactions for which any precedent could be shown. For the *seigneurs'* previous tyranny, see Murray's report, quoted p. 62, n. 5, above. Also Hey's letter to Lord Apsley (August 28, 1775, C. D., p. 671).

apprehension the Quebec Act had suddenly been thrown. It could not yet be judged in the light of its actual working. Its provisions could only be known to the *habitants* by hearsay ; they were framed in general and formal terms ; and the crudest perversions of their meaning and purpose could only be effectively disproved when they came into operation. Old men might doubt and wait, but there were some among the young and restless only too ready to believe that the British Government's main intention in the Act was to fasten the *seigneur's* collar more firmly than ever round their necks. ' What will be your lordship's astonishment ', wrote Hey to the Lord Chancellor, ' when I tell you that an Act passed for the express purpose of gratifying the Canadians and which was supposed to comprehend all that they either wished or wanted, is become the first object of their discontent and dislike.' [1]   To make matters worse, there were *seigneurs* foolish enough to hold this false opinion of the Act themselves and to try to recover some of their lost authority by proclaiming it abroad. ' They have been and are too much elated ', wrote Hey, ' with the advantages they supposed they should derive from the restoration of their old privileges and customs, and indulged themselves in a way of thinking and talking that gave very just offence as well to their own people as to the English merchants.' [2]   And then, to crown all, came Carleton's demand for that one feudal service which above any other the *habitants* regarded as an intolerable burden, which they had thrown off as they hoped for ever at the conquest, which they would never willingly resume again. Instantly the tales those ' sons of

---

[1] Hey to Lord Apsley, August 28, 1775, C. D., p. 670.

[2] Letter cited in preceding note. Writing at the height of the crisis Hey speaks too sweepingly of the whole class of *seigneurs* as of the whole class of *habitants*. He continues : ' The little I have seen of them in Council gives me no idea of their abilities or moderation. Inflexible to any arguments either of expediency or justice, they will admit no alteration in their ancient laws, particularly in the article of commerce which I insist upon and believe shall carry in favour of the English merchants.'

sedition ' had told them of the Government's intentions were confirmed ; instantly they determined to disobey the call. They might still pay the *seigneur* his annual dues, they might still labour for him in the fields, but they would never again entrust their lives to his command in war.[1]

One case, recorded by a British resident in the province at the time, may be cited by way of illustration. M. La Corne, a young man of some twenty-three years, was sent by Carleton to enrol the tenants of his *seigneurie* at Terrebonne. ' He addressed them in a very high tone and reminded them of the right which he had by the tenure of their lands to command their military service.' On their replying ' that they were now subjects of England and did not look upon themselves as Frenchmen in any respect whatever ', the young *seigneur* lost his temper ; and being ' imprudent enough to strike some to those who spoke loudest ', so provoked the crowd that he was obliged to hurry back to Montreal, threatening as he left that he would return with two hundred British soldiers to enforce obedience.

The people, hearing this, forthwith armed themselves, some with guns, others with clubs, and they all resolved to die rather than submit to be commanded by their seignior. General Carleton, hearing of the disturbance that Mr. La Corne's behaviour had occasioned, instead of complying with his desire of sending troops to enforce obedience to his authority, thought it advisable to send with him an English officer of merit, Captain Hamilton (late of the 15th Regiment, and now Lieutenant-Governor of Detroit) to pacify the people. Captain Hamilton asked them what they meant by assembling in that riotous, disorderly manner. They answered that their intentions were to defend themselves from the soldiers with whom they were threatened by Mr. La Corne, their seignior. " If General Carleton ", said they, " requires our services, let him give us Englishmen to command us ; such a man as you, for instance, we would

---

[1] Carleton foresaw that the calling out of the militia would confirm the American propaganda : see his letter of February 4, 1775, quoted p. 141, above.

follow to the world's end." " But ", replied Mr. Hamilton, " English military gentlemen are not to be found in sufficient numbers in the province to take the command of you." " Then ", said they, " give us common soldiers to lead us rather than those people. For we will not be commanded by *ce petit gars*." [1]

The behaviour of these people, the narrator naïvely adds, ' is the more remarkable because Mr. La Corne is a very pretty young man in his person and appearance, and not despicable in point of understanding, and not less than three-and-twenty years old ; so that nothing but his quality of seignior and the odious powers which they suppose to be connected with that character can have rendered him disagreeable to the people '.[2]

The attitude of the *habitants* of Terrebonne suggests an obvious question. Their hostility, it seems, was directed against the *seigneur* rather than the Government. They would not accept the leadership of young La Corne merely in virtue of his hereditary claims, but they were willing— so they said—to serve under British officers or even British private soldiers. Even from his scanty garrison Carleton could have spared one or two officers to take the chief command of a few thousand French-Canadians, and the subordinate posts could surely have been filled in accordance with their wishes. If, then, the refusal of the *habitants* to fight was simply due to their repudiation of the *seigneurs'* authority, why was it that the appeal for volunteers through-

---

[1] ' That is literally ', explains the narrator, ' by that little boy, but, in their sense of it, by that insignificant, raw young man.'

[2] A contemporary account of the disorders, &c., in Munro's *Documents relating to the Seigniorial Tenure in Canada*, pp. 242–244. Another case given in this narrative is that of Mr. Cuthbert, an English *seigneur* who ' made a peremptory demand of their (his tenants') services on the French system ' and was told that ' he had best retire to his own home and trouble them no more, for that not a man of them would follow him '. Munro warns the reader against some very palpable exaggerations in the narrative as a whole (p. 241, note).

out the country proved almost as complete a failure as the calling out of the militia ?

The truth is that the attack on the *seigneurs* was only a part and not the chief part of the revolutionist propaganda. Its agents had done their best to poison the *habitants'* minds against the Government as well. They had told them many strange things about the intentions of their British rulers towards them. They were to suffer the same fate as the Acadians : those transports lying in the St. Lawrence had been brought there for the very purpose of carrying them to Boston. ' Some amongst them ', wrote Hey, ' believe they are sold to the Spaniards (whom they abominate) and that General Carleton has got the money in his pocket ! ' [1] And, of course, in contrast with these dark designs the motives and intentions of the insurgent colonists were painted in the whitest colours. ' They are told ', says Finlay, ' that the people of Boston are fighting merely to prevent the return of the Stamps, which they seem to think a matter of great politeness and do not wish to see them disturbed in so good a work.' [2] ' They have the notion ', says Hey, ' that, if the rebels get entire possession of the country, they'll be for ever exempted from paying taxes.' [3] But ignorant and credulous as the *habitants* were, falsehood and cajolery were not enough to win their active support ; and the revolutionists soon had recourse to threats. Even in the Address from Congress there had been an undercurrent of intimidation. It had reminded the Canadians of their neighbours' power no less than of their goodwill. And John Brown already confesses in March 1775 that ' the weapons that have been used by our friends have been chiefly *in terrorem* '. [4] A few weeks later, Carleton

[1] Hey to Lord Apsley, August 28, 1775, C. D., p. 670.
[2] Finlay's letter of September 20, 1775, cited p. 150, n. 1, above.
[3] Hey's letter of August 28, 1775, cited above.
[4] John Brown at Montreal to Committee of Correspondence at Boston, March 29, 1775, iv A. A., vol. ii, pp. 243-245.

reports that the deputies from Massachusetts have threatened the Canadians that, if they would not side with the Americans, Canada would be invaded by an army of 50,000 men which would devastate the country with fire and sword.[1]

Yet all this second part of the American propaganda was, like the first, only half successful. The great majority of the *habitants* were ' terrified and corrupted ' into refusing to fight for the *seigneurs* or the Government : [2] but they refused as stubbornly to fight for the colonists. Even when the actual invasion revealed the weakness of the British garrison, when in quick succession the frontier forts surrendered, when the Americans entered Montreal, and when at last Carleton was cooped up with his small surviving forces in Quebec, scarcely more of the *habitants* took arms with the invaders than had answered the British call for volunteers.[3] The American commanders made every effort to win them to their side. Washington himself emphatically reminded Arnold that the prospects of the invasion were closely dependent on the attitude of the *habitants*. ' If they are averse to it ', he wrote, ' and will not co-operate or at least willingly acquiesce, it must fail of success.' [4] Acquiescence, more or less willing, the invaders obtained : the *habitants* received them generally with friendliness, here and there with enthusiasm, and hastened to make what profit they

---

[1] Kingsford, vol. v, p. 252. In the following August John Brown writes to Turnbull : ' Now, sir, is the time to carry Canada. It may be done with great ease and little cost, and I have no doubt but the Canadians would join us.' Large forces, he adds, will be needed which will ' turn the scale immediately. *The Canadians must then take up arms or be ruined* ' (August 14, 1775, iv A. A., vol. ii, p. 135). In September, when the invasion has begun, Finlay writes : ' General Schuyler, commanding the expedition against this country, has commanded the parishes on the Sorel or Richelieu River, &c., to send 50 men from each, armed and properly provided, under pain of having fire and sword carried among them on refusal ' (Letter of September 20, cited p. 150, n. 1, above).

[2] Hey, in the letter cited p. 159, n. 1, above.

[3] For the numbers see Coffin, *op. cit.*, pp. 501-502.

[4] Washington's Instructions to Arnold, iv A. A., vol. iii, p. 765.

could from selling them supplies.¹ But co-operation on any considerable scale the Americans could not obtain, even at the high tide of their success, when they seemed in a position to carry out, if they wished, all the pillage and devastation their emissaries had threatened. In the early stages of the campaign they made the most of the few hundred men who joined them out of a population of seventy thousand. ' I can have as many Canadians as I know how to maintain ', writes Montgomery in a sanguine mood after the occupation of Montreal : but he significantly adds : ' At least I think so, while affairs wear so promising a prospect.' ² The proviso was justified : for as soon as ever the final triumph of the invasion was checked by the obstinate defence of Quebec and before the decisive turning of the tide in the new year, the American commanders found that the sympathy of the Canadians was only skin-deep.³ And in the early months of 1776 their reports are very different from those of the previous autumn. The Canadians now are ' timorous and want encouragement', ' there is but little confidence to be placed in them ' : ' they are fond of being of the strongest party'.⁴ In April the newly arrived commissioners from Congress find a surprising change in their attitude : it is

¹ See the reports by John Brown, Ethan Allen, Schuyler, and Arnold in August and September, 1775, of the friendly attitude of the Canadians (Coffin, *op. cit.*, pp. 501–502). Evidence of British officials, p. 163, below. Maître Badeaux wrote in his diary of the passing of American troops through Three Rivers, ' Il n'est pas possible d'exprimer combien la canaille triomphe de la passée de ces gens là ; il semble que chaque brigade leur apporte une fortune ' (*ibid.*, p. 501). Cf. Berthelot's *Mémoire* (Verreau, p. 230).

² November 24, 1775, iv A. A., vol. iv, p. 1695. Meigs' Journal, November 16 : ' The Canadians are constantly coming in to express their satisfaction at our coming into the country ' (C. I. Bushell, *Crumbs for Antiquarians*, vol. i, p. 23, New York, 1864). Thayer's Journal, November 15 : ' The French seem for the most part in our favour ' (E. M. Stone, *The Invasion of Canada in 1775*, p. 19, Providence, 1867).

³ See the warnings of Schuyler and Montgomery to Washington *before* Christmas, 1775 (Coffin, *op. cit.*, p. 502).

⁴ Arnold, January 11, 1776 ; Wooster, about the same time (Coffin, *op. cit.*, p. 502) ; Arnold, February 27 (Stone, *op. cit.*, p. xvii).

now, they write, a question of *regaining* their friendship.[1]
And Washington now speaks of measures needed ' *as well to
defend our troops against the Canadians themselves* as to ensure
success to the expedition '. By May it has become difficult
to get supplies from them, and Arnold is convinced ' they
are in general our bitter enemies '.[2] A few Canadians
remained active in the American cause till the end came in
June and some of them left Canada with the retreating
invaders : but from first to last the great majority maintained an immovable neutrality.[3]

7

' How have we been deceived in the Canadians ! ' wrote
Postmaster-General Finlay : [4] and it was only natural that
Carleton and his colleagues, their high hopes utterly disappointed in the first hour of trial, should regard the mere
neutrality of the *habitants* as the basest ingratitude, and,
ready in the moment of reaction to believe the worst of
those they had once praised and championed before all the
world, should ascribe it to nothing more manly or more
complex than the cowardice of a people whose bravery
they had tested in war and honoured in peace. ' As to my
opinion of the Canadians ', wrote Carleton in 1776 to the
Secretary of State, ' I think there is nothing to fear from
them while they are in a state of prosperity, and nothing
to hope for when in distress. I speak of the people at large :
there are some among them who are guided by sentiments of
honour, but the multitude is influenced only by hopes of
gain or fear of punishment.' [5] ' Your lordship will remember ',

---

[1] Coffin, *op. cit.*, p. 503.   Franklin was one of the Commissioners : see
Garneau, vol. ii, p. 367.

[2] *Ibid.* ; C. H. Jones, *The Campaign for the Conquest of Canada in 1776*,
p. 38.

[3] Coffin quotes American General Orders of July 21, 1776, directing the
march to Albany of ' the regiment of Canadians with all the Canadian
families now at Ticonderoga ' (*op. cit.*, p. 504).

[4] Letter of September 20, 1775, cited p. 150, n. 1, above.

[5] Carleton to Germain, September 28, 1776, C. D., p. 675.

wrote Hey to the Lord Chancellor, ' how much has been said by us all of their loyalty, obedience and gratitude, of their habitual submission to Government . . . but time and accident have evinced that they were obedient only because they were afraid to be otherwise, and with that fear lost (by withdrawing the troops) is gone all the good disposition that we have so often avowed in their names and promised for them in ages to come.' ' Yet I am sometimes willing to think ', continued Hey, shrinking, as it were, from so sweeping a reversal of his old beliefs, ' that fear, joined with extreme ignorance and a credulity hardly to be supposed of a people, has been overmatched by the subtilty and assiduity of some colony agents who were very busy here last winter, and that they are not at bottom an ungenerous or disobedient people.' [1] And presently Carleton, too, remembers the revolutionist propaganda and makes allowance for its influence. When the crisis is safely over, his views are the same cooler views he had held just before it came. He tells the Home Government in 1777 that the defection of the Canadians was only to be expected : they had been too much affected by seditious agitation to be ' suddenly restored ' to their old subordination. And he recognizes now that the obligations of militia service and forced labour are ' a considerable burden upon the people and that, after the disuse of them for many years, it is not surprising they should forget the duty to which they were bound by the tenure of their lands and their original government '.[2]

[1] Hey to Lord Apsley, August 28, 1775, C. D., pp. 669–670.
[2] Carleton to Germain, May 29 and July 10, 1777, C. D., p. 677, nn. 1 and 2. Lord George Germain, who succeeded Dartmouth in 1776, had a grudge against Carleton, censured him, and superseded him in his military command in Canada by Burgoyne. Carleton sent in his resignation in June 1777 (see Lucas, *History of Canada, 1763–1812*, pp. 124–144). Hence the tone of these letters, which suggest that ministers ought not to be surprised at obvious facts, and Carleton's somewhat forced disclaimer that any information from him could have induced them to expect active assistance from the Canadians.

These second thoughts were fairer : for, all things considered—the decay of the seigniorial system ; the simplicity of the *habitants*, their detachment from the outer world and their ignorance of the broader issues involved in the Revolution ; the unconcealed disloyalty of a section of the British in the province ; the lies, promises, and threats of the colonial agents ; above all, the weakness of the British garrison and the invaders' swift and easy occupation of the country up to the walls of Quebec—there is little to be wondered at in the neutrality of the *habitants*. It might, indeed, seem almost more surprising that they did not take sides against their British rulers. Only some fifteen years ago, these Britons, who now stood on the defensive with their backs to the wall, had fought and conquered them. The traditional enemies of their race from the beginnings of Canadian history, they had won the day at last, torn down the flag of France from their old French citadels, cut them apart from their homeland, and set foreigners and heretics to rule them. And if many of the *habitants* by the end of that war had lost their ardour for the cause of France,[1] there were deeper and more personal reasons for not loving their conquerors overmuch. Every war leaves its bitter memories and obstinate longings for revenge : and these British redcoats, so few and feeble now and cut off by the winter ice from succour or escape, were the people who, only some fifteen years ago, had killed their fathers and brothers, their lovers and husbands and sons. Stirred by such memories and by the pride of a hardy, fighting stock, the *habitants* must surely have been tempted, especially when the invasion was actually in being, to raise the old battle-cry and reverse the judgement of the Plains of Abraham. Had a few thousand of them joined the besiegers,

---

[1] Towards the end of the Seven Years' War, the enthusiasm of the Canadians for the cause of France had steadily declined as its prospects became steadily more desperate (G. M. Wrong, *The Fall of Canada*, p. 262) ; but they had fought finely and with heavy casualties in its earlier stages.

Quebec must needs have fallen by assault. Had they risen
en masse, armed only with weapons of the chase and the
farm, they would have overwhelmed the meagre British
forces by sheer weight of numbers and been strong enough
in the hour of victory to dictate their own terms to their
American allies.[1]

Why, then, did they not seize their chance ? Because, in
the first place, to fight against the British Government
was to fight for the colonies : and, though British soldiers
had played the chief part in the conquest, the *Bastonnais*
were older, more constant, more hated enemies than they.
Threats came more naturally than fair promises from their
opponents in the long, savage blood-feud of the border.
' An eye for an eye and a tooth for a tooth ' had been the
cry in those days : and the echo of it could not easily be
stifled by these new professions of friendship and esteem.
And indeed, when the ill-disciplined colonial troops entered
their country, it could no longer be pretended that the old
hostility was dead or the old ' low-minded infirmities ' of
religious prejudice blown entirely away by the breath of
freedom. Washington had spared no pains to impress
upon the leaders of the expedition the vital need of treating
the Canadians as their friends and especially of avoiding
any offence to their faith. Arnold, for instance, was
instructed to punish with the utmost severity, even with
death itself, any man ' so base and infamous ' as to injure
the Canadians in person or in property, and to punish also
any man who ridiculed the Roman Catholic religion and its
ceremonies or affronted its ministers.[2] But, despite all
precautions taken by the commanders, there were several
cases of violence and insult. ' The peasantry in general ',

[1] Compare the loyalty to the Union and the British Commonwealth of the
great majority of the South African Dutch in 1914, only twelve years after the
close of the last ' Boer War '.
[2] Washington's Instructions to Arnold, Nos. 5, 6, 14, iv A. A., vol. ii,
pp. 765–767.

confessed Colonel Hazen, ' has been ill-used.' Food, fuel, and the use of vehicles were sometimes forced from them at less than current prices at the bayonet's point. One case is recorded of a man being run through the neck for demanding the payment of a debt. ' Their clergy ', reported the same observer, ' have been neglected and sometimes ill-used.' One village priest had his house broken open and his watch taken from him.[1] Such a record may be favourably compared with that of many other invasions in history, but not with that of the only other the Canadians of 1775 had experienced : and there must have been many *habitants* who recalled the firm discipline, the considerate conduct, the full payment given for goods and services, in the days of the British conquest.[2] And further resentment was aroused when the *habitants* discovered that the profits they were bent on making from the new-comers were by no means secure. The lack of specie figures as prominently as military insubordination in the story of the American Revolution as a whole ; and nowhere was the colonial paper-money more distrusted than in Canada. Nor was there an adequate supply even of paper to meet the local costs of the expedition. It was estimated by the Congress commissioners in May 1776 that £14,000 was then owing in Canada.[3]

But it was not only old causes for antipathy and new causes of resentment towards the *Bastonnais* that restrained the *habitants* from taking arms on their side. It was said at the time, it has been said since, that the policy pursued

---

[1] For details and authorities, see Coffin, *op. cit.*, pp. 518–521 ; J. H. Smith, *op. cit.*, vol. ii, pp. 225–226. Arguing that the *habitants* were completely alienated from British rule by the Quebec Act, Coffin considers the licentiousness of the American troops as the main reason for their passive attitude. But, as J. H. Smith suggests (p. 225), the outrages could scarcely have occurred if the *habitants* had been regarded as real sympathisers with the invasion and likely to join it in arms. For Washington's fears that ' the impudent conduct of our troops would create a disgust to our cause in Canada' and his judgement on the outcome, see Coffin, *op. cit.*, pp. 519, 520.

[2] See p. 20, with n. 1, above.   [3] Coffin, *op. cit.*, pp. 516–518.

by British statesmen in Canada since the conquest, the policy which culminated in the Quebec Act, had made no impression or, if anything, a bad impression on their minds. But this judgement is only true of the Act itself in so far as it was misrepresented and misunderstood : and of the general policy which had led up to the Act it is not true at all. Uneducated and ill informed as they were, the *habitants* could not have failed to feel the general spirit of conciliation and tolerance pervading the new *régime*. They could appreciate with a plain man's simplicity certain tangible facts in their everyday life. They had expected ruin and oppression—and this is what those glib revolutionists foretold if they continued to endure the British yoke—but so far, at any rate, their fears had proved ungrounded. It was currently reported that Governor Murray and Governor Carleton had betrayed such a whole-hearted sympathy with their race and its traditions as to provoke the angry and open opposition of the British business people in the towns. They could see for themselves that their new masters had not tampered with their faith. They could worship in their churches as freely as of old. Their priests were unmolested. Even their bishop was back in Quebec. They had been worried for a time by an attempt to decide their civil disputes by newfangled unintelligible rules and by the high fees the lawyers charged for failing to interpret them. But the rules they knew had never really been abolished, and the new Act (some said) would restore them in their entirety for good and all. Year by year, in fact, it had become more manifest that the conquest had left their old familiar ways of life unchanged. The agents from Boston, with an axe of their own to grind, might say what they liked, and many an impulsive simpleton might believe them, especially when they cleverly contrived to represent the Government as only the *seigneur's* friend ; but in the eyes of the average hard-headed peasant their lurid picture of intolerable despotism, of an unhappy people not only injured but insulted, simply did not square with the plain facts of his own experience.

But probably the strongest factor in restraining the *habitants* from joining the ranks of the invaders was the influence of their own kinsmen in the more educated classes. The *seigneurs*, it has been seen, no longer wielded their traditional authority ; many of them were personally unpopular ;' and few, if any, of the *habitants* were ready to obey their call to military service. But it does not follow that every *seigneur* had lost all his influence with all his tenants : and at least the more elderly and more conservative-minded among them must have been deeply impressed by the unanimous and unwavering loyalty of their old leaders. All the records are agreed that the *seigneurs* as a body supported the Government throughout the war. Carleton's tribute in the hour of crisis to their ' zeal ' and ' fidelity ' has been quoted ; and when in 1777 he drew up a ' list of the principal persons settled in the province who very zealously served the rebels in the winter 1775 and 1776 ', he included only one Frenchman in it and he was a subject of Old France.[1] The testimony of the invaders was the same. ' With respect to the better sort of people, both French and English ', wrote an American officer to his General, ' seven-eighths are Tories who would wish to see our throats cut.' [2] ' As the introduction of French laws will make room for the French gentry ', reported John Brown, ' they are very thick about the Governor.' [3] The *seigneurs* are loyal to the

[1] R. C. A., 1888, p. xiv. The name was Pelissier. Carleton, p. 142, above. Cramahé wrote : ' The justice must be done to the gentry, clergy, and most of the *bourgeoisie* that they have shown the greatest zeal and fidelity to the King's service and exerted their best endeavours to reclaim their infatuated countrymen ' (to Dartmouth, September 21, 1775, C. D., p. 667). The French-Canadian evidence naturally stresses the point : e. g. Badeaux and Sanguinet in their Journals (Verreau, pp. 167, 43) and various *seigneurs* in correspondence (*ibid.*, pp. 303–377).

[2] Colonel Hazen to General Schuyler from Montreal, April 1, 1776, quoted by Sir G. O. Trevelyan, *The American Revolution*, vol. ii, p. 81, note.

[3] John Brown to the Boston Committee of Correspondence, March 29, 1775, iv A. A., vol. ii, pp. 243–245. Cf. deposition of John Duguid,

Government, complained the Montreal Committee, because it respects their religion and offers them an equal share of office with the English. ' Of liberty or law they have not the least notion.'[1] And with the *seigneurs* went a part at least of the professional and *bourgeois* class.[2] But far more powerful than the influence of *seigneur* or lawyer or trader on the *habitant* was the influence of the priest. Social ascendancies and feudal ties might be weakened by time and conquest ; but the Church, which in the infancy of the old French colony had been practically its ruler, had never lost its hold on the conscience of its people.[3] The tragedy of Acadia had borne witness to the power of the priests in politics ; and now among the Canadian peasants, close cousins of the Acadian, they laboured for the British Government with the same ardour and with the same spiritual weapons as they then had laboured for the French.[4] For,

a Scotsman resident for the last sixteen months in Canada, August 2, 1775, vol. iii, pp. 12–13.

[1] Montreal Committee to Massachusetts Committee of Safety, April 8, 1775, iv A. A., vol. ii, pp. 305–306.

[2] See Cramahé's statement, p. 168, n. 1, above : and Coffin, *op. cit.*, p. 511, note.

[3] Coffin (*op. cit.*, p. 489) suggests that the authority of the Church had weakened ; but the only evidence is that legal provision was needed to ensure that all parishioners paid their tithes. It must be remembered that the main object of Coffin's valuable monograph is to show that the policy of the Quebec Act neither directly nor indirectly did anything but harm to the British cause among the *habitants*.

[4] The clergy are always classed with the *seigneurs* in Carleton's and other tributes : see pp. 142 and 168, n. 1, above. 'The Clergy are our bitter enemies', reported Arnold to Congress, January 24, 1776 (J. H. Smith, *op. cit.*, vol. ii, p. 214). A British officer who took part in the defence of Quebec noted in his journal that the refusal by the priests of the sacraments, especially that of extreme unction, acted as 'a most potent spell' in restraining the Canadians from joining the invaders (*Journal of the Principal Occurrences during the Siege of Quebec, &c.*, London, 1824). Sanguinet notes in his Journal that the *habitants* complain of the priests' refusal of absolution to those who join the Americans (Verreau, p. 95). Cf. Stone, *op. cit.*, p. xxi. See also Wooster's report quoted by J. H. Smith, *op. cit.*, vol. ii, p. 217 ; and authorities cited by Coffin, *op. cit.*, p. 505, n. 2. Hazen's report that every priest in the country except one refused absolution to any one who took up arms with the Americans can scarcely be as authentic as it sounds.

while their immediate object had thus been reversed, their ultimate cause was the same—the cause of their Church and its faith. Their leaders were closely in touch with Carleton ; they could not mistake the plain meaning of the Quebec Act ; and they never doubted for a moment from which of the two warring parties to expect the greater meed of tolerance and freedom. The bishop himself was quick to give the lead. In May 1775, at the time of the first American inroad into Canada, he issued a *mandement* in the following terms :

A troop of subjects in revolt against their lawful Sovereign, who is at the same time ours, have just made an irruption into this province, less in the hope of maintaining themselves here than with a view of dragging you into their revolt or at least preventing you from opposing their pernicious design. The remarkable goodness and gentleness with which we have been governed by his very gracious Majesty, King George the Third, since the fortune of war subjected us to his rule ; the recent favours with which he has loaded us, in restoring to us the use of our laws and the free exercise of our religion, and in letting us participate in all the privileges and advantages of British subjects, would no doubt be enough to excite your gratitude and zeal in support of the interests of the British Crown. But motives even more urgent must speak to your heart at the present moment. Your oaths, your religion, lay upon you the unavoidable duty of defending your country and your King with all the strength you possess.[1]

For the rank and file of the clergy this was a clear, unequivocal lead. But indeed they did not require to be led. Had the village *curés* ever questioned the liberality and sincerity of the Government's religious policy, the confirmation of their tithes by the Quebec Act must have convinced them ; and they knew from of old how very different was the temper and purpose of the militant Protestantism of New England. Congress itself, moreover, had gratuitously emphasized the contrast. In its Address to Quebec, while boldly confessing its antagonism to the *seigneurs*, it had tried indeed to cloak

---

[1] *Mandement* of May 22, 1775, H. Têtu, *Évêques de Québec* (Quebec, 1889), p. 326.

the religious quarrel with a phrase. But the Canadian priests had also read the Address by the same Congress to the British People ; and, set beside its unrestrained abuse of Popery, the special pleading of the later document was instantly transparent. So gross and plain, in fact, was the discrepancy that effective use could be made of it to counter the American propaganda among the *habitants* : at one meeting, when a French translation of the earlier Address was read aloud, the audience cried out against the perfidy of Congress.[1] It cannot, then, have been difficult for the priests to convince the *habitants* that on the question of their creed, at any rate, the *Bastonnais* were not their genuine friends, and that, even supposing that their British masters had proved themselves tyrants and persecutors as well as heretics, to escape from them by joining the Americans— unless indeed they could rise in such force as to hold their own against their allies—would be only to pass from the rule of King Log to the rule of King Stork. Yet, argue and exhort and threaten as they might, they could not persuade their parishioners to fight for the British Government : all they could do was to persuade them not to fight against it.[2]

From both sides, therefore, strong influences were brought to bear upon the *habitants*. Never before had they been exposed to such a gale of argument and counter-argument. Never had their quiet, uneventful lives been vexed by such conflicting appeals to their interests and their impulses. Small wonder, then, that, in the end, bewildered by the maze of contradictory assertions and desires, they withdrew, so to speak, into themselves and waited for the storm to pass. ' After all ', they told themselves, ' it is a domestic quarrel between Englishmen : it is not our business to interfere on

---

[1] iv A. A., vol. ii, p. 231.

[2] The clergy like the *seigneurs*, appealed for active defence of the country, not for mere neutrality only. See the bishop's *mandement* ; Carleton's statements already quoted. ' The clergy ', wrote Wooster from Montreal (January 6, 1776), ' preach damnation to all those who will not take up arms against us ' (J. H. Smith, *op. cit.*, vol. ii, p. 217).

either side.'[1] Inevitably both sides were disappointed and angrily expressed their disappointment ; for belligerents are rarely patient with the neutral standpoint in the heat of war. But in the event the neutrality of the *habitants* told in favour of the British. Carleton and his men could just save Canada without their help ; their help given to the enemy, they must have lost it. And so, since the major part of the influences which told in favour of the British cause were directly or indirectly due to it, Carleton's policy had not proved in fact the failure that it seemed.

8

It is time to return to the sequence of events and to describe briefly the course of the invasion.[2]

It is an open question which side actually began the fighting in New England ; but it was certainly the Americans who took the offensive as far as Canada and its British garrison were concerned. In May 1775 a few weeks after the affair at Lexington, a body of adventurous colonists, known as the ' Green Mountain Boys ' and settled in the district which afterwards took from them its name of Vermont, fell suddenly, under the leadership of Ethan Allen, on the New York border forts of Ticonderoga and Crown Point, completely surprised their unprepared defenders, pushed on over Lake Champlain and across the Canadian frontier, seized the dozen men in Fort St. John's and a Government ship at anchor there, and then, on the approach of reinforcements from Montreal, withdrew down

[1] Finlay wrote from Quebec, September 20, 1775 : ' Many of them have told me that they look upon this rebellion only as a quarrel among Englishmen, in which they are no way immediately concerned ' (*American Independence and the French Revolution* (Source Books), p. 51).

[2] A succinct account of the American War as it affected Canada is given by Lucas, *History of Canada, 1763–1812*, chap. iii. For details, see Kingsford, vols. v and vi, J. H. Smith, C. H. Jones, J. Codman, *op. cit.*, and the standard histories of the American Revolution.

the lake.[1] So far, though Benedict Arnold had been sent to accompany the expedition, Congress had not planned or taken charge of these proceedings in the North; but after the Battle of Bunker's Hill the capture of Canada became an essential part of the official plan of campaign. To Washington and his colleagues the strategic importance of Canada was as obvious as it had been to Carleton.[2] If the quarrel with the mother country was now to be settled by war, Canada in her hands would be once more the safe entry-port for troops from Europe and the dangerous menace to the flank and rear of the colonies which it had been in the hands of France. Montreal, indeed, was a better base than Boston for British operations. A strong force descending the Lake Champlain route to the River Albany and New York would cut the colonies in two. Carleton had recognized this at the outset of his governorship;[3] it was clear to his civilian colleague, Hey, in 1775;[4] but it was not till two years later that British ministers grasped it and in a half-hearted and disastrously unsystematic manner launched

---

[1] The ' Green Mountain Boys ' had recently declared their independence of New York in defiance of its local colonial Government and Legislature, which were supported by the Home Government. Allen had been declared an outlaw by the Governor. Ticonderoga fell on May 10, Crown Point on May 12, St. John's on May 13. Carleton had pointed out the decayed condition of the forts at Ticonderoga and Crown Point, and advised their repair in 1767 (Carleton to Gage, February 15, 1767, C. D., p. 280). For his report of this first invasion see his dispatch of June 7, 1775 (C. D., p. 663). He states that some of the invaders would probably have been cut off by the troops he dispatched from Montreal if they had not been warned by Bindon, a merchant of that town. This Bindon, he adds, brought back a letter from Allen ' addressed to one Morrison and the British Merchants of Montreal, Lovers of Liberty, demanding a supply of provisions, ammunition & spirituous liquors, which some of them were inclined enough to furnish had they not been prevented '.

[2] See p. 60, above.

[3] See his dispatch to Gage (February 15, 1767, C. D., p 280) in which he recommends ' a place of arms ' near New York, a citadel at Quebec, and the strengthening of the forts on the main line of communication.

[4] ' From this country they are more accessible, I mean the New England people (paradoxical as it may seem) than even from Boston itself ' (Hey to Apsley, August 28, 1775, C. D., p. 669).

Burgoyne's ill-fated expedition. It was to anticipate such a move that Washington decided to take the offensive at the very beginning of the war. His strategical scheme for the invasion was simple and effective. Two columns were to march on the St. Lawrence valley—one by the old direct line of Lake Champlain and the Richelieu to Montreal, the other by a more arduous canoe-route up the Kennebec, over a *portage* through the mountains, and down the Chaudière to Quebec.[1] A force of 8,000 men was nominally assigned by Congress to the western column under Schuyler ; but it is doubtful whether half that number were eventually scraped together. About 1,100 made up the eastern column under Arnold.[2] But the difficulty of raising adequate forces was felt in every field of the American operations : and the invasion of Canada was not by any means regarded in official circles as of merely secondary importance. ' You are entrusted with a command ', wrote Washington in his Instructions to Arnold, ' of the utmost consequence to the interest and liberties of America. Upon your conduct and courage and that of the officers and soldiers detached on this expedition . . . the safety and welfare of the whole continent may depend.'[3] ' It appears to me ', wrote R. H. Lee, when the advance on Canada had begun, ' that we must have that country with us this winter, cost what it may ' :[4] and when the winter came and the complete success of the invasion was delayed by the defence of Quebec, Washington vigorously exhorted Arnold to make every effort to take it. ' To whomsoever it belongs ', he wrote,

[1] See Washington's Memorandum to Congress, September 21, 1775, iv A. A., vol. ii, p. 761.

[2] For the numbers see J. H. Smith, *op. cit., passim.* There seems to be no authentic official record of the exact size of the western army; it varied from time to time as scanty reinforcements dribbled in or as, when the severities of winter came on, men refused to renew their short period of enlistment or openly deserted. See p. 185, below.

[3] iv A. A., vol. ii, p. 765. Similar language in Instructions to Schuyler, p. 1196.

[4] R. H. Lee to Washington, October 1775, iv A. A., vol. ii, p. 1137.

' in their favour probably will the balance turn. If it is in ours, success, I think, will most certainly crown our virtuous struggles. If it is in theirs, the contest at least will be doubtful, hazardous and bloody.' [1]

To defeat this prompt and determined effort to capture Canada the forces at Carleton's disposal seemed desperately inadequate. It will be remembered that in the previous autumn he had weakened his small garrison by promptly acceding to Gage's request that he should send two regiments to Boston. But he was confident that reinforcements would arrive from England in the spring. ' Left to my own speculations in this retired corner ', he wrote to Gage in February, ' without intelligence of what passes in Europe till long after the event. . . . I entertain no doubt that, as soon as the navigation opens, some troops from Britain will be sent up this river, and in my opinion it should not be an inconsiderable force.' [2] But he had not made allowance for the crass military incompetence of the Home Government. The expectations Carleton had fostered of raising a large French-Canadian force were not a sufficient excuse for its neglect throughout the open season of that critical year—a neglect to send a body of British regulars to Canada which very nearly cost the British Commonwealth the loss of its last inch of ground in North America. Even when Carleton reported the first raid into the province in the spring and suggested that the arrival of an adequate force would not only secure Canada but also ' assist General Gage in extinguishing the flames of rebellion in the other provinces more speedily ', not a man was sent him.[3] Left

---

[1] iv A. A., vol. iv, p. 874.

[2] Carleton to Gage, February 4, 1775, C. D., p. 662. ' If we are to have a French War ', he continues, ' this corps will become indispensably necessary here ; if not, it might effectually second your intentions.' Thus Carleton is still thinking at least as much of the danger of a new outbreak of war with France as of the trouble in the colonies.

[3] Carleton to Dartmouth, June 7, 1775, C. D., p. 665. Carleton admitted that it might already be too late in the year ; but a Chatham would have

in the lurch by Whitehall, he turned to Boston. Gage had never acted up to his own suggestion that the two regiments he had borrowed in the previous autumn should be returned in the spring ; and at the beginning of September, when invasion in force was imminent, Carleton begged him to make good the debt. General Howe, who had just taken over the command from Gage, at once ordered one regiment to be in readiness to sail, but Admiral Graves characteristically refused to supply the transports on the ground that the passage from Boston to Quebec was very dangerous in October.[1] So Carleton was left to his own depleted resources.

Of British regulars, he had, in June 1775, 859 officers and men of the 7th Fusiliers and the 26th Foot and 130 of the Royal Artillery.[2] Many of these were necessarily scattered over the province on garrison duty. A small new regiment, about 100 strong, called the Royal Highland Emigrants, was raised by Colonel Maclean among the British soldier-settlers at Murray Bay, and presently increased by 100 recruits from Newfoundland.[3] Of volunteers some 300 at most could be reckoned on from among the British residents at Quebec and Montreal. As to the French-Canadians, Carleton probably obtained from 300 to 500 volunteers mostly, no doubt, from the small body of *seigneurs* and *bourgeois* ; [4] and at one time as many as 1,000 *habitants* rallied to the militia, but their numbers declined with the decline of the British fortunes. [5]

With these meagre resources Carleton did all that could be done. His first object was to bar the American advance on Montreal. Depleting, therefore, to a minimum the garrison at Quebec and retaining only a small reserve at

got reinforcements through before the winter, if he had not sent them before.

[1] Kingsford, vol. v, p. 432.   [2] *Ibid.*, p. 453.
[3] *Ibid.*, p. 482. For the Murray Bay Settlement, see p. 42, above.
[4] See Coffin, *op. cit.*, p. 510, note. It is impossible to fix the number.
[5] See p. 182, below.

Montreal, he concentrated the strongest possible force—
about 550 regulars and 120 French-Canadian volunteers—at
Fort St. John's, which lay on the Richelieu River twenty
miles inside the frontier and about the same distance from
Montreal. At Fort Chambly, lower down the river, midway
between the city and St. John's, he posted 80 regulars.
He remained himself at Montreal, in touch by the
St. Lawrence with Quebec where he had left Cramahé in
charge. He knew nothing as yet of the intended invasion
by the eastern route. The immediate danger lay in the west :
and if only the pass could be held at St. John's through the
winter, reinforcements from England in the spring might
save the situation.

But, if St. John's should fall, what hope was there of
stemming the invasion ? Little could be expected, much
indeed might be feared, from the civilian population if the
invaders penetrated deeply into Canada. The mass of the
habitants seemed clearly disaffected. If the British were
forced back down the St. Lawrence valley, the whole
countryside might rise and wipe them out. And if the
' better class ' of British residents, mostly at Quebec and
Montreal, were ready, like the *seigneurs,* to fight for the
Government, the disloyal minority could be counted on to
aid the invaders by all means in their power. The Montreal
Committee had been in constant touch with Boston since
the winter. They had refused, it is true, to send delegates
to the next Congress unless the agreement of the colonies
to import no British goods should be waived in their case.
For them to join in it, they had explained, would mean
that the French-Canadians would capture all their trade.[1]
They had declared, too, that, cordially as they sympathized
with the colonial cause, they could not fight for it till their

[1] John Brown at Montreal to Committee of Correspondence at Boston,
March 29, 1775, iv A. A., vol. ii, pp. 243–245 ; Montreal Committee to
Committee of Safety of Massachusetts, April 8, 1775, iv A. A., vol. ii,
pp. 305–306.

friends in the South marched in to save them. 'Few in this colony dare vent their griefs,' they wrote, 'but groan in silence and dream of *lettres de cachet*, confiscations, and imprisonment.'[1] But if Carleton regretted for the moment that the English criminal law and the right of *habeas corpus* had ever been introduced into the province 'to be used as arms against the state' and that he could not use the arbitrary powers of repression enjoyed by the old French Government, he refrained, even after his declaration of martial law in June, from arresting the extremist leaders.[2] His object, doubtless, was to avoid exacerbating still further the hostility of their faction and giving it a new cry against the tyranny of Government : but it was a risky policy and it enabled them to convey secret information to the invaders as to the condition of the defence and the movements of troops. 'Some of the King's old subjects have joined the rebels', wrote Cramahé when the invasion had begun ; 'and it were to be wished that all of them inclined to that cause had done the same ; we should be the safer for it.'[3]

9

Thus the British cause in Canada was endangered from within as well as from without when, at the beginning of September, the invaders crossed the frontier and encamped at the Île aux Noix a few miles from St. John's. Carleton at once hastened back to Montreal from Quebec whither he had gone to summon the first Legislative Council under the

---

[1] Letter to Committee of Safety, cited in preceding note. This letter was signed by Walker and three others. Carleton was described to John Brown by his Montreal friends as 'no great politician, a man of sour morose temper, a strong friend to Administration and the late Acts of the British Parliament'.

[2] See Carleton to Dartmouth, June 7, 1775, C. D., p. 665.

[3] Cramahé to Dartmouth, September 21, 1775, C. D., p. 667. He encloses an intercepted letter from a grain merchant in the Richelieu district.

new Act. At first the news was good. A rash attempt by
Ethan Allen and some 150 men to seize Montreal by
surprise on the night of September 24 was beaten back and
its leader captured. The *habitants*, moreover, seemed at last
to be rallying to the British side. No less than a thousand
were at this time under arms at Montreal. ' Courage,
loyalty and cheerfulness ', wrote a sanguine observer to
Finlay at Quebec, ' are conspicuous in their countenances
and they do their duty cheerfully.' [1] But the danger-point
was at St. John's, closely besieged on September 24 by
Montgomery who had succeeded to the command of the
western column on the breakdown of Schuyler's health : [2]
and who could tell how long its garrison could hold out ?
Chief Justice Hey, at any rate, had quite lost heart. He had
already on September 11 added a pessimistic postscript to
a letter written a fortnight earlier to the Lord Chancellor—
' Everything seems to be desperate, and I cannot but fear
that before this reaches your lordship Canada will be as
fully in the possession of the rebels as any other province
upon the continent.' ' St. John's and Montreal ', he writes
in yet another postscript six days later, ' must soon fall into
their hands, and I doubt Quebec will follow too soon. In
this situation I hold myself in readiness to embark for
England.' [3]

Hey's pessimism was nearly justified. On October 15 an
American detachment laid siege to Fort Chambly, and only
two days later it unexpectedly surrendered. Thus, at a stroke,
Montgomery not only replenished his failing stock of provisions—for the fort had been well furnished—but also

[1] Finlay's letter of September 20, 1775, cited p. 172, n. 1, above.
[2] Unlike Schuyler or Arnold, Montgomery (born in Ireland in 1736)
had been an officer in the regular British army. He had taken part in the
British conquest of Canada, but in 1772 retired from the army and afterwards settled in New York and married into the Livingstone family.
He was well known and greatly esteemed by Burke, Fox, and other
eminent men in England. See Lucas's comments, *op. cit.*, pp. 116–118.
[3] Hey to Lord Apsley, August 28 to September 17, 1775, C. D., p. 672.

obtained the guns and ammunition the lack of which had hitherto crippled his operations against St. John's. The siege of this main stronghold was now pressed with renewed vigour ; and the prospects of its garrison, greatly out-numbered, cut off from reinforcements and supplies, and now exposed to effective bombardment, soon became desperate. On October 30 Carleton sallied out with his small force from Montreal in an attempt to break the siege, but he was beaten back. On November 2, St. John's capitulated.[1]

The way to Montreal was now open and Carleton recog-nized at once that it was impossible to defend the town. It was practically unfortified and he had only about 100 regulars to hold it. More than half his little army had been taken prisoner at St. John's, and his only chance now was to seek shelter within the walls of Quebec. He knew, moreover, from an intercepted message that Arnold would soon be threatening his line of retreat. On November 11, therefore, having dismissed the militia to their homes, Carle-ton embarked with the regulars and left the town to its fate. Of his ' unmoved temper and firmness ' at this humiliating moment an eye-witness has left an admiring record. ' A general without troops, and at the eve of quitting Montreal to give entrance to lawless rebels, his mind appeared unshaken . . . though undoubtedly wrung to the soul.'[2] He had indeed delayed the inevitable retreat too long. One of his ships went aground near Sorel and a change of wind held up the rest of his flotilla for three days. The Americans,

[1] Kingsford (vol. v, p. 452) severely censures Major Stopford for surren-dering Chambly, but, as Lucas points out (op. cit., p. 108), Carleton declared he had no charge to bring against the garrison of either fort. A narrative of the siege of St. John's by Major Preston, who commanded there, is printed in R. C. A., 1914–1915, Appendix B. The Articles of Capitulation are given in Kingsford, vol. v, p. 465.

[2] Lieutenant-Governor Hamilton to Dartmouth, August 29, 1776, quoted by Coffin, op. cit., p. 370, n. 2. For Bindon's further services to the invaders, see Kingsford, vol. v, p. 468.

who had entered Montreal on the 13th and at once started to pursue Carleton's party along the river banks, were thus able to overtake them. Batteries were raised farther down the river commanding their descent, and they were summoned to surrender. Nor were these the only enemies between them and Quebec. After a seven-weeks' journey through the wilderness, Arnold had brought the eastern column of invasion to its goal. On November 8—five days after the fall of St. John's—he reached Point Levis on the bank of the St. Lawrence opposite Quebec.[1] On November 14—three days after Carleton's departure from Montreal— he crossed the river to the Heights of Abraham and sent a message to Cramahé demanding the surrender of the city. No reply was given ; and he withdrew to Point aux Trembles, nineteen miles up the river, to await a junction with Montgomery's column according to plan. To all appearance Carleton was thus caught in a net. His flotilla indeed was doomed, and after a few days it surrendered with more than a quarter of his tiny residue of regulars on board.[2] But Carleton himself had slipped through the meshes. A council of war had decided that, whatever happened to the rest, the Governor must not be taken prisoner, and a hardy French-Canadian, Captain Bouchette, had offered to attempt the passage in a whale-boat. The offer was accepted, and on the night of the 16th Bouchette took Carleton on board his boat and dropped quietly down stream. The oars were muffled : at the most dangerous points the rowers paddled only with their hands : and the boat passed

---

[1] For a full record of the journey see J. H. Smith, *op. cit.*, vol. i, and also *Arnold's March from Cambridge to Quebec* (New York and London, 1903), in which Arnold's own journal is printed.

[2] Walker, the moving spirit of the Montreal Committee, was on board and thus escaped from imprisonment. As he had been actively tampering with the *habitants* in the country north-west of Montreal and was implicated in Allen's surprise attack on the town, Carleton had at last arrested him. Extracts from letters describing Walker's conduct and arrest are given in iv A. A., vol. ii, pp. 1185–1187.

undetected through the enemy's lines. Below Three Rivers a British sloop was met with, and on the 19th Carleton safely reached Quebec.[1]

10

The general was once more in command of soldiers, but the last defenders of British Canada, now gathered in the old French city, only numbered between 1,200 and 1,300 fighting men. Colonel Maclean, who had marched up the river to join Carleton, but finding the way blocked by the enemy had retreated, was there at the head of the Royal Highland Emigrants, now 200 strong. The only other regulars were some 60 men of the 7th Fusiliers and six Artillerymen. About 460 seamen, marines, and artificers from the ships in the harbour were enrolled among the garrison. The British militia were about 200 strong, the French-Canadian militia about 300. The total population sheltering in the city was about 5,000. Of these a certain number were more or less disaffected, and Cramahé, following Carleton's example at Montreal, had hitherto taken no action against them. But in a state of siege open enemies could not be tolerated within the gates, and Carleton issued a proclamation ordering those who ' will not serve in arms ' to ' quit the town within four days '. The extremist party, headed by John McCord and other leaders of the Quebec Committee, accordingly crossed over to the American lines ; and from that time, it is said, ' cabals ceased '. Meanwhile, a ship had been dispatched to England with a letter from Carleton informing the Government that he would defend Quebec to the last.[2]

It was now the last entrenchment of British rule in Canada ;

---

[1] Kingsford, vol. v, p. 462.

[2] On May 1, 1776, the regulars numbered 269, marines, &c., 457, British militia 257, F.-C. militia 508. Official figures, vol. ii, pp. 130, 147, of *History of Forces of Canada since 1763* by Historical Section of General Staff, which contains a full account of the invasion and siege with documents.

five months at least must elapse before reinforcements could be expected to make their way up the St. Lawrence ; and whether Carleton could hold out till then was desperately uncertain. The new fortifications he had recommended seven years before had never been erected ; but the natural strength of the historic city on the cliff had been proved by several sieges, and in the last of them, when Murray had held it through the winter of 1759–1760 against the French, Carleton had acquired experience of its defence. Yet, with such a handful of troops to man the walls, no skill or courage could avail against a greatly superior force. The issue depended on the numbers, spirit, and equipment of the besiegers : and in point of numbers at any rate there was reason for the gravest anxiety. Now was the golden moment for the *habitants* to rise.

But they did not rise. Less than 500 of them, perhaps not more than 300, took part in the siege—about the same number in fact as took part in the defence. Thus Montgomery was dependent almost solely on the colonial troops ; and when he had brought his men down from Montreal in the ships he had so fortunately captured and joined up with Arnold's column, the combined American force was not above 2,000. Montreal had surrendered without resistance : Three Rivers had declared for the invaders as he passed it on his way down the river ; and he hoped that Carleton, deserted by the great mass of the French-Canadians, his little body of regular troops already reduced by two-thirds, would think it no less hopeless to defend Quebec. But when he landed above the city on December 5 and summoned him to surrender, no answer was returned ; so, camping himself on the plains of Abraham and placing Arnold on the low ground by the River St. Charles north of the city, he sat down to the arduous task of investment. The establishment of a close blockade was almost automatic ; for Carleton could expect no more assistance than Montgomery from the neigh-

bouring peasantry ; and the river way to the outer world was
soon blocked with floating ice. But Montgomery could not
rely on starving out the garrison. Time was in Carleton's
favour, not in his. The advance of the bitter northern winter
would expose his unseasoned troops, quartered on open
ground, to ever-increasing hardships. For many of them
the term of enlistment would expire at the New Year ; and
he feared, with good reason, that under such conditions they
would refuse to renew their service. Thus pressed for time
and lacking adequate artillery to reduce the city rapidly by
an intensive bombardment, he decided to risk a direct surprise assault. About two o'clock in the morning of December 31, in the midst of a wintry blizzard, two storming
parties—one, 900 strong, led by Montgomery himself, the
other, 700 strong, led by Arnold—advanced along the water's
edge from west and north with the object of forcing the
barricades, meeting in the centre of the lower town and thence
fighting their way up to the heights. The attempt failed
disastrously. The western party was caught under
a concentrated fire at the first barricade ; Montgomery fell
dead at its head, twelve others were killed, and the rest
retreated in dismay. The northern party carried the first
barricade, not without losing Arnold, who was carried away
with a wound in his leg, pushed on down a narrow street,
and was there ' caught as it were in a trap ', as Carleton
put it, before the second barricade and under fire from the
houses. Its retreat was soon cut off and 431 surrendered.[1]

These few hours' fighting had decided the fate of the siege.
Disheartened by the loss of their leader and the disablement
of Arnold, severely tried by bitter frost and snow and
driving wind, ill equipped and ill sheltered, and for a final
trial stricken with an epidemic of small-pox, the besiegers
stayed sullenly within their lines, their numbers fluctuating
from day to day as reinforcements straggled down from

[1] For details of the siege, see Series 7 and 8 of *Historical Documents*,
Lit. and Hist. Soc. of Quebec (1905–1906).

Montreal and as those who had finished their time or openly deserted made off for some less rigorous field of service or for home.   Every day it became clearer that the invaders would be robbed of the prize which had once seemed so well within their grasp, unless a new column, large and well-found, could come to the rescue through the snow and ice of the Champlain route.   And if Congress had hitherto failed them, Washington at least had never lost sight of the importance of the Canadian expedition.   Early in January he wrote to Arnold urging him to press the siege ; [1] and, when the news of the fiasco of December 31 arrived, Congress, spurred to a vigorous, if tardy, effort to save the situation, voted reinforcements to the number of 6,000. But the vote did not materialize.   Only a few score men struggled up into the frozen North.   The strength of the force before Quebec in the last months of the siege seems never to have exceeded 2,500, and at one time there were less than 1,000 fit to fight.   A sally, indeed, by the garrison might well have proved successful ; but Carleton's supplies of ammunition, food, and fuel, though running low, were not exhausted, and ignorant of the exact strength of the enemy he chose the more prudent and more certain course.   So the siege dragged on till with the coming of spring the end came quickly.   In the early morning of May 6, three British ships, the first of a convoy of eighteen bringing help at last from England, having made their way up river through the ice, cast anchor in the basin.   Nine hundred men were aboard them, and when these had been landed and drawn up on the heights to attack the American lines, the besiegers had no spirit left for resistance.   Retirement broke quickly into rout and panic, and the tide of flight was only stayed when it had reached Sorel.   Nor were the invaders strong enough to hold their earlier gains against the growing number of British troops now fast disembarking at Quebec.   In a few

[1] See p. 174, above.

weeks' time Three Rivers was reoccupied, and Arnold evacuated Montreal, Chambly, and St. John's in quick succession. By the end of June the invasion of Canada was over. That the retreat was not followed up, that the course of the war in the South was so long protracted and terminated in such disaster, was no fault of Carleton's. If Carleton, indeed, had controlled the whole campaign, the disaster might well have been avoided. As it was, it was limited in its scope by the stubborn courage with which he and his men had held Quebec. If the South was lost, at any rate they had saved the North.

II

It is difficult in any history of British Canada to exaggerate the importance of the crisis through which Carleton's soldiership, crowning his statesmanship, had safely carried her. If the issue had been different—if the *habitants* had risen, if Quebec had fallen, if the Americans, stimulated to new efforts by its capture, had occupied it in sufficient force to repel all attempts at its recovery in 1776—only sixteen years of that history would have remained for the students of a later age. After 1775 the history of Canada would probably have been merged in the history of the United States. But, as it was, while Saratoga and York Town created a new American nation, the defence of Quebec made it possible for Canada to remain outside it and build up a nation of her own, distinct but not separate from the other nations of the British Commonwealth. And the foundations of it were laid when French and British fought side by side in the darkness and the driving snow of that December night. With a true insight into its historic meaning a later generation has commemorated the event. On the site of the Sault au Matelot barricade the inscription reads :

HERE STOOD HER OLD AND NEW DEFENDERS
UNITING, GUARDING, SAVING CANADA.

CONCLUSION

I

THE American invasion occurred in the first year of an eight years' war; and, though the British position in Canada was never again quite so critical as in the winter of 1775, the policy of the Quebec Act was put to a further and, in some ways, a severer proof by the entry of France into the war as the ally of the Americans in 1778. Forbidden by the treaty of alliance from openly aiming at the restoration of Canada to France, all that the French could honourably do was to appeal to the French-Canadians to side with their kinsmen in driving the common enemy of by-gone days from North America. But by the *habitants* at any rate, if not by the *seigneurs* and the priests, this appeal could only be interpreted as a call to reunite New France with Old. And the French Admiral's manifesto, a copy of which appeared on the door of every French-Canadian parish church, was far more seductive than the Address from Congress. Unlike Congress, D'Estaing could outbid Carleton. He could hold out to the *seigneurs* a more certain continuance of their status and rights than the Quebec Act promised, especially in view of the continued agitation of the British minority in Canada. Obviously— since no one in Canada could suspect the impending French Revolution—the maintenance of a feudal aristocracy would be better safeguarded by the absolutist monarchy of France than by the constitutional monarchy of Britain: and restored to the bosom of the *ancien régime* and freed from contact with British ideas of liberty, the *seigneurs* might well hope to recover some of their lost authority with their tenants. To the Roman Church in Canada, similarly the most Christian King could offer far more than any Protestant King of England, however generously tolerant. He alone could fully satisfy her secular ambitions ; make her once more the close comrade, almost the colleague, of the Government ; repair without disguise or compromise the broken links between her hierarchy and the See of Rome. And for the *habitants*, though some of them might realize that as regards their feudal obligations their lot would certainly be no lighter if King Louis should return to his own in Canada, the call of France went deeper than social or material interests : it was for every French-Canadian the call of the blood.

Inevitably, therefore, the concluding years of the war were anxious years for Haldimand, the practical Swiss professional soldier who had succeeded Carleton as Governor of Quebec. His British garrison was not so dangerously weak as Carleton's had been in 1775 ; and the French-Canadians, without any burning hatred of their rulers to spur them to a desperate venture, were not likely to attempt a rebellion of their own accord ; but the crossing of Lake Champlain by French troops or the arrival of a French fleet in the St. Lawrence would in all probability be the signal for a general rising. With unconcealed anxiety, Haldimand referred in his dispatches to evidence of secret preparations among the *seigneurs* to assist a French invasion and of wavering or changed opinions among the priests, though he could rely, as Carleton had relied, on the loyalty of Bishop Briand, who in 1781 addressed a *mandement* to his clergy ' well worthy of the occasion ' and a ' proof of his good disposition '.[1] There was, indeed, only one thing Haldimand could do to stem the drift towards France— make the best of the Quebec Act, the sole fault in which, as he complained, was that, ' unfortunately for the British

[1] Haldimand to Germain, July 6, 1781, R. C. A. 1885, p. 360: Kingsford, vii, p. 241.

Empire, it was enacted ten years too late '. He was naturally, therefore, as obstinate as Carleton in opposing any
tampering with it in the interests of the British merchants.
' It requires but little penetration to discover ', he told the
Secretary of State, ' that, had the system of government
solicited by the old subjects been adopted in Canada, this
Colony would in 1775 have become one of the United States
of America. . . . On the other hand the Quebec Act alone
has prevented, or can in any degree prevent, the emissaries
of France and the rebellious Colonies from succeeding in
their efforts to withdraw the Canadian clergy and *noblesse*
from their allegiance to the Crown of Great Britain. For
this reason amongst many others, this is not the time for
innovations, and it cannot be sufficiently inculcated on the
part of Government that the Quebec Act is a sacred charter,
granted by the King in Parliament to the Canadians as
a security for their religion, laws and property.' [1] But the
power of the Quebec Act was never tested by the appearance of the French in Canada. Washington effectively discouraged an invasion by land under French leadership ;
and when, in 1781, De Grasse had secured the command of
the West Atlantic, and having dealt the decisive blow
of the war by cutting the communications between York
Town and New York, might have decided to take his fleet
and 3,000 troops up the St. Lawrence in the following
spring, he chose instead to strike at the British West Indies,
and sailed south to meet his fate at Rodney's hands. The
Battle of the Saints saved Canada for good and all from
French reconquest.

   Thirty years later the loyalty of the French-Canadians
was again put to the proof. Once more the United States
and France were in alliance against Britain. Once more
Canada lay open to invasion. Once more, since Britain was
now at death-grips with Napoleon in Europe, the regular

---

[1] Haldimand to Germain, October 25, 1780, C. D., p. 720 [K., p. 166].

garrison was absurdly small. And this time the ground
had been better prepared. Skilful and continuous propaganda had been organized in Canada by successive
French diplomatists at Washington ; and a new class of
French-Canadian politicians, called into being by the grant
of representative institutions under the Constitutional Act
of 1791, had already begun to embitter their political
disputes with the British executive by appeals to race-
antagonism. ' The acquisition of Canada ', thought Jeffer-
son, not without some excuse, ' as far as the neighbourhood
of Quebec, will be a mere matter of marching.' [1] But he
under-estimated certain factors that told against the American
cause. On the one hand, the French-Canadians no more
desired annexation to the United States in 1812 than in
1775 ; and, on the other hand, the old ties of sentiment
with France had been weakened almost to breaking-point
by the French Revolution. The *habitants* might chafe
against the seigniorial system, but they had experienced
nothing comparable to the sufferings of the peasantry in
Old France, and they were quite incapable of understanding
the bitter memories or the passionate hopes that inspired
the great uprising of the French people. As for the *seigneurs*
and the priests, their sympathies were with the *ancien
régime* to which they belonged ; their kin were not the victors
of the Revolution, but its victims, the clergy and the nobles
of Old France ; and the Jacobins seemed to them as criminal
a gang of atheists and assassins as to any British Tory.
Nor was the rule of the Corsican upstart and the despoiler
of the Holy City any more palatable than that of the Committees, until Napoleon's shrewd attempt by the ' Con-
cordat ' to disarm the hostility of Roman Catholics all the
world over softened the hearts of some at least among the
French-Canadian parish priests. But the hierarchy remained
loyal. As in 1799 on the news of the Battle of the Nile,

---

[1] T. C. Smith, *Wars between England and America* (London, 1914), p. 217.

Bishop Denant of Quebec had ordered a general thanks-
giving ' for the just laws and protecting arms of the Imperial
British Crown ', so in 1812 Bishop Plessis issued a *mandement* congratulating his fellow Catholics in Canada on their
ready response to the calling out of the militia in anticipa-
tion of a breach with the United States. There was much,
therefore, to set against the influence of French propaganda.
The British Government, moreover, for its part, had been
true to the promise of the Quebec Act. The Act of 1791,
while superseding its constitutional provisions, had re-
affirmed its policy of national toleration. In the first
place, it had dealt with the problem created by the immigration of the British loyalists from the old thirteen colonies
by providing for the division of the Province of Quebec
into Upper and Lower Canada, so that the British minority,
now so much increased in numbers and in moral weight,
might develop a province of their own, so to speak, on
British lines, while the old French community along the
banks of the St. Lawrence could continue its traditional
life. And, secondly, to make still more definite this rough-
and-ready solution of the old crux, it was enacted that in
Lower Canada, while precisely the same measure of representative government was introduced as in Upper Canada,
the French-Canadian law should still prevail. Very justly,
therefore, had Bishop Plessis praised his people for their
readiness to sacrifice everything rather than lose the protection of a Government that had both granted them
a liberal constitution and preserved to them their ancient
law. And so, despite the friction between the politicians
and the executive at Quebec, when the American invasion
came, there was no question this time of neutrality. The
French-Canadians served willingly and fought bravely in
the militia ; and, if it was on the citizen-soldiers of Upper
Canada together with the British regulars and the colonial
regiments newly raised in the Maritime Provinces and

Newfoundland that the brunt of the fighting fell, their heroism would have been of no avail if the French-Canadians had not held the flank in Lower Canada. The *voltigeurs* at Chateauguay take rank in history beside the British at Queenstown Heights and Lundy's Lane. As at the siege of Quebec, so in 1812, on a larger scale and against worse odds, the Canadians of both races joined in creating a common national tradition for the Dominion of a future day.[1]

Twenty-five years later came the third and the last crisis —the tragic rebellions of 1837–8. But the futile rising of a few hundred French-Canadians in Lower Canada was concurrent with—it was even ineffectively concerted with— the equally futile rising of a few hundred British-Canadians in Upper Canada. It is clear, therefore, that the former was not wholly due to the spirit of nationalism in revolt against alien rule, nor merely a test of the gratitude or loyalty of French-Canadians as such. Both rebellions had a common origin in the fact that the constitution of 1791 had served its time, in the intractable deadlock between legislative chambers composed of the elected representatives of the people and irresponsible and irremovable executives, in the incapacity of British statesmen to foresee that a fuller extension of self-government to the colonies would not disrupt the second British Empire but bind it all the more closely together. In Lower Canada, it is true, the constitutional dispute had soon become steeped in nationalism ; and the misguided peasants who took up arms in 1837 were dreaming of a French-Canadian republic. But the rebellions were no great national uprising of French-Canada. The Church, the bulk of the propertied class, the great majority of the *habitants* took no part in it. Even in 1837 it cannot be said that the policy of the Quebec Act had been proved a failure.

[1] Lucas, *The Canadian War of 1812* (Oxford, 1906) ; W. Wood, in *Canada and its Provinces* (Toronto), vol. iii ; Kingsford, vol. vii ; Têtu, *Les Évêques de Québec*, p. 481.

Yet Lord Durham thought so. Deeply impressed by the evidence of the cleavage between French and British, too close to the grim fact of rebellion to believe that French-Canadians could remain French and yet be loyal, he decided that the policy of toleration had been mistaken and advised that an attempt should be made to submerge French-Canadian nationality in British. Accordingly, in 1840, Upper and Lower Canada were re-united in one province. But that was all. The idea of ' anglicization ' was soon abandoned, and within a generation British-Canadian states-men were forced to recognize as clearly as their French-Canadian colleagues that the political fusion of the two races was impracticable. By the federation of 1867, United Canada was re-divided into the provinces of Ontario and Quebec. Once more the French-Canadians were free to control their own domestic life in their old home on the St. Lawrence. By federation, in fact, Canadian public opinion adopted and endorsed the policy of the Quebec Act : for the creators of federal Canada were not the British Government but the leaders of the Canadian people.

2

The issue, then, has been decided, but the controversy in which the Quebec Act was born has never quite died out. It would be idle to pretend that federation has resulted in a perfect harmony between the races. The overflow of French-Canadians from Quebec into other provinces has led to difficulties, not yet everywhere or finally solved, in such matters as the use of the French language in schools. There are some, moreover, who argue that, in general, the existence of two distinct major races in Canada, two great rival languages, two disparate cultures prevents the growth of a strong, coherent, independent sense of national unity ; and for Canada, stretched so loosely over such vast spaces from sea to sea, with new-comers moreover, of other European stocks continually pressing in, national unity seems the first and greatest need. Ought not the political framework of the Canadian nation—it is sometimes asked—to have been unitary rather than federal ? Did not South Africa wisely avoid the Canadian precedent ? Was not that great South African lawyer, de Villiers, right when he said that the result of federation had been ' to establish a distinctly French province without any prospect of its being ever merged into a Canadian as distinguished from a purely French nation ' ? [1] And if so, was not the decision of 1774 the initial and irremediable mistake ? Did not the Quebec Act, like some ghastly injury of childhood, stunt and spoil the future life of Canada ?

If the facts of that distant time have been truly stated in this essay, the first answer to such doubts and questions is evident. It is probable, in the highest degree, that, if the policy of the Quebec Act had not been adopted, Canada would have been lost to the British Empire in 1775, and no distinct Canadian nation could ever have come into being.

And the second answer is also clear. The contrary policy —the suppression of French-Canadian nationality—was in its essentials precluded by the terms of the Capitulations and the Treaty of Paris. The Roman Catholic religion and, in part at least, the French-Canadian civil law could not have been suppressed without a violation of public faith.

Apart, moreover, from the antecedent treaty-rights and apart from the subsequent dangers of the American invasion, it is difficult to believe that the policy of suppression was really practicable. The French-Canadians might have been deprived of their law, their Church of its legalized tithes, and their language of all official recognition. But would such measures, would even harsher measures, have succeeded in destroying French-Canadian nationality ? There are

[1] E. A. Walker, *Lord de Villiers and His Times* (London, 1925), p. 434.

many examples in history, and some in very recent history, to show how hard it is for one nation to fuse another nation's life into its own, unless indeed the fusion be mutual and voluntary. For nationality is at root a spiritual thing and difficult to kill. Nor was it in New France in 1774 a young and tender growth : the French-Canadians had been rooted there for a century and a half. Nor, again, were they, like the French of Louisiana when it was annexed to the United States, a small minority in a great English-speaking state : the position was precisely the reverse. Under these circumstances, the French-Canadians might have been compelled to obey the English law ; but, once the spirit of national revolt had been aroused, no power could have compelled them to speak the English tongue. Nor could penal laws have forced the French-Canadians, any more than they could force the Irish, to abjure their faith ; and so long as their Church survived, the mainspring of their nationality would have remained unbroken. Forcible fusion, in fact, must have proved, if it had ever been adopted, a futile policy.

A futile and—let it be frankly said—a vicious policy. Public opinion in these days will not readily accept the doctrine of inevitable national antagonism, that nationality must fight or die, must kill or be killed ; that, if two nationalities exist within a single state, ' one is the hammer and the other is the anvil '. To the modern mind, indeed, it would seem a crime to have tried to stamp out French nationality in Canada, a crime not only against the French-Canadians but against all Canadians of all time. For it cannot be questioned that, whatever the transient drawbacks and difficulties may be, Canada is the richer for its twofold national heritage, for being peopled from a Celtic as well as an Anglo-Saxon stock, for its pride in French as well as British customs and traditions, for its use of the two greatest languages and its access to the two greatest literatures of the modern world. A multi-national state, moreover, is not merely richer, in its complexity and variety, than a uni-national state : it is, as Acton argued long ago, a higher species of political organism, a greater achievement in civilized life, provided that its component nationalities are at once free and united.

Nor, lastly, can it be admitted that freedom in Canada is a permanent obstacle to unity. These are still early days in the life of the Dominion, and such a final judgement as de Villiers's is almost absurdly premature. Already, indeed, since he uttered it, the prospect has grown fairer ; there is a better understanding, a closer concord in the recognition of a common patriotism, between French and British-Canadians to-day than there has ever been since 1837 ; and only the blackest pessimists can refuse to believe that, in due course of time, Canada will grow into a unity as real and lasting as the unity of Britain. When that day comes, the last doubt as to the statesmanship of the authors of the Quebec Act will have faded away. No one will claim, then or now, that Carleton and North and the rest were gifted with superhuman foresight or inspired by the ideals of a later age. They were only concerned to meet the needs of their own day : they were simply trying to honour their treaty-pledges and to conciliate a conquered people. Practical men, they achieved those practical ends ; but their achievement was greater and more lasting than they knew. For they had acted in accordance with political principles of permanent force and universal application— that, in the long run, the unity of the whole is all the stronger for the diversity of its parts, and that on fidelity to the old, deep loyalties of local or provincial or national life, and only indeed on that sure foundation, can be built, if men are wise and patient, a broader and more generous communion of human fellowship and service.

Appendix A

BRITISH TREATY OBLIGATIONS
1759–1763

I. *Capitulation of Quebec* (1759) [1]

Article VI

French Request

Que L'Exercice de La relligion Catholique apostolique & romaine sera conservé, que L'on Donnera des sauve gardes aux maisons des Ecclesiastiques, relligieux & relligieuses particulierement à Mg^r L'Evêque de Quebec qui, rempli de zele pour La relligion Et de Charité pour le peuple de son Diocese desire y rester Constamment, Exercer Librément & avec La Decense que son Etat et les sacrés mysteres de la relligion Catholique Apostolique & Romaine, Exigent, son Authorité Episcopale dans La ville de Quebec Lorsqu'il Jugera à propos, Jusqu'à ce que la possession Du Canada ait Eté decidée par vn traité Entre S. M. T. C. & S. M. B.

That the exercise of the Catholic, Apostolic and Roman religion shall be maintained ; and that safeguards shall be granted to the houses of the clergy, and to the monasteries, particularly to his Lordship the Bishop of Quebec, who, animated with zeal for religion, and charity for the people of his diocese, desires to reside in it constantly, to exercise, freely and with that decency which his character and the sacred offices of the Roman religion require, his episcopal authority in the town of Quebec, whenever he shall think proper, until the possession of Canada shall be decided by a treaty between their most Christian and Britannic Majesties.

---

[1] As printed in C. D., pp. 3–7. It will be observed that the translation though sufficiently accurate on the main points, is not perfect.

British Reply

libre Exercice de la Religion Romaine, sauves gardes accordées a toutes personnes Religieuses ainsi qua Mr Leveque qui pourra venir Exercer Librement et avec Deçence Les fonctions de son Etat lorsqu'il le Jugera a propos jusqu'a ce que la possession du Canada ayt été Decidée entre Sa Majesté B. et S. M. T. C.

The free exercise of the Roman religion is granted, likewise safe-guards to all religious persons, as well as to the Bishop, who shall be at liberty to come and exercise, freely and with decency, the functions of his office, whenever he shall think proper, until the possession of Canada shall have been decided between their Britannic and most Christian Majesties.

II. Capitulation of Montreal (1760) [1]

Article XXVII

French Request

Le Libre Exercice de la Religion Catholique, Apostolique et Romaine Subsistera En Son Entier ; En Sorte que tous Les Estats et les peuples des Villes et des Campagnes, Lieux et postes Eloignés pouront Continuer de S'assembler dans les Eglises, et de frequenter les Sacremens, Comme Cy devant, Sans Estre Inquietés, En Aucune Maniere directement, ni Indirectement.

Ces peuples seront Obligés par le Gouvernement Anglois à payer aux prestres qui en prendront Soin, Les Dixmes, et tous les droits qu'ils avoient Coutume de payér sous le Gouvernement de Sa M^{té} tres Chretienne.

The free exercise of the Catholic, Apostolic, and Roman Religion, shall subsist entire, in such manner that all the states and the people of the Towns and countries, places and distant posts, shall continue to assemble in the churches, and to frequent the sacraments as heretofore, without being molested in any manner, directly or indirectly. These people shall be obliged, by the English Government, to pay their Priests the tithes, and all the taxes they were used to pay under the Government of his most Christian Majesty.

[1] As printed in C. D , pp. 7–36.

British Reply

Accordé, pour le Libre Exercise de leur Religion. L'Obligation de payer la Dixme aux Prêtres, dependra de la Volonté du Roy.

Granted, as to the free exercise of their religion, the obligation of paying the tithes to the Priests will depend on the King's pleasure.

Article XXVIII

French Request

Le Chapitre, Les Prestres, Curés et Missionaires, Continueront avec Entiere Liberté leurs Exercises et fonctions Curiales dans les paroisses des Villes et des Campagnes.

The Chapter, Priests, Curates and Missionaries shall continue, with an entire liberty, their exercise and functions of cures, in the parishes of the towns and countries.

British Reply

Accordé.

Granted.

Article XXX

French Request

Si par Le Traitté de paix, Le Canada restoit au pouvoir de Sa M^{té} Britanique, Sa M^{té} Tres Chretieñe Continueroit à Nomer L'Evesque de La Colonie, qui Seroit toujours de la Comunion Romaine, et Sous L'Autorité duquel les peuples Exerceroient La Religion Romaine.

If by the treaty of peace, Canada should remain in the power of his Britannic Majesty, his most Christian Majesty shall continue to name the Bishop of the colony, who shall always be of the Roman communion, and under whose authority the people shall exercise the Roman Religion.

British Reply

Refusé.

Refused.

Article XXXI

French Request

Poura Le Seigneur Evesque Etablir dans le besoin de Nouvelles paroisses, Et pourvoir au rétablissement de Sa Cathedrale et de Son Palais Episcopal ; Et Il Aura En Attendant la Liberté de demeurer dans les Villes, ou paroisses, Comme Il le Jugera àpropos.—Il poura Visiter son Dioceze avec les Ceremonies Ordinaire, Et Exercer toute La Jurisdiction que son predecesseur Exerçoit sous la domination francoise ; sauf a Exiger de Lui Le Serment de fidelité, ou promesse de ne rien faire, ni rien dire Contre Le Service de Sa M^{té} Britanique.

The Bishop shall, in case of need, establish new parishes, and provide for the rebuilding of his Cathedral and his Episcopal palace ; and, in the mean time, he shall have the liberty to dwell in the towns or parishes, as he shall judge proper. He shall be at liberty to visit his Diocese with the ordinary ceremonies, and exercise all the jurisdiction which his predecessor exercised under the French Dominion, save that an oath of fidelity, or a promise to do nothing contrary to his Britannic Majesty's service, may be required of him.

British Reply

C'est Article est compris sous le precedent.

This article is comprised under the foregoing.

Article XXXII

French Request

Les Comunautés de filles Seront Conservées dans leurs Constitutions et privileges. Elles Continüeront d'Observer leurs règles—Elles seront Exemptes du Logement de Gens de Guerre, Et Il Sera fait deffenses de Les Troubler

The communities of Nuns shall be preserved in their constitutions and privileges ; they shall continue to observe their rules, they shall be exempted from lodging any military ; and it shall be forbid to molest them in their reli-

dans Les Exercices de pieté qu'Elles pratiguent, ni d'Entrer chez Elles ; On leur donnera même des Sauves Gardes, Si Elles En demandent.

gious exercises, or to enter their monasteries : safe-guards shall even be given them, if they desire them.

British Reply

Accordé.

Granted.

Article XXXIII

French Request

Le precedent Article Sera pareillement Executé à L'Egard des Comunautés des Jesuites et Recolets, et de la Maison des prestres de St Sulpice à Montreal ; Ces derniers et Les Jesuites Conserveront Le droit qu'ils ont de Nomer à Certaines Cures et Missions, Comme Cy devant.

The preceding article shall likewise be executed, with regard to the communities of Jesuits and Recollects and of the house of the priests of St. Sulpice at Montreal ; these last, and the Jesuits, shall preserve their right to nominate to certain curacies and missions, as heretofore.

British Reply

Refusé Jusqu'a ce que le plaisir du Roy soit Connu.

Refused till the King's pleasure be known.

Article XXXIV

French Request

Toutes les Comunautés, Et tous les prestres Conserveront Leurs Meubles, La proprieté, Et L'Usufruit des Seigneuries, Et Autres biens que les Uns et les Autres possedent dans la Colonie de quelque Nature qu'ils Soient, Et Les d: biens seront Conservés dans leurs priviléges, droits, honeurs, et Exemptions.

All the communities, and all the priests, shall preserve their moveables, the property and revenues of the Seignories and other estates, which they possess in the colony, of what nature soever they be ; and the same estates shall be preserved in their privileges, rights, honours, and exemptions.

British Reply

Accordé.

Granted.

Article XXXV

French Request

Si Les Chanoines, Prestres, Missionaires, Les Prestres du Seminaire des Missions Etrangeres Et de St Sulpice, ainsi que les Jesuites et Les Recolets, Veulent passer En france, Le passage leur sera Accordé sur les Vaisseaux de Sa Majesté Britanique ; Et Tous auront la Liberté de Vendre, En total ou partie, Les biensfonds, Et Mobiliers qu'ils possedent dans la Colonie, soit aux francois, ou aux Anglois, sans que le Gouvernement Britanique puisse y mettre le moindre Empeschement ni Obstacle.

Ils pouront Emporter avec Eux, ou faire passer En france Le produit de quelque Nature qu'il soit, des d^s biens Vendus, en payant Le fret, Comme Il est dit à L'Article 26.

Et Ceux d'Entre Ces Prestres qui Voudront passer Cette Année, Seront Nouris pendant La Traversée aux dépens de Sa M^{té} Britanique, Et pouront Emporter avec Eux leurs bagages.

If the Canons, Priests, Missionaries, the Priests of the seminary of the foreign Missions, and of St. Sulpice, as well as the Jesuits, and the Recollects, chuse to go to France, a passage shall be granted them in his Britannic Majesty's ships, and they shall have leave to sell, in whole, or in part, the estates and moveables which they possess in the colonies, either to th French or to the English, without the least hindrance or obstacle from the British Government.—They may take with them, or send to France, the produce of what nature soever it be, of the said goods sold, paying the freight, as mentioned in the XXVIth article ; and such of the said Priests, who chuse to go this year, shall be victualled during the passage, at the expence of his Britannic Majesty ; and they shall take with them their baggage.

British Reply

Ils seront les maitres de disposer de leurs biens, et d'en passer le produit, ainsi que leurs personnes, et tout ce qui leur appartient, En france.

They shall be masters to dispose of their estates and to send the produce thereof, as well as their persons, and all that belongs to them to France.

Article XXXVI

French Request

Si par Le Traitté de Paix, Le Canada reste à Sa M^{té} Britanique, Tous Les Francois, Canadiens, Accadiens, Comerçant, et Autres personnes qui Voudront se retirer En france, En Auront la permission du Général Anglois qui leur procurera le passage.—Et Néantmoins Si d'icy à Cette décision Il Se trouvoit des comerçans françois ou Canadiens, ou Autres personnes qui Voulussent passer En france, Le Général Anglois Leur En donneroit Egalement la permission Les Uns et les Autres Emmeneront avec Eux leurs familles domestiques et bagages.

If by the treaty of Peace, Canada remains to his Britannic Majesty, all the French, Canadians, Acadians, Merchants and other persons who chuse to retire to France, shall have leave to do so from the British General, who shall procure them a passage : and nevertheless, if, from this time to that decision, any French, or Canadian Merchants or other persons, shall desire to go to France ; they shall likewise have leave from the British General. Both the one and the other shall take with them their families, servants, and baggage.

British Reply

Accordé.

Granted.

Article XXXVII

French Request

Les Seigneurs de Terres, Les Officiers Militaires et de Justice, Les Canadiens, Tant des Villes que des Campagnes, Les francois Etablis ou Comerçant dans toute l'Etendue de La Colonie de Canada, Et Toutes Autres personnes que ce puisse Estre, Conserveront L'Entiere paisible

The Lords of Manors, the Military and Civil officers, the Canadians as well in the Towns as in the country, the French settled, or trading, in the whole extent of the colony of Canada, and all other persons whatsoever, shall preserve the entire peaceable

proprieté et possession de leurs biens, Seigneuriaux et Roturiers Meubles et Immeubles, Marchandises, Pelleteries, et Autres Effets, même de Leurs batimens de Mer ; Il n'y Sera point touché ni fait le moindre domage, sous quelque prétexte que ce Soit :—Il leur Sera Libre de les Conserver, Loüer, Vendre, Soit aux François, ou aux Anglois, d'En Emporter Le produit En Lettres de Change, pelleteries Especes Sonantes, ou autres retours, Lorsqu'ils Jugeront à propos de passer en france, En payant le fret, Comme à L'Article 26.

Ils Joüiront aussi des pelleteries qui sont dans les postes d'En haut, & qui leur apartiennent, Et qui peuvent même estre En Chemin de se rendre à Montreal. Et à cet Effet, Il leur Sera permis d'Envoyer dès cette Année, ou la prochaine, des Canots Equipés pour Chercher Celles de ces pelleteries qui auront restées dans ces postes.

property and possession of the goods, noble and ignoble, moveable and immoveable, merchandizes, furs and other effects, even their ships ; they shall not be touched, nor the least damage done to them, on any pretence whatever. They shall have liberty to keep, let or sell them, as well to the French as to the British ; to take away the produce of them in Bills of exchange, furs, specie or other returns, whenever they shall judge proper to go to France, paying their freight, as in the XXVIth Article. They shall also have the furs which are in the posts above, and which belong to them, and may be on the way to Montreal ; and, for this purpose, they shall have leave to send, this year, or the next, canoes fitted out, to fetch such of the said furs as shall have remained in those posts.

British Reply

Accordé comme par L'Article 26.

Granted as in the XXVIth article.

Article XLI

French Request

Les francois, Canadiens, Et Accadiens, qui resteront dans La Colonie, de quelque Estat et Condition qu'ils Soient, ne Seront, ni ne pouront Estre forcés a prendre les Armes Contre Sa M^té très Chretienne, ni Ses Alliés, directement, ni Indirectement, dans quelque Occasion que ce Soit. Le Gouvernement Britanique ne poura Exiger d'Eux qu'Une Exacte Neutralité.

The French, Canadians, and Acadians of what state and condition soever, who shall remain in the colony, shall not be forced to take arms against his most Christian Majesty, or his Allies, directly or indirectly, on any occasion whatsoever; the British Government shall only require of them an exact neutrality.

British Reply

Ils deviennent Sujets du Roy.

They become Subjects of the King.

Article XLII

French Request

Les francois et Canadiens Continueront d'Estre Gouvernés Suivant la Coutume de Paris et les Loix et Usages Etablis pour ce pays; Et Ils ne pouront Estre Assujettis à d'Autres Impots qu'a Ceux qui Estoient Etablis sous la domination françoise.

The French and Canadians shall continue to be governed according to the custom of Paris, and the Laws and usages established for this country, and they shall not be subject to any other imposts than those which were established under the French Dominion.

British Reply

Répondu par les Articles précedents, et particulierement par le dernier.

Answered by the preceding articles, and particularly by the last.

III. *Treaty of Paris* (1763) [1]

Article IV

Sa Majesté Très Chretienne renonce à toutes les Pretensions, qu'Elle a formées autrefois, ou pû former, à la Nouvelle Ecosse, ou l'Acadie, en toutes ses Parties, & la garantit toute entiere, & avec toutes ses Dependances, au Roy de la Grande Bretagne. De plus, Sa Majesté Très Chretienne cede & garantit à Sa dite Majesté Britannique, en toute Proprieté, le Canada avec toutes ses Dependances, ainsi que l'Isle du Cap Breton, & toutes les autres Isles, & Côtes, dans le Golphe & Fleuve St Laurent, & generalement tout ce qui depend des dits Pays, Terres, Isles, & Côtes, avec la Souveraineté, Proprieté, Possession, & tous Droits acquis par Traité, ou autrement, que le Roy Très Chretien et la Couronne de France ont eus jusqu'à present sur les dits Pays, Isles, Terres, Lieux, Côtes, & leurs Habitans, ainsi que le Roy Très Chretien cede & transporte le tout au dit Roy & à la Couronne de la Grande Bretagne, & cela de la Maniere & d[e] la Forme la plus ample, sans Restriction, & sans qu'il soit libre de revenir

His Most Christian Majesty renounces all pretensions which he has heretofore formed or might have formed to Nova Scotia or Acadia in all its parts, and guaranties the whole of it, and with all its dependencies, to the King of Great Britain : Moreover, his Most Christian Majesty cedes and guaranties to his said Britannick Majesty, in full right, Canada, with all its dependencies, as well as the island of Cape Breton, and all the other islands and coasts in the gulph and river of St. Lawrence, and in general, every thing that depends on the said countries, lands, islands, and coasts, with the sovereignty, property, possession, and all rights acquired by treaty, or otherwise, which the Most Christian King and the Crown of France have had till now over the said countries, lands, islands, places, coasts, and their inhabitants, so that the Most Christian King cedes and makes over the whole to the said King, and to the Crown of Great Britain, and that in the most ample manner and form, without restriction, and without any liberty to depart

[1] As printed in C. D., pp. 97–122.

sous aucun Pretexte contre cette Cession & Garantie, ni de troubler la Grande Bretagne dans les Possessions susmentionnées. De son Coté Sa Majesté Britannique convient d'accorder aux Habitans du Canada la Liberté de la Religion Catholique ; En Consequence Elle donnera les Ordres les plus precis & les plus effectifs, pour que ses nouveaux Sujets Catholiques Romains puissent professer le Culte de leur Religion selon le Rit de l'Eglise Romaine, en tant que le permettent les Loix de la Grande Bretagne.—Sa Majesté Britannique convient en outre, que les Habitans François ou autres, qui auroient eté Sujets du Roy Très Chretien en Canada, pourront se retirer en toute Sûreté & Liberté, où bon leur semblera, et pourront vendre leurs Biens, pourvû que ce soit à des Sujets de Sa Majesté Britannique, & transporter leurs Effets, ainsi que leurs Personnes, sans être genés dans leur Emigration, sous quelque Pretexte que ce puisse être, hors celui de Dettes ou de Procés criminels ; Le Terme limité pour cette Emigration sera fixé à l'Espace de dix huit Mois, à compter du Jour de l'Echange des Ratifications du present Traité.

from the said cession and guaranty under any pretence, or to disturb Great Britain in the possessions above mentioned. His Britannick Majesty, on his side, agrees to grant the liberty of the Catholick religion to the inhabitants of Canada : he will, in consequence, give the most precise and most effectual orders, that his new Roman Catholick subjects may profess the worship of their religion according to the rites of the Romish church, as far as the laws of Great Britain permit. His Britannick Majesty farther agrees that the French inhabitants, or others who had been subjects of the Most Christian King in Canada, may retire with all safety and freedom wherever they shall think proper, and may sell their estates, provided it be to the subjects of his Britannick Majesty, and bring away their effects as well as their persons, without being restrained in their emigration, under any pretence whatsoever, except that of debts or of criminal prosecutions: The term limited for this emigration shall be fixed to the space of eighteen months, to be computed from the day of the exchange of the ratification of the present treaty.

Appendix B

THE QUEBEC BILL

(with the Commons' amendments) [1]

A BILL

Intituled

An Act for making more effectual Provision for the Government of the Province of *Quebec*, in *North America*.

NB.—The words within square brackets are those omitted by the Commons : the words within curved brackets are those inserted by them. As the Lords accepted the Commons' amendments and made no further changes, this text gives the text of the Act, 14 George III, c. lxxxiii.

Preamble.
Whereas His Majesty, by His Royal Proclamation, bearing Date the Seventh Day of *October*, in the Third Year of His Reign, thought fit to declare the Provisions which had been made in respect to certain Countries, Territories, and Islands in *America*, ceded to His Majesty by the definitive Treaty of Peace concluded at *Paris*, on the Tenth Day of *February*, One thousand seven hundred and sixty-three :

And whereas, by the Arrangements made by the said Royal Proclamation, a very large [Part of the Territory of Canada], (Extent of Country), within which there were several Colonies and Settlements of the Subjects of *France*, who claimed to remain therein under the Faith of the said Treaty, was left, without any Provision being made for the Administration of Civil Government therein, and [other] (certain) Parts of the [Said Country] (Territory of Canada), where sedentary Fisheries had been established and carried on by the Subjects of *France*, Inhabitants of the said Province of *Canada*, under Grants and Concessions from the Government thereof, were annexed to the Government of *New-*

[1] C. D., pp. 554–560.

foundland, and thereby subjected to Regulations inconsistent with the nature of such Fisheries :

May it therefore please Your most Excellent Majesty,

That it may be enacted ; and be it enacted by the King's most Excellent Majesty, by and with the Advice and Consent of the Lords Spiritual and Temporal, and Commons, in this present Parliament assembled, and by the Authority of the same. That all the [said] Territories, Islands, and Countries, [heretofore Part of the Province of *Canada*], in *North America*, [extending Southward to the Banks of] (belonging to the Crown of *Great Britain*, bounded on the South by a Line from the Bay of *Chaleurs*, along the High Lands which divide the Rivers that empty themselves into the River *Saint Lawrence*, from those which fall into the Sea, to a Point in Forty-five Degrees of Northern Latitude, on the Eastern Bank of the River *Connecticut*, keeping the same Latitude directly West, through the Lake *Champlain*, until, in the same Latitude, it meets the River *Saint Lawrence* ; from thence up the Eastern Bank of the said River, to the Lake Ontario ; thence through the lake *Ontario*, and the River commonly called *Niagara* ; and thence along by the Eastern and South Eastern Bank of Lake *Erie*, following the said Bank, until the same shall be intersected by the Northern Boundary, granted by the Charter of the Province of *Pensylvania*, in case the same shall be so intersected ; and from thence along the said Northern and Western Boundaries of the said Province, until the said Western Boundary strike the *Ohio* : But in case the said Bank of the said Lake shall not be found to be so intersected, then following the said Bank, until it shall arrive at that Point of the said Bank which shall be nearest to the North Western Angle of the said Province of *Pensylvania*, and thence by a right Line to the said North Western Angle of the said Province ; and thence along the Western Boundary of the said Province, until it strike) the River *Ohio*, (and along

The Territories, Islands, and Countries in North America, belonging to Great Britain.

the Bank of the said River) Westward, to the Banks of *Mississippi*, and Northward to the Southern Boundary of the Territory granted to the Merchants Adventurers of *England* trading to *Hudson's Bay*; and [which said] (also all such) Territories, Islands, and Countries, [are not within the Limits of some other *British Colony*, as allowed and confirmed by the Crown or] which have, since the Tenth of *February*, One thousand seven hundred and sixty-three, been made Part of the Government of *Newfoundland*, be, and they are hereby, during His Majesty's Pleasure, annexed to, and made Part and Parcel of, the Province of *Quebec*, as created and established by the said Royal Proclamation of the Seventh of *October*, One thousand seven hundred and sixty three.

Annexed to the Province of Quebec.

(Provided always, That nothing herein contained relative to the Boundary of the Province of Quebec, shall in any wise affect the Boundaries of any other Colonies.)

Not to affect the Boundaries of any other Colony

(Provided always, and be it enacted, That nothing in this Act contained shall extend, or be construed to extend, to make void, or to vary or alter, any Right, Title, or Possession, derived under any Grant, Conveyance, or otherwise howsoever, of or to any Lands within the said Province, or the Provinces thereto adjoining, but that the same shall remain and be in Force, and have Effect, as if this Act had never been made.)

nor to make void other Rights formerly granted.

And whereas the Provisions made by the said Proclamation, in respect to the Civil Government of the said Province of *Quebec*, and the Powers and Authorities given to the Governor and other Civil Officers of the said Province, by the Grants and Commissions issued in consequence thereof, have been found, upon Experience, to be inapplicable to the State and Circumstances of the said Province, the Inhabitants whereof [amounting] (amounted) at the Conquest, to above [One hundred] (Sixty-five) thousand Persons, professing the Religion of the

Former Provisions made for the Province to be null and void after *May* 1, 1775.

Church of *Rome,* and enjoying an established Form
of Constitution and System of Laws, by which their
Persons and Property had been protected, governed,
and ordered, for a long Series of Years, from the first
Establishment of the said Province of *Canada* ; be
it therefore further enacted by the Authority aforesaid, That the said Proclamation, so far as the same
relates to the said Province of *Quebec,* and the Commission under the Authority whereof the Government
of the said Province is at present administered, and
all and every the Ordinance and Ordinances made by
the Governor and Council of *Quebec* for the Time
being, relative to the Civil Government and Administration of Justice in the said Province, and all Commissions to Judges and other Officers thereof, be,
and the same are hereby revoked, annulled, and
made void, from and after the first Day of *May,*
One thousand seven hundred and seventy five.

And for the more perfect security and Ease of the
Minds of the Inhabitants of the said Province, it is
hereby declared, That His Majesty's Subjects professing the Religion of the Church of *Rome,* of, and in the
said Province of *Quebec,* [as the same is described
in and by the said Proclamation and Commissions,
and also of all the Territories, Part of the Province
of *Canada,* at the time of the Conquest thereof, which
are hereby annexed, during His Majesty's Pleasure,
to the said Government of *Quebec*], may have, hold,
and enjoy, the free Exercise of the Religion of the
Church of *Rome,* subject to the King's Supremacy,
declared and established by an Act made in the
First Year of the Reign of Queen *Elizabeth,* over all
the Dominions and Countries which then did, or
thereafter should, belong to the Imperial Crown of
this Realm ; and that the Clergy of the said Church
may hold, receive, and enjoy their accustomed Dues
and Rights, with respect to such Persons only as
shall profess the said Religion.

Provided nevertheless, That [nothing herein contained shall extend, or be construed to extend, to

Marginal notes:

Inhabitants of *Quebec* may profess the *Romish* Religion, subject to the King's Supremacy, as by Act I *Eliz.* ;

and the Clergy enjoy their accustomed Dues.

Provision may be

the disabling] (it shall be lawful for) His Majesty, His Heirs or Successors, [from making] (to make) such Provision (out of the rest of the said accustomed Dues and Rights,) for the Encouragement of the Protestant Religion, and for the Maintenance and Support of a Protestant Clergy within the said Province, as he or they shall, from Time to Time, think necessary and expedient.

made by His Majesty for the Support of the Protestant Clergy.

(Provided always, and be it enacted, That no Person professing the Religion of the Church of *Rome*, and residing in the said Province, shall be obliged to take the Oath required by the said Statute, passed in the First Year of the Reign of Queen *Elizabeth*, or any other Oaths substituted by any other Act in the Place thereof, but that every such Person, who by the said Statute is required to take the Oath therein mentioned, shall be obliged, and is hereby required, to take and subscribe the following Oath before the Governor, or such other Person in such Court of Record as His Majesty shall appoint, who are hereby authorised to administer the same; *videlicet*,

No Person professing the Romish Religion obliged to take the Oath of I Eliz. ;

but to take, before the Governor, &c., the following Oath.

The Oath.

' I A. B. do sincerely promise and swear, That
' I will be faithful, and bear true Allegiance to His
' Majesty King *George*, and Him will defend to the
' utmost of my Power, against all traiterous Con-
' spiracies, and Attempts whatsoever, which shall be
' made against His Person, Crown, and Dignity ; and
' I will do my utmost Endeavour to disclose and make
' known to His Majesty, His Heirs, and Successors,
' all Treasons, and Traiterous Conspiracies, and
' Attempts, which I shall know to be against Him, or
' any of Them ; and all this I do swear, without any
' Equivocation, mental Evasion, or secret Reserva-
' tion ; and renouncing all Pardons and Dispensa-
' tions from any Power or Person whomsoever to the
' Contrary.
' So help me God.'

Persons refusing the

And every such Person who shall neglect or refuse to take the said Oath before mentioned, shall incur and be liable to the same Penalties, Forfeitures, Disabilities, and Incapacities, as he would have incurred and been liable to, for neglecting or refusing to take the Oath required by the said statute, passed in the First Year of the Reign of Queen *Elizabeth*.) Oath to be subject to the Penalties by Act I *Eliz.*

And be it further enacted by the Authority aforesaid, That all His Majesty's *Canadian* Subjects within the Province of *Quebec*, the Religious Orders and Communities only excepted, may also hold and enjoy their Property and Possessions, together with all Customs and Usages, relative thereto, and all other their Civil Rights, in as large, ample and beneficial Manner, as if the said Proclamation, Commissions, Ordinances, and other Acts and Instruments, had not been made, and as may consist with their Allegiance to His Majesty, and Subjection to the Crown and Parliament of *Great Britain*; and that in all Matters of Controversy relative to Property and Civil Rights, Resort shall be had to the Laws of *Canada*, (as the Rule) for the Decision of the same; and all Causes that shall hereafter be instituted in any of the Courts of Justice, to be appointed within and for the said Province by His Majesty, His Heirs and Successors, shall, with respect to such Property and Rights, be determined [by the Judges of the same], agreeably to the said Laws and Customs of *Canada*, [and the several] (until they shall be varied or altered by any) Ordinances that shall, from Time to Time, be passed in the said Province by the Governor, Lieutenant Governor, or Commander in Chief for the Time being, by and with the Advice and Consent of the Legislative Council of the same, to be appointed in Manner herein-after mentioned. His Majesty's *Canadian* Subjects (religious Orders excepted) may hold all their Possessions, &c.

and in Matters of Controversy, Resort to be had to the Laws of *Canada* for the Decision.

(Provided always, That nothing in this Act contained shall extend, or be construed to extend, to any Lands that have been granted by His Majesty, or shall hereafter be granted by His Majesty, His Heirs and Successors, to be holden in free and common Soccage.) Not to extend to Lands granted by His Majesty in common Soccage.

Owners of Goods may alienate the same by Will, &c. .
    Provided [always] (also) That it shall and may be lawful to and for every Person that is Owner of any Lands, Goods, or Credits in the said Province, and that has a Right to alienate the said Lands, Goods, or Credits, in his or her Lifetime, by Deed of Sale, Gift, or otherwise, to devise or bequeath the same, at his or her Death, by his or her Last Will and Testament ; any Law, Usage, or Custom heretofore or now prevailing in the Province, to the Contrary hereof in any-wise notwithstanding.

    [Provided also, That nothing in this Act contained shall extend, or be construed to extend, to any Lands that have been granted by His Majesty, or shall hereafter be granted by his Majesty, his heirs and Successors, to be holden in free and common

if executed according to the Laws of Canada.
Soccage :] (Such Will being executed either according to the Laws of *Canada*, or according to the Forms prescribed by the laws of *England*.)

Criminal Law of England to be continued in the Province.
    And whereas the Certainty and Lenity of the Criminal Law of *England*, and the Benefits and Advantages resulting from the Use of it, have been sensibly felt by the Inhabitants from an Experience of more than Nine Years, during which it has been uniformly administered ; be it therefore further enacted by the Authority aforesaid, That the same shall continue to be administered, and shall be observed as Law, in the Province of *Quebec*, as well in the Description and Quality of the Offence, as in the Method of Prosecution and Trial, and the Punishments and Forfeitures thereby inflicted, to the Exclusion of every other Rule of Criminal Law, or Mode of Proceeding thereon, which did or might prevail in the said Province before the Year of our Lord One thousand seven hundred and sixty-four ; any Thing in this Act to the Contrary thereof in any Respect notwithstanding ; subject nevertheless to such Alterations and Amendments, as the Governor, Lieutenant Governor, or Commander in Chief for the Time being, by and with the advice and Consent of the Legislative Council of the said Province, here-

after to be appointed, shall, from Time to Time, cause
to be made therein, in Manner herein-after directed.

And whereas it may be necessary to ordain many
Regulations, for the future Welfare and good Government of the Province of *Quebec*, the Occasions of
which cannot now be foreseen, nor without much
Delay and Inconvenience be provided for, without
intrusting that Authority for a certain Time, and
under proper Restrictions, to Persons resident there :

His Majesty may appoint a Council for the Affairs of the Province ;

And whereas it is at present inexpedient to call
an Assembly ; be it therefore enacted by the
Authority aforesaid, That it shall and may be lawful
for His Majesty, His Heirs and Successors, by
Warrant under His or Their Signet, or Sign
Manual, and with the Advice of the Privy Council,
to constitute and appoint a Council for the
Affairs of the Province of *Quebec*, to consist of such
Persons resident there, not exceeding Twenty-three,
nor less than Seventeen, as His Majesty, His Heirs
and Successors, shall be pleased to appoint ; and,
upon the Death, Removal, or Absence of any of the
Members of the said Council, in like Manner, to constitute and appoint such and so many other Person
or Persons as shall be necessary to supply the Vacancy
or Vacancies ; which Council, so appointed and
nominated, or the major Part thereof, shall have
[full] Power and Authority to make Ordinances for
the Peace, Welfare, and good Government of the
said Province, with the Consent of His Majesty's
Governor, or, in his Absence, of the Lieutenant
Governor, or Commander in Chief for the Time being.

which Council may make Ordinances, with Consent of the Governor.

Provided always, That nothing in this Act contained shall extend to authorise or impower the said
Legislative Council to lay any Taxes or Duties
within the said Province, (such Rates and Taxes
only excepted, as the Inhabitants of any Town or
District within the said Province, may be authorised
by the said Council to assess, levy, and apply,
within the said Town or District, for the Purpose
of making Roads, erecting and repairing publick

The Council are not impowered to lay Taxes, Publick Roads or Buildings excepted.

Buildings, or for any other Purpose respecting the local Convenience and Oeconomy of such Town or District.)

Ordinances made to be laid before His Majesty for His Approbation.   Provided also, and be it enacted by the Authority aforesaid, That every Ordinance so to be made shall, within Six Months, be transmitted by the Governor, or, in his Absence, by the Lieutenant Governor or Commander in Chief for the Time being, and laid before His Majesty, for His Royal Approbation ; and if His Majesty shall think fit to disallow thereof, the same shall cease and be void from the Time that His Majesty's Order in Council thereupon shall be promulgated at *Quebec*.

Ordinances touching Religion not to be in Force without His Majesty's Approbation.   Provided also, That no Ordinance touching Religion, or by which any Punishment may be inflicted greater than Fine or Imprisonment for Three Months, shall be of any Force or Effect, until the same shall have received His Majesty's approbation.

When Ordinances are to be passed by a Majority.   Provided also, That no Ordinance shall be passed, at any Meeting of the Council (where less than a Majority of the whole Council is present, or at any Time) except between the First Day of *January* and the First Day of *May*, unless upon some urgent Occasion ; in which Case, every Member thereof, resident at *Quebec*, or within Fifty Miles thereof, shall be personally summoned by the Governor, or, in his Absence, by the Lieutenant Governor or Commander in Chief for the Time being, to attend the same.

Nothing to hinder His Majesty to constitute Courts of Criminal, Civil, and Ecclesiastical Jurisdiction.   And be it further enacted by the Authority aforesaid, That nothing herein contained shall extend, or be construed to extend, to prevent or hinder His Majesty, His Heirs and Successors, by His or their Letters Patent, under the Great Seal of *Great Britain*, from erecting, constituting, and appointing, such Courts of Criminal, Civil, and Ecclesiastical Jurisdiction, within and for the said Province of *Quebec*, and appointing, from Time to Time, the Judges and Officers thereof, as His Majesty, His Heirs and

Successors, shall think necessary and proper, for the
Circumstances of the said Province.

(Provided always, and it is hereby enacted, That
nothing in this Act contained shall extend, or be
construed to extend, to repeal or make void, within
the said Province of *Quebec*, any Act or Acts of
the Parliament of *Great Britain* heretofore made, for
prohibiting, restraining, or regulating the Trade or
Commerce of His Majesty's Colonies and Plantations
in *America* ; but that all and every the said Acts,
and also all Acts of Parliament heretofore made,
concerning or respecting the said Colonies and Plantations, shall be, and are hereby declared to be, in
Force, within the said Province of Quebec, and every
Part thereof.)

All Acts for-
merly made
are hereby
inforced
within the
Province.

Finis.

INDEX